Sports Journalism

SPORTS
JOURNALISM

A History of Glory, Fame, and Technology

PATRICK S. WASHBURN and CHRIS LAMB

University of Nebraska Press | Lincoln

Portions of this manuscript originally included
in Pat Washburn's "New York Newspaper
Coverage of Jackie Robinson in His First Major
League Season." *Western Journal of Black
Studies* 4, no. 3 (Fall 1980): 183–92.

Library of Congress
Cataloging-in-Publication Data
Names: Washburn, Patrick Scott, author. |
Lamb, Chris, 1958– author.
Title: Sports journalism: a history of glory,
fame, and technology / Patrick S. Washburn
and Chris Lamb.
Description: Lincoln: University of Nebraska
Press, [2020] | Includes bibliographical
references and index.
Identifiers: LCCN 2019054496
ISBN 9781496220233 (hardback)
ISBN 9781496221223 (paperback)
ISBN 9781496221896 (epub)
ISBN 9781496221902 (mobi)
ISBN 9781496221919 (pdf)
Subjects: LCSH: Sports journalism—United
States—History.
Classification: LCC PN4784.S6 W39 2020 |
DDC 070.4/49796—dc23
LC record available at
https://lccn.loc.gov/2019054496

Set in Minion Pro by Laura Buis.
Designed by L. Auten.

This book is dedicated to our wives, Glenda Washburn and Lesly Lamb, who have always supported our passion for researching and writing history.

Contents

Preface

PATRICK S. WASHBURN

Sports became a permanent part of the American psyche centuries ago. Ever since, nothing has captured the imagination, affection, and free time of Americans the way sports has, whether we're sitting in a ballpark, a stadium, or an arena; watching games on television; listening to them on radio; following them on Twitter or tweeting about them; or checking updates on smartphones to see if anything happened since we last checked a short time ago. Quite simply, Americans are obsessed with sports—not just one or two sports as in many countries but far more, including those that are watched by millions of fans on a nightly basis. You can fill much of the Library of Congress with what has been written about sports in the past few centuries and much of the blogosphere with what has been written about sports in the past twenty-four hours. And we have always looked to sports journalists to learn not only who won but why and how.

Sports have changed enormously over time in the United States, and just as sports have changed so has sports journalism. It is part and parcel of the new technologies that have brought seismic changes to society. Where once Americans read in the shipping news about a sports event a week, a month, or more after it occurred in America and maybe in England, now a soccer game half a world away is as immediately accessible as the phone in the palm of our hand. Never before have sports—any sport—been more accessible to us and, because of advances in technology, never before is so much being reported, written, and said about sports.

But as technology has changed sports reporting, it has not necessarily improved it—though in some cases it has by making it possible to produce stories and updates in real time and by including links that provide additional information about the subject of the story. A generation or so ago we relied mainly on newspapers for most of our information about sports. But papers now give us only a fraction of what is said about sports. Because of ever-developing technology we can read and watch sports wherever we are. Because of technology there has been an increase in the number of people who identify themselves as sports journalists and in how sports are reported. And because of technology sports news has become more and more prominent, competing sometimes with politics, crime, and natural disasters in a national news cycle.

What has been the effect of the digital age on sports journalism and how and why has that changed from the 1700s when the major technology was hand-powered printing presses? It is with those things in mind that this book was written. It is about the past, the present, and, to some extent, the future of American sports journalism. But it is more than just a journalism history; it is a tale of who we are as Americans and how we spend our leisure time. In chronicling sports, journalists can reveal our mores and social conditions and give us insights into such things as nationalism, individualism, capitalism, racism, and sexism. Most Americans are aware of sports stories that went far beyond what happened in a game: concussions in football, drugs in baseball and track and field, cheating by colleges and universities to get the best football and basketball players, and the sexual abuse by coaches of female gymnasts and other athletes. Not long ago these types of sports stories were rarely tackled by the media and almost never in depth. Now, such stories have become commonplace.

We wrote this book about the history of American sports journalism because we are lifelong fans of sports, having grown up as kids avidly reading newspaper sports pages and listening to games on radio and seeing them on television. Sports stars were our heroes whom we hoped one day to emulate. I began researching and writing this book more than ten years ago because I was curious how sports journalism had changed since its beginning in the first half of the 1700s and why those changes had occurred. As a historian, I had written only one scholarly article on sports about how three New York City newspapers covered Jackie Robinson, the first black baseball player in the modern major leagues, in his first season with the Brooklyn Dodgers in 1947. That study, which was done in my first semester as a doctoral student at Indiana University in the early 1980s, was sparked by reading what I consider to be the best sports book ever written: Roger Kahn's *The Boys of Summer*. While I enjoyed studying sports history my areas of expertise as a researcher for various reasons became the history of the black press and the First Amendment struggle between the press and government in World War II. That led to books on those subjects and invitations to speak at numerous universities as well as the Smithsonian and the National D-Day museum.

But while my research on this book is a new subject of sorts for me I have had extensive experience with sports. I lettered in tennis and swimming in high school, and in the latter I was on an undefeated state championship team in my senior year and placed in two free-style events in the state finals. After captaining the swimming team at Baylor University I spent the next four years as a sportswriter on daily newspapers in Texas, Virginia, and Georgia before switching to college sports information, in which I worked for four years at Harvard University and the University of Louisville. Later, as a graduate student at Indiana University, I worked in the sports information office and wrote sports for a local newspaper. And, finally, I was an NCAA faculty athletic representative while teaching journalism at Ohio University from 1984 to 2012.

Over the years my progress on the book slowed considerably, partly because of health issues (the worst time was a sixteen-week period in which my hundred-year-old mother died, my wife had a stroke, her ninety-five-year-old mother died, and I had a knee replaced). It became obvious after a while that I needed help to complete this book, so I invited Chris Lamb to join me as a coauthor. I was glad when he agreed to do it. He was an excellent choice for several reasons: he not only writes well but is an experienced historian with a well-deserved national reputation for research excellence.

And, most importantly, his research expertise is sports.

Chris was thrilled to get the call to help finish the book although he never thought he would become a relief pitcher of sorts in late middle age, thirty years after tearing his rotator cuff playing softball. He also grew up playing sports and continued playing softball—with an impaired right shoulder—until he turned fifty. He spent his boyhood reading everything he could about baseball, and no statistic appeared too trivial to put in his memory. He worked as a sports reporter for a radio station in Knoxville, Tennessee, while he attended college. After graduation he was hired as a sports editor for a small daily in Tennessee. He later worked for newspapers in Knoxville, Dayton, Ohio, and Daytona Beach, Florida.

In 1993, while working as a columnist for the *Daytona Beach News-Journal*, he interviewed Billy Rowe, a former sportswriter for the prominent black weekly newspaper, the *Pittsburgh Courier*. Rowe had accompanied Jackie Robinson during the ballplayer's first spring training with the Brooklyn Dodgers organization in Daytona Beach in 1946. From that interview came Chris's interest in Robinson and how the press covered the integration of baseball, which he began examining more closely while in a doctoral program at Bowling Green State University.

Working as a journalism professor for nearly a quarter-century Chris has written a number of books on sports, media, and race, including *Blackout: The Untold Story Behind Jackie Robinson's First Spring Training*; *Conspiracy of Silence: Sportswriters and the Long Campaign to Desegregate Baseball*; *From Jack Johnson to LeBron James: Sports, Media, and the Color Line*; and *Jackie Robinson: A Spiritual Biography*. He also has written columns and articles about sports for *Sports Illustrated*, the *New York Times*, the *Wall Street Journal*, ESPN .com, and New Republic.com.

And so this book was written.

Among those who deserve credit for how it turned out were two master's students in the E. W. Scripps School of Journalism at Ohio University, Joe Lowe and Brian Boesch. They did considerable research and writing on chapters 1 and 2 respectively, and the chapters are better because of what they did. We also would like to thank David Abrahamson of Northwestern University for his encouragement and help with the manuscript. And finally, and certainly not least, we are particularly appreciative of the assistance we have received from Rob Taylor of the University of Nebraska Press, whose professionalism, conscientiousness, and support have been invaluable. Others at the Press who have been extremely helpful in putting the manuscript in its final form are Courtney Ochsner, John Wilcockson, and Joeth Zucco.

In closing I recall a recent trip to a large Ohio antique mall in search of old fishing lures, which I look for ardently and collect seriously. As I walked through the mall I saw a nearby mother look at a painting and say to her thirty-something daughter, "That's interesting." The daughter retorted with disdain in her voice, "That's not interesting. That's ugly. In fact, it is beyond ugly!" Chris and I are storytellers who work hard to be interesting in what we write, and we agree that there is no boring history, just boring historians (and sometimes boring professors). So, like the mother, we urge readers to have a positive attitude when they read this book, and we guarantee they will not be disappointed. The history of American sports journalism is not boring. Instead, it is filled with what famed twentieth-century sportswriter Grantland Rice used as the title of his 1954 book, *The Tumult and the Shouting*. So, enjoy.

Introduction

Print is dead. Sportswriting is not dead. Sportswriting is
moving to the internet. It is how it is disseminated.

—Jay Mariotti, AOL.com sports columnist, 2009

On April 2, 1995, HBO debuted *Real Sports with Bryant Gumbel*. The
host of the show said it was "spawned by the fact that sports have
changed dramatically, that it's no longer just fun and games, and that
what happens off the field, beyond the scores, is worthy of some serious
reporting." By the end of 2017 the excellence of the ongoing program
was shown by the awards that it had received—thirty-two Emmys,
three Duponts, and two Peabodys.[1]

The 150th show on September 15, 2009, had a thirteen-minute segment on what Gumbel described as the "rapidly changing world of
communications." He noted that the internet, which provided free
sports news on computers, had resulted in newspapers losing readers
and advertising as sports sections slowly died. "That's the reality," he
said. "The question is: Should we care?"[2] To answer that, which fit
into his desire to look at something "off the field . . . worthy of some
serious reporting," he turned the program over to one of the country's
most respected sports journalists, seventy-year-old Frank Deford.
By the time that he died in May 2017 Deford had written more than
thirty years for *Sports Illustrated*, appeared on Gumbel's show for
twenty-two years, done 1,656 weekly sports commentaries on National
Public Radio's *Morning Edition*, and had been the first sportswriter to

receive the National Humanities Medal, which was presented to him by President Barack Obama.[3]

Deford began Gumbel's 2009 show by recalling that he had been the editor in chief of the *National Sports Daily*, a tabloid newspaper that went out of business in 1991 after it lost $150 million in only eighteen months due to reporting, printing, and delivery expenses. And he noted that was before papers "had to contend with the power and the immediacy of the internet."

To look at how things had changed for newspapers by 2009 Deford interviewed Jay Mariotti, who had been a sports columnist for sixteen years at the *Chicago Sun-Times* before leaving in 2008 for the same position at AOL.com. Mariotti said the immediacy of sports made them a perfect fit for the internet because people did not want to wait twelve or thirteen hours to read in a newspaper about what had occurred. "Print is dead," he said bluntly. "Sportswriting is not dead. Sportswriting is moving to the internet. It is how it is disseminated." Deford admitted that the quickness of the internet could make newspapers feel "stale and irrelevant." Mariotti added: "[On the internet] you eliminate the ink, you eliminate the [newspaper] trucks, . . . you eliminate the unions, you eliminate bing, bing, bing. Why wouldn't a newspaper want to cut all those newsprint costs . . . and do it on the internet and you'll eventually make more money? Why would you want to pour all this money into this archaic system where people aren't really reading it this much anymore?"

Deford countered that he had been reading newspapers while he ate breakfast since he was a child and wondered what he was going to do if sports sections continued to decline. Mariotti replied that there would always be a need for newspapers—by people, for instance, on trains— but he believed papers would have little usefulness in the future. At the end of the segment, Deford joined Gumbel for a candid conversation:

GUMBEL: Is there any evidence to suggest that the public, whose standards have been lowered by the internet, really care one way or another how they get it [sports news]?

DEFORD: It's not so much the public. . . . it's the young people who don't seem to have the interest in reading those investigative pieces. It's a different mind-set.

GUMBEL: But also people don't differentiate between a blog or an investigative report.

DEFORD: That's the problem because a blog is just bloviating, it's just somebody's opinion, whereas investigative reporting is— the objective word [is] reporting—going out and discovering things. And we all know the bulk of that through the years has come from newspapers, from day-to-day hard reporting, and in the case of sports, traveling with the team, being on top of things at all times.

GUMBEL: The bottom line: Is it possible you and I are just dinosaurs who resent change?

DEFORD: Yes.

GUMBEL: I agree.[4]

The comment about becoming "dinosaurs" because of the internet is as true today as when Gumbel and Deford were talking in 2009. Quite simply, technological changes in media—some would call it progress—continue to occur rapidly and are viewed as a major threat to the viability of the established conveyors of sports news in the U.S. When radio arose in 1920 and quickly became a nationwide success, newspapers were wary of it although the editor in chief of the *Detroit News* said in 1922 that he did not believe it would supplant daily newspapers as a major information source. Two years later, RCA's David Sarnoff noted that radio made a listener a "participant" in whatever was being broadcast, but he said people would still want to read papers because of the amount of information they offered.[5] Nevertheless, *Editor & Publisher*, the trade journal for newspapers, was concerned. "There is no question that radio reporting of a prize fight, ball game, President's speech, is in many respects superior to any reporting possible on the printed page," it wrote in 1924. "It is instantaneous. You feel in actual contact with the event. A clever observer tells you more than a reporter could write or a newspaper print. You get color, atmosphere and a sense of miraculous presence."[6]

Although newspapers learned to live with radio and were not appreciably hurt by it, a more serious challenge to not only papers but also radio and magazines was the advent of television. Introducing it at the 1939 New York World's Fair, Sarnoff predicted it would "become an important factor in American economic life."[7] It grew slowly at first, but in 1952 the Federal Communications Commission allowed numerous new television stations to begin broadcasting, and the number grew from 105 that year to 422 in 1955 and 559 in 1960. Antennas quickly sprouted on rooftops, and by the end of the decade there were fifty million sets in the U.S. with nearly 90 percent of the country's households having at least one TV.[8] Sports programming was common on television from the beginning, which created the same problem for newspapers that they would face later from the internet—what should be reported when some of the readers, maybe the majority of them, had already seen a sports event on TV on the previous day? And that was not the only concern. Budd Schulberg, the boxing editor of *Sports Illustrated*, complained in 1954 about the large number of sports events appearing on television: "One of the problems of television is that it is so much with us. It is not only a hungry giant but a Gargantua with an oversized tapeworm of an appetite."[9] In the mid-1970s both novelist James Michener and writer David Halberstam made the same observation with the latter partially blaming viewers for the continuing growth of TV sports programming. "We have, for some fifteen years or so, simply seen too much," said Halberstam. ". . . Football was there every Sunday, it was free, or almost free, and so we watched it. One game was not enough, so we watched two."[10]

The problems that radio, television, and the internet posed for newspaper and magazine sports coverage have been examined by numerous historians. However, that is only a small part of the story of American sports journalism. This book, which is a chronological, in-depth examination of the history stretching back to 1733, is the most thorough account yet produced.[11]

This is not to say that the history of sports journalism has been ignored. Books and articles about it generally fall into six areas: autobiographies by sports journalists; biographies of notable persons in the field; sports journalism in specific media, such as radio and television; the history of individual media, such as *Sports Illustrated* and ESPN; notable journalists in one sport, such as baseball; and the history of certain types of sports journalists, such as women and black newspaper baseball writers. While all of these provide important details about specific periods in sports journalism history, none of them by themselves, unlike this book, tells the entire historical story.

Because the history of American sports journalism is too encyclopedic to cover adequately in one book, our research was focused on two central questions:

1. What changes occurred in American sports journalism over time?
2. Why did those changes occur?

In addressing those questions we made a careful distinction between "journalism" and "media." Journalism refers to what is written and broadcast while media is a reference to the print and broadcast outlets that produce journalism.

The end result is that this book is an overall, general history of American sports journalism. It is what might be called an "institutional" history that emphasizes the beginnings of the field, its practitioners and a few famous athletes who influenced what was written and broadcast, notable events, and the media and technological changes that have shaped the relationship between the press and sports over almost three hundred years. This was never meant to be a history of the craft of sports journalism, which could be the subject of another book, although there are places in the history where the way that sports was written about and broadcast resulted in notable changes.

The major theme that emerged in the research for this book was the significance of technology in determining historical changes that occurred in sports journalism. In the 1700s, the main technology affecting newspapers as well as magazines was hand-powered presses, which made publishing a time-consuming job. But in 1812 the first steam-driven press was invented, and the speed at which papers could be printed increased dramatically. As larger and faster presses came on the market throughout the nineteenth century, newspaper circulations rose rapidly and so did the number of pages, which resulted in more news being printed and the number of sports-related stories increasing markedly. While this was occurring, steamboats and then trains made it possible for reporters to get to distant sporting events quicker, and with the telegraph and telephones, their stories could appear in print considerably sooner than before, sometimes on the next day. Then, in 1886, the linotype machine was invented. This led to even larger papers and more sports news because it speeded up the setting of type, which allowed reporters to get more immediate news because deadlines were set back.

Another important piece of technology for the press in the 1800s was photography. Newspapers started using illustrations, made from woodcuts, in the early 1700s, and although photography began in the 1830s, papers did not use pictures for more than forty years because of technical and reproduction problems. In contrast, by the Civil War in 1861–65, more and more magazines were running photographs because they attracted readers and led to higher circulations, and by the late 1880s and early 1890s, photos of athletes and outdoorsmen were common. The *New York Daily Graphic*, in 1880, was the first daily newspaper to publish a picture, and by 1897 photography was common in metropolitan dailies. Sports scenes were included among the pictures as the American public showed a penchant for wanting to see athletes and athletic competition, not just read about them, and this desire would mushroom in the media in the twentieth century.

Meanwhile, newspapers' stranglehold on being the first to report sports events began being challenged by different uses of existing technologies as well as the rise of new ones. Starting in the 1890s telegraphic accounts of baseball games were recreated, pitch by pitch and out by out, on small diamonds around the country. By the time of the 1919 World Series more than a hundred thousand miles of telegraph lines were used to bring the games "live" to crowds in smoke-filled rooms in 250 U.S. cities as well as Winnipeg, Canada, and Havana, Cuba. A different threat came from motion picture newsreels, starting with silent film in 1911. They began regularly featuring sports highlights, and, in 1927, the first newsreel with sound showed a college football game and a rodeo.

And then there was wireless telegraphy, which would lead to radio. In 1898 more than seven hundred messages were sent in Morse code from a boat following a British yacht race to an operator on shore; he transcribed the messages and telephoned them to a newspaper, which posted them outside of its office for an excited crowd to see. A year later the *New York Herald* used the same method of reporting to cover an America's Cup yacht race off the New Jersey coast and put out an edition that scooped its competitors before the ships returned to shore. That led to more demonstrations of wireless telegraphy in the following years and then the establishment of experimental radio stations before the first ones were licensed by the government in 1920, with sports quickly becoming a regular part of programming.

While radio suddenly brought sports live into listeners' homes and accentuated the experience with announcers and the sounds of an event, television went further because now viewers could see the action too, first in black-and-white and then in color by the 1950s. Technology played a big part in TV's success. Satellites made it possible to show sports events from anywhere in the world; blimps could provide novel views from above; and producers quickly began utilizing such things as instant replay, reverse angle replay, zoom camera lenses, and electronic yard lines on football fields that only showed up on television screens. As for the announcers, computers fed them constant updated statistics about the game. Thus, television added an excitement to sporting events that newspapers and magazines found difficult, if not impossible, to match.

And then a new piece of technology—the internet—arrived and dramatically changed sports journalism. During much of the last half of the twentieth century, fans could only learn what was happening in sports when they read it in newspapers or heard it on television or radio. But the internet meant that those interested in sports could receive updates in real time from websites, blogs, and social media networks, where journalists expressed their opinions and interacted with fans, athletes, and other reporters. Thus, anyone with a computer could find out quickly what was happening in sports—and anyone with a computer and a blog could become a sportswriter or at least claim to be one. Instead of the internet being the end of established sports journalism, as some predicted, it became a new way to present content that had never before existed. But it also raised ethical concerns. As one sportswriter noted: "The biggest problem with sports journalists shifting mostly to the internet is that it has become like talk radio; some people are writing gossip and have no integrity. . . . This really hurts the reputation and credibility of all of us."[12]

While the overriding importance of technology in determining the history of American sports journalism was the most significant finding in our research, it was surprising that only a small number of people played large, pivotal roles in the changes that occurred. This book, with its focus on change, was never envisioned as an exhaustive examination of noted sports journalists. Thus, many famous sports journalists do not appear in this book or are rarely mentioned; while they demonstrated excellence in writing or broadcasting, they were responsible for little or no important changes. A few, however, through their journalistic skill, and sometimes being at the right place at an opportune moment, did far more than others in contributing to the evolution of sports journalism.

One of them, for example, was Grantland Rice. A newspaper sportswriter and columnist in New York City from 1912 to 1954, he was the leader of what became known as the "Gee-Whiz" school of writing, which basically praised and glorified athletes in contrast to the "Aw Nuts" writers, who were far more skeptical in attributing greatness to anyone. "When a sportswriter stops making heroes out of athletes," Rice said, "it's time to get out of the business."[13] Columnist Arthur Daley of the *New York Times*, who in 1956 became the first sportswriter to win a Pulitzer Prize, wrote two days after Rice's death in 1954 that it was doubtful that anyone had had a greater impact on sportswriting. "He gave it fire and enthusiasm and sparkle," he said. "He could reflect the drama and the excitement as few men could. There was an era in the 1920s when every young writer tried to emulate Grantland Rice."[14]

Another example was Roone Arledge. In the second half of the twentieth century, his impact on sports broadcasting was as large as Rice's on newspaper writing. Named the producer of ABC television's college football games in 1960, Arledge declared before the first game in a memorandum that he was going to bring "excitement and color" to viewers to make them feel like they were present at a game. He added: "WE ARE GOING TO ADD SHOW BUSINESS TO SPORTS!" Using blimps for different views of a stadium, he not only showed the game but also zoomed in with extra cameras on cheerleaders, bands, spectators in the stands including pretty women, and coaches on the sidelines.[15] Then, a year later, he introduced ABC's *Wide World of Sports*, which in thirty-seven years won numerous awards for broadcasting sports events, some of them for the first time ever on TV, from fifty-three countries and forty-six states.[16] All of that led in 1970 to Arledge starting *Monday Night Football* for pro games. What was particularly notable was his selection of two of the three announcers because he felt they would create controversy by teasing and needling each other; by the end of the first season, he said he was pleased with the result because the announcers had made the broadcasts more important than what happened in a game. All of this led to some calling him a television "legend" and an historian labeling him "the dominant figure in sports television" by the mid-1970s.[17]

As this book shows, there also occasionally were periods in American history when a group of sports journalists, rather than just one individual, brought about changes collectively. The most significant involved women.

While the lineage of female sports journalists in the U.S. stretches back to 1869 it was not until the 1980s that their numbers increased rapidly. Prior to then few women had high-profile sports jobs, such as columnists, anchors, or beat reporters in either print or broadcast, and the ones who did sometimes faced discrimination or sexual harassment. In the early 1970s a woman was not allowed in the press box at a National Football League game and was forced to cover it while standing on the roof of the stadium. Women reporters, unlike their male counterparts, also were barred from locker rooms. In baseball, that changed on September 25, 1978, when a federal judge ruled that the major league policy of only allowing male reporters in locker rooms gave them an unfair advantage over women, which violated the Equal Protection Clause of the Fourteenth Amendment.[18]

By the mid-1980s, with women continuing to push hard for equal treatment, professional football, basketball, and hockey joined baseball in opening their locker rooms to female reporters. But harassment continued. The women were accused of being voyeurs who wanted to gawk at nude male athletes, and sometimes they were thrown out of locker rooms. And if they did get in, it sometimes was not only a bad experience but a scary one. One woman was hit in the head with a sweat-soaked jockstrap, and another had a naked tight end stand in front of her and say, "Is this what you want? Do you want to take a bite out of this?" Meanwhile, several other players crowded around her and made lewd comments. She called it "premeditated mind rape."[19]

By 2010 more women were working in sports journalism than ever before although they lagged behind in prestigious media jobs. The Institute for Diversity and Ethics in Sports at the University of Central Florida gave the print and broadcast media an "F" grade for gender representation among columnists and editors. It reported that 94 percent of sports editors were white, as were 88 percent of sports columnists, and 93 percent of columnists were male.[20] The *Hartford Courant*'s Claire Smith, who in 1983 had become one of the first female major league beat writers, was among the women journalists who pushed for equality. She later worked for the *New York Times*, the

Philadelphia Inquirer, and ESPN, and in 2017 was the first woman to receive the J. G. Taylor Spink Award from the Baseball Writers Association of America "for meritorious contributions to baseball writing." In her acceptance speech, she mentioned the long fight for equality by female sports journalists and thanked "the women who walked the walk and fought the battles and got all of us to this point." She added: "No one does this by themselves."[21]

As this book shows the persistence of the women who pushed for equal rights was just one of the many forces that have molded the history of American sports journalism. Besides the overriding importance of technology other factors have included: religion in the 1700s; urban pride and competition between cities in the 1800s along with the expanding sizes and circulations of metropolitan newspapers; sportswriters on black newspapers covering black athletes and pushing for equality well before the civil rights movement of the 1950s; ethical concerns faced by journalists; and the effects of advertising and business economics in determining not just what sports news would be covered by the media but how it would be covered. Thus, the history of sports journalism is a far more complex story than it appears at first glance, and this is its first comprehensive, chronological account.

After the preeminent sports and political historian David Halberstam died in 2007, Glenn Stout wrote a year later about why his friend had cared so deeply about sports:

> He once wrote of his sports titles [books] that "[they] are my entertainments, fun to do, a pleasant world and a good deal more relaxed venue," less pressured and more enjoyable than his heavier and more lengthy books about what he termed "society, history and culture." Yet I do not think he viewed writing about sports as necessarily something lesser, for he also wrote that sports were "a venue from which I can learn a great deal about the changing mores of the rest of the society." He recognized that sports are important because sports matter to people, and that sports, and how we relate to sports, say something of value

about ourselves, our society, and our history and culture, one of the rare places where citizens of differing creeds, classes, and races come together.[22]

Halberstam unquestionably understood the importance of history. And if he was still alive, he would appreciate what this book offers. It talks about how and why sports journalism has changed and been shaped by numerous factors over almost three centuries of American history. It is a rich, interesting story that, in Halberstam's view, has "value."

Sports Journalism

The Beginning of American Sportswriting

1

> Yesterday the Prize of Forty Pounds, was run for on our
> Race Ground, by Col. *Tasker's* Mare *Selyma*, and Capt.
> *Butler's* Mare *Creeping Kate*; and won by the former.
>
> —Horse race story in the *Maryland Gazette*, 1752

On March 5, 1733, Americans on the northeastern Atlantic coast had yet to see reassuring signs of the approaching spring. All the way down to Annapolis in the colony of Maryland, rivers remained frozen, and sledges still ran snowy routes between Boston and other New England towns. Bostonians, many of whom undoubtedly lingered near their fireplaces to escape the bitter gusts off Boston Bay, found a small piece of novel news buried that day on the second page of the city's four-page newssheet, the *Boston Gazette*: five months earlier in England, alehouse owner Bob Russel had sparred with carpenter John Faulconer in a boxing match on a London bowling green. This drew "as great a Concourse of People as ever was known on such an Occasion." In a roped off, impromptu ring, with horses carefully tied out of the way and heavy wagering, spectators watched as Faulconer, the favorite, lost in about eight minutes. Readers of the ninety-nine-word account, which dealt principally with the event's size and social significance, may have been disappointed. Other than noting in half a sentence that Russel was the winner, nothing that occurred in the fight was described, leaving the details totally to the readers' imagination.[1]

Published forty-two years before the start of the Revolutionary War the *Gazette*'s account of the bout was one of the earliest examples of sports journalism on the American continent.[2] From the year of its publication until 1857, when America finally had its first full-time sports reporter, the growth of sports journalism roughly followed that of the United States.[3] Constrained by technological, social, and religious factors, sports coverage during the colonial period remained relatively small. Although sports and their importance began to grow at the end of the 1700s and the beginning of the 1800s as capitalism and market production started to flourish in the new United States, it was not until the 1830s that conditions were favorable for a flowering of American sports journalism. Then, a determined group of pioneering journalists began navigating uncharted territory to deliver increased sports coverage to a country learning to play.

***

Like many aspects of early American culture colonial attitudes toward sports and recreation can be traced back to England. In 1618, two years before the pilgrims landed at Plymouth Rock in what is now Massachusetts, King James I, reacting to anti-sport measures by Puritans in Lancashire, issued "The Book of Sports," a national proclamation ordering that "no lawfull Recreation bee barred to Our good People."[4] In doing so, he condemned puritanical attempts to limit recreation and urged his subjects to enjoy the pleasures of sports and recreation, even on the Sabbath. His motives were both cynical (a means of controlling his subjects and providing a benign safety valve for political discontent) and utilitarian (martial sports helped potential soldiers prepare for combat). England's Puritans, who considered sporting activity and revelry to be sinful, especially on the Sabbath, were not pleased. In fact, they often associated the word "sport" with loud, Sabbath-wrecking ball games or other violent sports.[5]

Puritanical belief, grounded in the Calvinistic doctrine of divine predetermination, emphasized an ascetic lifestyle and viewed sports as unholy and sin-inducing activities. This anti-sport belief sprang not so much from an inherent dislike of sports as from the vices that they were thought to promote, which included gambling, drunkenness, and the deliberate inflicting of pain or the causing of injuries.

Also troublesome was the gory, raucous, and excessive nature of English sports. For example, the "butcherly sports" of bull and bear baiting, which were popular with both the upper and the lower classes, involved people teasing and then killing the animals as crowds cheered. Even Elizabeth I, like many in England's gentry, was enamored with bear baiting. Bull baiting, a tradition particularly liked by the lower classes, originated in the Middle Ages and was founded on the belief that bulls baited before slaughter produced a more tender meat. By the seventeenth century, that notion had vanished, but the popularity of the sport remained. Besides bull and bear baiting, cockfights and dogfights, which lasted until one of the participants was dead, also were well attended. Another deadly sport was called gander pulling. This involved tying up a goose and then having a horseback rider gallop past and try to decapitate it with his hand.[6]

Historian Thomas Altherr has noted that it was "hardly surprising" that the English brought such "blood sports" to colonial America, where they flourished both in the North and in the South. "'If animals were going to die or meet the butcher's blade, why not subject them to some torture or combat to provide humans with spectacle and sport?' went the logic," he wrote. "If one could win some money gambling all the better. Drink, perhaps some fisticuffs, and other immoralities would attend the merriment. At the very least it would be a social occasion."[7]

English fans were not restricted to blood sports, however, to satisfy their sporting desires. Early forms of soccer stirred communities into such festive spirits that shops were closed and homes were boarded up to avoid damage. Opposing teams, which typically represented parishes or villages, were not required to be equal in size and sometimes contained upward of a hundred men. They competed on loosely demarcated playing fields, sometimes several miles in length, in both towns and in the country with local landmarks serving as goals. Despite a few local rules, matches were violent, resulting in property damage and, more often than not, bodily injury, especially to participants' shins. Boxing and wrestling, which also could lead to bodily injuries, were favorite English pastimes as well; and, for the wealthy and privileged, hunting and fishing served as sporting outlets along with horse racing, tennis, handball, and bowling. While the latter originated in England's upper class, by the end of the seventeenth century, it was enjoyed by the middle class, too.[8]

When Puritans settled New England, they were determined, in their desire to create a godly society, to stamp out sinful activities, and many of the sports that they opposed in England fell into this category. However, not everyone in the northern colonies shared such convictions, and occasional confrontations occurred. One of the earliest was on Christmas Day in 1621 when Massachusetts Governor William Bradford came home and found some of the colony's newcomers "in the streete at play, openly; some pitching the barr, and some at stool-ball and shuch like sports." After taking away their "implements" he told them that there would be no "gameing or revelling in the streets," and anyone wishing to continue those types of activities was advised to do so at home.[9]

Cotton Mather, a noted Congregationalist minister in Boston, drew a distinction between acceptable and unacceptable forms of sport in a 1726 treatise: "Men and Brethren, We would not be misunderstood, as if we meant to insinuate, due Pursuit of Recreation is inconsistent with all manner of Diversion; No, we suppose there are Diversions undoubtedly innocent, yet profitable and of use, to fit us for Service, by enlivening & fortifying our frail Nature, Invigorating the Animal Spirits, and that a brightening the Mind, when tired with a close of Application to Business."[10] Thus, opposition to sports in the northern colonies was not always simply objections to the "woeful spectacle[s]" associated with these contests because they violated the Sabbath. For example, the dubious historical origins of some sports, which could be traced back to impure pagan or catholic "papist" sources, inspired puritanical distrust. In addition, Puritans believed sports should serve as "refreshment," and ones that led to bodily fatigue, such as soccer, were deemed foolish.[11]

With many Puritans loosely equating hard work with religious virtue, recreation unsurprisingly was idealized as a moderate and useful activity that promoted man's industrious responsibilities. Thus, activities that kept villagers busy while minding their religious duties and the Sabbath, such as house and barn raisings, were viewed favorably.

In addition, many Puritans, amazed at the seemingly endless bounty offered by the new world, fished with zeal, perhaps believing tales that circulated widely about legendary waters where the fish were so thick that one could walk on their backs from one side to the other and never get wet. With such abundance, both real and imagined, fishing quickly became one of the major industries in New England in the seventeenth and eighteenth centuries as well as the most popular sporting pastime. It not only provided refreshment, but it did not require excessive exertion and could be done quietly and privately without spectators; and, best of all, it was an industrious activity that provided food. Fishing's widespread popularity—one historian noted that "[a]ll males seem to have fished in seventeenth-century New England"—led eventually to the formation of early sporting clubs, whose members planned trips and contests. Apparently, the first such organization in New England was the Shad & Salmon Club, which was established in Hartford, Connecticut, in the 1780s.[12]

The popularity of hunting, which also met with approval from the religious authorities because it was a source of food, never equaled fishing although it was still enjoyed widely. The vast, unrestricted American wilderness was far different from England, where the best hunting was reserved for the nobility on royally protected land and trespassing was punishable by castration, dismemberment, or death. But in America, despite plentiful game and numerous opportunities for both the rich and the poor to engage in the sport without any restrictions, there were a number of reasons why people were somewhat wary of hunting. Many were unwilling to brave a trip into the wilderness, which was viewed with terror because, both literally and figuratively, it was considered the devil's dwelling place. Furthermore, hunting could be dangerous, with people occasionally getting lost or having accidents, and there was the possibility of encountering unfriendly Indians, whom the Puritans regarded as "men transformed into beasts." As time passed the sport also declined somewhat as settlements grew, which resulted, unlike fishing, in a rapidly decreasing game population and thus poorer hunting.[13]

While sports may have met with disapproval from many Puritans, recreation did have a few allies. Like their English counterparts American inn owners used sporting activities to attract patrons, and common tavern recreation included shooting contests, boxing, wrestling, cockfighting, and bear baiting, all of which probably angered Puritans. Taverns were not the only place that colonists in New England could enjoy sports, however. Horseracing tracks, modeled on ones in the southern colonies, were built in Newport, Rhode Island. By the 1730s the tracks became increasingly sophisticated as professional, uniformed jockeys began to race on specially bred horses, sometimes up to a dozen times daily. Leading up to the American Revolution, ball sports, played primarily by soldiers and children, were not overly popular, but soldiers continued to bowl during the war, using cannonballs when the regular balls were unavailable. Finally, by the early 1780s, attitudes were slowly changing, and there was a growing trend toward the acceptance of all sports.[14]

This gradual acceptance owed a debt to forward-thinking colonists like Benjamin Franklin and Philadelphia physician Benjamin Rush, both of whom publicly advocated sports and the benefits derived from them. Franklin impressed admirers with his swimming abilities, and Rush wrote that horseback riding "is the most manly and useful species of exercise for gentlemen."[15] In addition, the printing of rulebooks and the creation of early clubs, such as the Shad & Salmon Club and other institutions offering athletic instruction, helped infuse sports with a modest amount of validity.[16]

While Puritans in the northern colonies managed successfully for the first hundred years to restrain sporting activities that they deemed

unfit, almost solely through contempt for those who participated in them, and to maintain a strict "industrious" ethic toward recreation and leisure, a different sporting philosophy evolved in the South. In the early seventeenth century, when colonists began arriving in Virginia and the Carolinas, a strict social hierarchy did not exist, but within a generation, a southern aristocracy began to emerge, modeled after England's ruling class. This meant not only a lifestyle of conspicuous consumption but also one that viewed leisure, regardless of its productive merits, as an important social activity. At the same time, puritanical beliefs began to erode among the southern ruling class as Anglican preachers, dependent upon those with wealth for support, tended to be more accepting of sports than their northern counterparts. Even southern legal courts, which recognized gambling debts as legitimate, did little to dissuade gamblers, who flocked to horse races, sometimes staking entire fortunes on one race. Meanwhile, in contrast to the views of the hardworking Puritans, labor in the South was considered a brutish, menial task, fit only for African slaves.[17]

Southerners enjoyed an assortment of sports. Attending horse races, which for the aristocracy helped solidify social standing, was a popular pastime, and cudgeling, a military sport in which competitors fought with long staffs, was bloody but widely practiced. Cockfighting, fox hunting, fishing, boating, wrestling, fencing, and bowling also were popular. In this stratified society, slaves held their own cockfights while poor whites organized horse races, cockfights, and bear baiting. For those on the less settled frontier, recreation took on some of the same forms as in New England with barn and house raisings accompanied by celebrations afterward. But when time permitted, log rolling, wrestling, boxing, and horse racing occurred.[18]

As sports slowly gained acceptance colonists arrived on the new continent with an old-world hunger for news. James Parker, the editor of the *New-York Gazette*, wrote in 1750 that newspapers were "an Amusement we can't be with out." However, the colonial press, which did not begin until 1690 in Boston, was responsible for more than entertainment. Early papers provided merchants and the general populace with shipping and other important commercial information as well as serving as a window to the outside world by providing news, albeit outdated, from Europe, other colonies, and other parts of the Americas. In addition, they kept colonists informed about births, deaths, and other local news.[19]

Sports stories in the colonial press, written with the sole intention of reporting an event, rarely appeared. However, there were occasional accounts, typically a paragraph or two in length, describing cockfights, cricket matches, horse races, or hunts.[20] A typical horse racing account, from the *Maryland Gazette* on May 14, 1752, reported tersely: "Yesterday the Prize of Forty Pounds, was run for on our Race Ground, by Col. *Tasker*'s Mare *Selyma*, and Capt. *Butler*'s Mare *Creeping Kate*; and won by the former." Then, there was a cricket match in the *Maryland Gazette* on August 1, 1754: "Saturday last the Cricket Match, between Eleven from Prince George's County and Eleven from Annapolis was play'd near Mr. Rawlings cool Spring, and Won by the former, the Difference being very few."[21]

For a sports event to merit reporting there typically had to be significant public interest, such as a long-awaited match of regional rivals whose outcome was socially relevant to many in a community.[22] For example, the *Virginia Gazette* wrote on March 23, 1755, that "a great cock match" took place at the courthouse in New Kent, pitting the roosters of three communities against one another with numerous wagers.[23] Sports also appeared in the papers if their practice led to a tragic or unusual result; accordingly hunting, fishing, swimming, and ice skating were reported.[24] Conversely, news of good hunting was sometimes noted, too. The *Boston Gazette* on November 15, 1733, published a short piece describing the successful hunt of a Newbury man who found "a great number of wild Geese, which being so fatigued and tired by a Storm, that they were not able to fly, he with a Club kill'd sixty of them, besides some which he shot."[25]

The most common mention of sports in the press were advertisements for such things as upcoming cockfights, cricket matches, bull baiting, horse races, shooting matches, and foot races, all of which became common in the colonies.[26] An example was an advertisement for a horse race in the *South Carolina Gazette* in March 1739: "On Tuesday the 2d Day of *April* next, will start at Mrs. *Sureau's*, two Horses, viz. *Ja Abercromby* Esq's Horse *Cherokee*, against *Wm. Walter* Esq's Colt call'd *Bright*, the first two Heats . . . to start exactly at four o'Clock. . . . Any Persons inclinable to bring their Horses to proof, may meet with Opportunity for any Sum not exceeding the [approved] Bett."[27]

Sports journalism grew and flourished in the early nineteenth century, when the Industrial Revolution resulted in changes that dramatically altered America's social, technological, and economic landscape. Those living in the colonies during the Revolutionary War had become painfully aware of their continuing dependence on English manufacturers when severe shortages of manufactured goods became common. In response to this and other factors a burgeoning manufacturing industry in New England sought to provide Americans with domestic alternatives. The rise of this industry, founded on the capitalist model, brought about dramatic changes, including urban migration, dissolution of the traditional guild system, and ultimately a growth in the amount of leisure time available to many Americans. The simultaneous increase in the urban population and more leisure time combined to create an urban sub-culture, which slowly began to embrace sporting activities.[28]

Another factor affecting sports at this time was the change in America's agricultural system. With the construction of canals and then railroads access to distant markets improved rapidly and America's agricultural system shifted from semi-subsistence to one centered on market production. The result was not only greater national wealth but also a more effective transportation system, both of which contributed to the growth of sports. With the aid of steamboats and then trains, journalists began traveling to distant sporting events, a practice that was unimaginable earlier.[29]

In addition, the invention of the telegraph in 1844 made rapid communication possible over long distances, which was an obvious advantage for correspondents relaying sports reports from distant corners of the country. This became increasingly important when national sporting journals, such as the *Spirit of the Times* in New York City, began to cover events from the horse-rich South and the far-scattered sites where championship boxing matches took place. Another important development was the steam-powered cylinder press, which speeded up newspaper production, making larger circulations possible. The result was an expanded newspaper readership in the United States and the creation of new audiences for sports journalists.[30]

However, technological and economic improvements were not the only factors contributing to the growing popularity of sports in the nineteenth century. It was obvious to many observers, both foreign and domestic, that Americans generally were not in good shape, and prominent foreign visitors to the United States, including Charles Dickens, noted the poor health that they found. Oliver Wendell Holmes Sr., the best-known physician of his time, agreed with Dickens. He lashed out in an 1858 *Atlantic Monthly* article that he was "satisfied that such a set of black-coated, stiff-jointed, soft-muscled, paste-complexioned youth as we can boast in our Atlantic cities never before sprang from the loins of Anglo-Saxon lineage."[31]

Reformers, alarmed by what they saw, set out to improve the country's health by constantly recommending exercise, self-control, fresh air, regular bathing, and vegetarianism to anyone who would listen. Reworking the principles that had once led Puritans to denounce sports as either unwholesome or a waste of time, they now began to imbue them with the old values of self-improvement, hard work, and godliness. The Muscular Christianity movement, which began in the 1850s with a handful of educators and physicians, along with other groups espousing athletic ideals, began to postulate that "reformed" sports, such as baseball, were vehicles for temperance, spiritual growth, and moral improvement. Thus, one's physical, mental, and moral health were related, and virtues such as self-reliance and self-improvement could not be supported by impure or unhealthy bodies. Mary Lyon, the founder of Mount Holyoke College, wrote that "those who enjoy bodily idleness sin. Exercise is part of the very constitution of man." As historian Elliott J. Gorn noted, "Taking charge of one's own physical condition became a prerequisite for a virtuous, self-reliant, spiritually-elevated life." Not only was athletic prowess a means to keep the mind and the spirit fresh, proponents claimed, but it was useful in the competitive business world and in the "unnatural" and ever-growing, American urban environment.[32]

Organized sports, which had been suspended temporarily during the Revolutionary War, quickly revived in the years following it with old favorites, such as bull and bear baiting and cockfighting, reemerging in the South and then in the North. Thoroughbred horse racing followed suit and during the early decades of the nineteenth century enjoyed increased popularity. Nothing could build more excitement or guarantee a big turnout than a match between regional thoroughbred rivals, and few matches received more acclaim than the "Great Match Race" of May 27, 1823, between the southern favorite, Sir Henry, and the northern champion, American Eclipse. The event, which drew about sixty thousand to Long Island's Union racetrack, had a paralyzing effect on the nation as business was halted on Wall Street and a recess was called in Congress. The *New York Evening Post* considered the race so important that it suspended publication of its May 27 edition so it could bring out the country's first sports extra.[33]

During the mid-1800s boxing matches, especially between American and British rivals, gained such popularity that the popular press felt compelled to report on them even while denouncing the sport's brutality. For example, *Harper's Weekly* called prize fighting "one of those exhibitions ever dear to degraded hearts." But the legendary April 17, 1860, bout in England between American John Heenan and Englishman Tom Sayers, which lasted forty-three rounds and ended in a draw, caused such a sensation that the *Spirit of the Times* printed 100,000 copies devoted to the fight, and *Frank Leslie's Illustrated Newspaper* outdid that by publishing 347,000.[34]

Boxing, although outlawed in many places and scorned by many in high society, remained a popular pastime, especially among the "fancy" as its urban fans were known, many of whom were young bachelors.[35] Its coverage in the press reflected the ambiguous relationship that the sport had with mainstream America as bouts were publicized only occasionally when they were of special interest. A few papers came out in support, such as the *National Intelligencer* in Washington DC, which promoted boxing in 1828 as a relatively safe alternative to dueling.

But support for the sport declined quickly in 1842 after Christopher Lilly killed Thomas McCoy in a bloody, 119-round match that lasted two hours and forty-one minutes near Hastings, New York. By the seventieth round McCoy's face was badly bruised and swollen, blood gushed from facial cuts onto his chest, and he was vomiting blood when he took deep breaths. Someone in the audience shouted, "For God's sake, save his life," but McCoy refused to quit. Then, in round 119, he walked out of his corner and fell dead. People were so outraged at what had occurred that eighteen of those involved with the fight were arrested (but not Lilly, who fled the country), and three were found guilty of fourth-degree manslaughter and were jailed for up to two years and fined up to $500.[36]

Newspapers also expressed widespread disgust. A writer for the *New-York Daily Tribune* labeled it a "murder" and lashed out in sensational fashion at the fifteen hundred spectators, whom he called "a festival of fiends":

> They were in raptures as the well-aimed, deadly blows descended heavily upon the face and neck of the doomed victim, transforming the image of God into a livid and loathsome ruin; *they* yelled with delight as the combatants went down— often on their heads—with a force that made the earth tremble around them—as the blood spirted [*sic*] in rills from the fated sacrifice, or as his conqueror came down heavily upon him and lay there to beat the breath out of him, until taken off by the seconds! They enlivened the shocking scene, as McCoy's eyes closed beneath the blows of his antagonist, with "Shutters up! There's a death in the family!", "Finish him, Chris!", "Knock

out his eye!" and &c., and still as the work of death went on rung out at intervals the infernal chorus, "2 to 1 on Lilly!" "100 even on McCoy!"[37]

As a result of McCoy's death, which was the first in an American boxing match, coverage of the sport by the press was largely suspended until the *Spirit of the Times* once again embraced it in the late 1840s.[38]

In addition to a flourishing of America's older sports, new ones, such as horse trotting, rowing, baseball, and yachting, were added to the country's sporting tradition. Rowing, a sport traditionally for sailors, made news in 1824 when a group of British mariners challenged New York's Whitehall Aquatic Club to a race. This caused a stir, and about fifty thousand New Yorkers watched from the banks of the North River (aka, the Hudson River) as the Americans prevailed. Then, in 1852, rowers from Harvard and Yale organized a regatta, which was America's first intercollegiate sporting event.[39] The popularity of yachting also began to grow at the same time, driven by the efforts of John C. Stevens, an American sailing pioneer. On June 30, 1844, aboard his boat in New York Harbor, nine yacht owners formed America's first yachting club and, in the next year, the New York Yacht Club held its first regatta. In the years that followed other clubs popped up, including the Southern Yachting Club in New Orleans (1849) and the Carolina Yacht Club (1853). In 1851 Stevens won the first America's Cup, proving to his English competitors that the "uncivilized" Americans were a force with which to be reckoned.[40]

A children's game, which was called "basteball," "roundball," "townball," and "goal ball," also gained in popularity with adults. Baseball, as it eventually came to be known, grew rapidly in the first decades of the nineteenth century and took on organized characteristics in the 1820s, but it was not until 1845 that a club team lasting more than a few years, the Knickerbockers, was established in New York City. In the 1850s dozens of similar fraternally minded clubs sprouted up, occasionally attracting crowds of more than a thousand to their games. The players, mostly respectable artisans and clerks, shunned the drunkenness and unruliness often associated with boxing and other blood sports, instead embracing the emerging values of health and self-restraint.[41]

The most popular of all antebellum sports, however, was harness racing, which was hailed as a democratic alternative to the exclusive and expensive tradition of thoroughbred racing. Also known as trotting, it increased rapidly as road conditions improved at the beginning of the nineteenth century, making racing feasible outside the established thoroughbred tracks. As it grew in popularity middle-class owners of trotting horses, or "roadsters" as they were called, realized that convenience, low costs, and the possibility of participating rather than watching helped make harness racing an appealing alternative to thoroughbreds. Except for the *Spirit of the Times*, however, the sport received little press coverage until the stock market crash of 1837, which brought about a decline in thoroughbred racing. In 1847 the *New York Herald* noted the changing landscape of horse racing: "While one specie of amusement has been going into decay, the other has risen to heights never before attained." By the 1850s more people were watching harness racing than any other American sport and seventy tracks had been built to accommodate the sport's increasing popularity.[42]

The lack of sports coverage in American newspapers created an opportunity for enterprising magazine editors as the interest in sports grew during the early decades of the nineteenth century. The first editor to see and exploit this was John Stuart Skinner, who in 1829 founded the *American Turf Register and Sporting Magazine*, which was the country's first publication with sporting coverage as its chief interest.[43]

Skinner was born on February 22, 1788, grew up on his family's large plantation in Maryland's prosperous Tidewater region, and as a youth learned many of the practical skills involved with plantation management, becoming particularly fascinated with early scientific efforts to increase agricultural productivity. After overseeing military spending in the War of 1812 he served as the postmaster of Baltimore.

His boyhood interest in farming remained strong, however, and when agricultural production in the state stagnated, he founded the *American Farmer* in 1819 to improve productivity.[44]

It was a successful enterprise, carving a niche in the emerging field of agricultural journalism and encouraging the founding of nearly a dozen similar publications. But the magazine was not devoted entirely to agricultural pursuits; on many occasions it featured small segments dedicated to "field sports," called "The Sporting Olio." Skinner frequently used this to discuss, offer advice, and report on horse racing and hunting, which were among the most popular sports of the time. Perhaps expecting reader opposition, he explained, "There is a decided and growing taste for such amusements," which provide "healthful diversions that necessarily conduct gentlemen from the bar-room and the gaming-table into the open air. It is, however, as we trust, well understood, that we would not inculcate a fondness for rural sports, to an extent that would involve the neglect of any man's cardinal duties."[45]

Skinner's interest in sports continued to grow, and in 1829 he sold the *American Farmer* and embarked on a new journalistic venture, the *American Turf Register and Sporting Magazine*, a weekly journal devoted primarily to purebred horse racing. In its first issue he explained that he would not only cover horse racing but report on "various rural sports, as RACING, TROTTING MATCHES, SHOOTING, HUNTING & FISHING." And in contrast to the long-held and widely accepted tradition of reproducing English news he said his journal would have "an original American cast."[46] He wanted to run locally written stories that would reinforce American cultural identities.[47]

One of his major reasons for founding the *American Turf Register and Sporting Magazine* was neither literary nor financial: he hoped to repeat his success with the *American Farmer* by providing horse owners and racing fans with systematic information that was lacking in the sport. This included precise records of weights and race times as well as betting standards and bloodline documentation. Few horse owners or breeders kept accurate lineage documentation, so Skinner's encouragement of this dramatically increased the value of many horses.

Besides wanting to remedy the records problem he had other reasons for choosing horseracing as his principal subject. While his intended audience, the land-owning gentry in the South and the urban rich in the North, still harbored social reservations about many sports, thoroughbred racing was the closest thing to a national sport in the United States. In both the North and the South, racetracks attracted large audiences, and wealthy southerners invested large amounts of money in its pursuit. Thus, he had a ready-made, highly interested audience.[48]

The first issue of the *Turf Register*, a "neatly-printed pamphlet," had fifty pages and was bound with an "ornamental" cover that featured engraved animals. Although it cost a rather pricey five dollars annually, its readership grew and included President Andrew Jackson. In addition to thoroughbred racing, it continued covering the same rural sports, such as fishing, hunting, and shooting, that had been in the *American Farmer*.[49]

In August 1835 the restless Skinner sold the *Turf Register* for $10,000 and focused his attention on publishing foreign books. The magazine changed owners twice before being bought by an up-and-coming New York sports editor, William T. Porter, who would leave his mark on early American sports journalism. Meanwhile, Skinner was replaced as Baltimore's postmaster in 1837 when Martin Van Buren assumed the presidency and in the following year he received an even heavier blow when he lost most of his savings in a fraudulent land deal, forcing him to survive for a while by writing articles for the *American Farmer* and editing agricultural-related publications. But his fortunes revived; he was third-assistant postmaster general of the U.S. from 1841 to 1845, and in 1848 he launched the *Plough, the Loom and the Anvil*, a monthly journal promoting home industries and agriculture. The *Plough*, however, was his last success. In the spring of 1851 Skinner died from a fall.[50]

While the *American Turf Register and Sporting Magazine* never had the large readership or influence enjoyed by its journalistic successor, the *Spirit of the Times*, it played an important role in sports journalism by paving the way for others. This was due largely to Skinner's pioneering spirit, ingenuity, and desire to improve and promote the sports that he enjoyed.[51]

Carrying on Skinner's groundbreaking work was Porter, the founder of the *Spirit of the Times* and arguably sport's greatest promoter in the first half of the nineteenth century. His editorial genius was matched only by his notoriously poor business sense, which eventually forced him to relinquish ownership of the *Spirit* in 1843. However, his sporting knowledge and editorial abilities were so valuable that the new owner, Englishman John Richards, kept him on as editor until he abruptly quit in the summer of 1856. He then teamed up with fellow editor George Wilkes and founded *Porter's Spirit of the Times*, which they co-owned until Porter's death in 1858.[52]

Like Skinner, Porter was born in rural America and grew up on his family's estate. Born in 1809, he was nine when his father died, leaving his mother in charge of the family, which she moved to Hanover, New Hampshire. He enrolled in Moore's Indian Charity School, but he disliked it despite his obvious academic abilities and instead spent the next nine years as an apprentice to a printer in Andover, Massachusetts, eventually earning journeyman status. In 1830, ready for a change, he quit his job as an editor at the *Farmer's Herald* in St. Johnsbury, Vermont, and traveled to New York City, likely seeking a metropolitan escape from the provincial world of his youth. He became a press shop foreman, but his ambition soon led him to found a sporting journal, the *Spirit of the Times*. With the help of James Howe, another youthful printer, and Horace Greeley, who set type, the first issue was published on December 10, 1831.[53]

Conveniently ignoring the *Turf Register,* Porter argued in the journal's prospectus that his sporting journal was dedicated to "a field unoccupied by others, and one which is deemed important to be filled." The *Spirit*, he said, would provide "SCENES OF REAL LIFE" as well as coverage of "SPORTS OF THE TURF, the RING, the PIT, of the FISHER and the FOWLER." He also extolled sports and their healthy, redeeming values, finding them to be a beneficial antidote for "the care-worn and sedentary citizen" because they allowed him "to strengthen his body by periodical healthful exercise." To stir interest in this, he pointed to the example set by the Romans, who had exhibited a "firmness of nerve and sinew" that was lacked by their contemporaries, the "palsied artisan and the pale manufacturer." Thus, "[m]anly exercises [will] confer the luxury of health upon the individual." As for the *Spirit*, he said the journal's purpose was not to serve merely as food for the "literary gourmand" but it "should be assisting in the great work of building up the physical frame for the Republic."[54]

The physical appearance of the *Spirit*, however, paled beside Porter's high-blown idealism. According to Greeley, the first issue, which was printed in a tiny attic press shop, was "a moderate sized sheet of indifferent paper, with an atrocious wood-cut for the head—about as uncomely a specimen of the 'fine arts' as our 'native talent' has produced." The contents of the four-page journal, which was consciously modeled on a respected London journal, *Bell's Life*, was mostly like "the average paper of 1830 . . . made up of a jumble of market and ship-movement items, [and] 'Foreign Intelligence' paragraphs lifted from European journals," according to historian Norris Yates. Only the last page, which was dedicated to sports, differentiated the paper from its contemporaries. Early sporting articles dealt primarily with hunting and horseracing, including random stories about "horse breaking, game laws, and coon hunts," noted Yates.[55]

Despite its humble origins the *Spirit* grew quickly, amassing an estimated readership of three to six thousand within a year. Considering New York's highly competitive journalistic market, which already supported thirty-one weekly newspapers and eleven semi-weeklies, this was no small feat. However, success was short-lived. A cholera outbreak in 1832 struck a deadly blow to the city and undoubtedly lowered both the journal's circulation numbers and Porter's income. This led Howe to quit in the summer of that year and Greeley followed him in September. Porter was then forced to sell the journal and spent the next two years editing the *New-Yorker* and the *Constellation* before buying back the *Spirit*, possibly with the help of several partners, in 1835.[56]

Porter's years on the *New-Yorker* and the *Constellation* were invaluable because they provided him with important business contacts. These contacts, along with future ones that he cultivated in popular horse racing regions in the South and the West, were essential to the success of the *Spirit*. National correspondents were necessary if he wanted to move beyond the confines of New York's sporting scene to provide accounts of great southern horse tracks and far-flung hunting expeditions, all of which his readers wanted. Improvements in transportation and communication, especially the telegraph in 1844, made it possible for the *Spirit* to provide coverage on a scale unimaginable by the *Turf Register*. In 1837 he proudly described the extent of his network of correspondents, although he undoubtedly embellished the truth: "From Maine to Florida, from the St. Lawrence to the Missouri, a thousand gifted pens are employed in imparting novelty and interest in our columns."[57]

Making contacts was not difficult for Porter, who was noted for his amiability and charm. A friend of his recalled that his "personal popularity and genial magnetism exceeded that of any man I ever knew." Standing six feet, four inches tall, which earned him the familiar nickname of "Tall son of York," and having snobbish tastes and dressing like a dandy "in all the luxury of white kids [gloves] and diamond studs," he was remembered by Greeley as "kind to those younger and less favored than himself, and a capital workman."[58]

During the 1830s Porter's fame as a sporting authority grew. Fans sought his opinion not only on thoroughbred matters, for which he was most well-known, but on everything from "catching a trout with a fly and shooting a canvas-back [duck] on the Delaware, to the capture of Buffalo on the prairies," according to historian Frederic Hudson. When he purchased and assumed editorial responsibility of the *Turf Register* in 1839, his reputation as America's foremost sports authority was cemented.[59]

The *Spirit*, however, was not for everyone at first. In 1837, Porter announced his journal was designed to "promote the views and interests of but an infinitesimal division of those classes of society composing the great mass." However, an economic panic that year and the following depression not only damaged the financial prospects of his hard-sought elite audience but also seriously harmed the health of thoroughbred racing. The large amount of cash necessary to breed and race horses, to maintain large stables, and to place bets was no longer available, and the sport's popularity sagged. Forced to find paying readers beyond "the very Corinthian columns of the community," he diversified sport coverage in his journal and increased the amount of backwoods humor, a move clearly intended to court middle-class readers.[60]

In 1839, hoping for more readers, Porter hired Henry William Herbert, a vain and aristocratic Englishman, to write a series of hunting pieces for his newly acquired *Turf Register*. Raised in England's upper society, Herbert wrote poetry while hoping to become famous for historical romances, but because his career had not yet met his expectations and he needed money he accepted the offer. With his literary talents meshing well with the work that he hesitantly accepted, he became the first sportswriter to attain national fame. Using the pen name of Frank Forester, his first series, "A Week in the Woodlands," has been described by one historian as a "watershed in American sports coverage."[61] In the opening story he described an upstate New York landscape in his typically ornate style: "The country became undulating with many and bright streams of water; the hill sides clothed with luxuriant woodlands, now in their many colored garb of autumn beauty; the meadow-land rich in unchanged fresh greenery—for the summer had been mild and rainy—with here and there a buck-wheat stubble showing its ruddy face, replete with a promise of quail."[62]

However, Herbert's national success and the diversified coverage were not enough to offset the consequences of Porter's calamitous business dealings. In 1839, in the middle of a deep, five-year economic depression, he raised the annual price of the *Spirit of the Times* to ten dollars, effectively limiting sales to all but its wealthiest readers. In addition, his purchase of the *Turf Register* and the decision to simultaneously edit both journals spread his time and money precariously thin. He fell $40,000 in debt, forcing him in 1842 to sell the *Spirit of the Times* and content himself with the exclusive role of editor.[63]

The change in ownership did little to hurt the *Spirit*'s popularity, and by the end of the 1840s, the journal had a circulation of a hundred thousand, making it the second most popular journal in the country. It seemed to be everywhere. Copies reached the Californian goldfields, the bayous and swamps of Louisiana and Florida, and even London, where the *Spirit* had a sales agent. Porter must have been pleased to learn that the London papers, which he had consciously emulated, had begun reprinting material from his journal. Meanwhile, the *Spirit*'s readership had become as diverse as its distribution. Gamblers, horsemen, horse breeders, boxers, ball players, bartenders, farmers, college students, army officers, and congressmen were attracted to the masculine sports coverage and read the journal avidly.[64]

Porter continued to edit the *Spirit* until 1856 with coverage remaining diverse as boxing and other lesser-known sports, such as foot racing, rowing, baseball, card-playing, and yachting, were added to the old standards of hunting and horseracing. His one memorable failure of the 1850s was his attempt to promote cricket and raise it to the status of a national pastime, a role that baseball was beginning to assume. This, however, did not prove a serious problem because he soon began promoting baseball. The *Spirit* was the first publication to publish the rules of the game, the first picture from a game, the first box scores, and the first personality profiles, which he referred to as "dope stories." He also is credited with being the first person to refer to baseball as the national game.[65]

In 1856 Porter left the *Spirit*, possibly because of the deaths of his brothers, gout, drinking, or simply a lack of interest. Whatever the reason, he and Wilkes, the founder of the *Police Gazette*, established *Porter's Spirit of the Times* with Porter handling the editorial duties while Wilkes occupied himself with the journal's business aspects. According to the paper, its circulation leapt to forty thousand by the eighth edition. However, Porter's health was declining, and by 1858 his only contribution was an occasional article, which frequently was an obituary of old friends, including Herbert. On July 19, he died at age forty-eight and left the journal to his partner, who changed its name to *Wilkes' Spirit of the Times* in the following year.[66]

Twenty-five years earlier, on September 3, 1833, Benjamin Day, a New Englander who had come to New York City four years before and had worked as a printer, began publishing a new paper, the *Sun*. He is credited with starting what became known as the penny press era, which signaled the beginning of an irrevocable shift in American newspapers. Writing for the masses in a paper that sold for a penny and producing stories that fed popular and sensationalistic interests, he quickly attracted new, middle-class readers rather than wealthier citizens, who historically had been the primary consumers of American newspapers.[67]

Newspapers of the day never covered sports with the same regularity of the sports journals, such as the *Spirit* and the *Turf Register*; none of them had a sports column or a daily sports page, and their sports coverage remained erratic before the Civil War. But their sports content was subtly changing. Previously, what little they had carried about sports in newspapers had come largely from British sporting periodicals, but by the end of the 1830s they were producing most of their own stories. Sports articles in the penny press began early in the decade when the *Sun* and the *Transcript* in New York, along with the *Public Ledger* in Philadelphia, began to cover prizefights and horse races, and this spread to other papers, including the *New York Tribune* and the *New York Herald*. Through these papers, the reading public became acquainted not only with the heroes and villains of boxing but also with the deeds of rower James Lee and famous foot-racing champions such as "Jackson" and "Deerfoot."[68]

Of all of the penny press editors none did more for sports than Scottish-born James Gordon Bennett Sr., the founder and editor of the *New York Herald*, who came closer than anyone else to equaling the "encouragement and promotion" of Porter and Skinner. Known for his competitiveness, he built the paper's readership with controversial, sensationalistic coverage, noting in the second issue of his paper that he would not shy away from reporting when "human nature and real life display their freaks and vagaries." Therefore, it was not surprising that he was willing to cover sports, especially boxing, even if they were looked down upon or deemed unworthy of publication by others. In addition to meeting his sensationalistic standards sports coverage was profitable, which made it particularly attractive. When Heenan fought Sayers in 1860, the *Herald*'s presses ran for four days to provide an enthusiastic public with news of the match.[69] Sales on this scale unquestionably netted him a decent profit.

Bennett's competitive nature proved a valuable asset for the *Herald* in other ways, too. Determined to scoop his competitors, he demonstrated a continual willingness to adopt and embrace the newest and fastest means to report on sports. For example, the paper quickened the reporting process by frequently sending out "Uncle Joe" Elliott, the delivery room superintendent, to cover local sports events. Seated at either ringside or trackside, he would dictate his story to a stenographer, who transcribed it before delivering it to a copyreader for final revisions. During the 1840s, as the *Herald*'s sports coverage grew to include horse races, yacht races, baseball games, and boxing matches, the need to report quickly on distant events became even more important. Bennett improved and sped up his news delivery system by using horseback riders and the newly invented telegraph, which quickly spread east of the Mississippi River in the 1840s and 1850s.[70]

Bennett enjoyed horse racing and was a regular proponent of it in his paper, feeling the sport was an expedient means to both test and improve breeds. Thus, in 1845, he sent eight reporters to cover the eagerly awaited race between Fashion and Peytona, which pitted the respective thoroughbred champions from the North and the South. The *Herald* printed four "extras," and the front page was covered with a lengthy description of the race.[71] The report began by explaining that the event's excitement was partly "because the contest was between the North and the South for the dominion of the turf," and it noted "the vast sums of money pending on the race" were "quite proportionate" to the event. That was followed by a description of the large, diverse crowd, which flowed in all morning from New York City to the Union Course racetrack on Long Island: "Here was the magnificent barouche [horse drawn carriage] of the millionaire, full of gay, laughing, dark-eyed demoiselles, jammed in between a Bowery stage and a Broadway hack—there were loafers and dandies, on horseback and on foot—sporting gentlemen in green coats and metal buttons—Southerners from Louisiana, Mississippi and Alabama with anxious faces, but hearts full of hope."[72]

After describing the heavy drinking, eating, and the "loungers, rowdies, gamblers, and twenty other species of the genus loose fish" loitering outside the track, the end of the first heat was reported dramatically: "Round the bottom they kept well together, but owing to dust, &c, there was no seeing further, until they had reached the draw-gate towards home, where Fashion appeared to have the lead, but it was immediately taken from her and Peytona came home two lengths in front, making the first heat in 7 m. 39 s., amid the most unbounded cheers."[73] When Peytona, the southern champion, also won the second heat, "The southerners appeared perfectly besides themselves with joy and afforded a striking contrast to the northerners, whose lengthened faces were indicative of the shortening their purses and fame had undergone within the last few minutes."[74]

The innovative Bennett employed "pony express" riders in 1847 to rush news of the Yankee Sullivan-Ben Caunt boxing match to New York City from Harpers Ferry in western Virginia. Then, to report on the 1849 championship bout between Tom Hyer and Sullivan in Maryland, Elliott used the telegraph. His report, steeped in bloody details of the fight, marked the first time that the new technology was used to report a prizefight. Later, Bennett dispatched boats to New York Harbor to intercept the first English ship in order to obtain news about the much-anticipated London bout between Heenan and Sayers. Reports of the fight received as much space as the upcoming presidential conventions.[75]

Bennett's successful boxing coverage compelled numerous penny press editors to follow his lead despite expressing a dislike of the sport in their papers. Even the chaste *New-York Daily Tribune*, edited by Greeley, covered important boxing matches, although not without critical comments. The Heenan-Sayers fight, he wrote, was entertainment worthy of "grog shops and the brothels and the low gaming hells," but he devoted six columns to it. Similarly, Henry Raymond, the editor of the *New York Times*, wrote it was "inexplicable, deplorable, [and] humiliating that an exhibition such as the contest between John Morrissey and Sullivan could have occurred." Like, Greeley, though, Raymond was not blind to the popularity of racing and boxing and covered them in the *Times*.[76]

Thus, Bennett's popular sports coverage not only spurred on sportswriting in the penny press but also helped make the use of new technology, such as the telegraph, a standard means of covering it. He showed sports could be successful front-page news, holding its own with political stories of the day, and by reporting on it in the *Herald* he helped introduce sports coverage to an audience not entirely composed of sporting fans.

That set the stage for an explosion of sports coverage in the American press, which commenced in 1857 when the *New York Clipper* hired Henry Chadwick as the country's first full-time sportswriter.[77] Sports and the media were now firmly locked together for all time in a dance that translated into big circulation gains.

***

While the rise of sports journalism would not have been possible without the large-scale transformations that reshaped America and American society in the early nineteenth century, the work of early sporting editors and writers helped bring about those changes. Feeling America's pulse and sensing that athletics was becoming more important, they delivered into the homes of thousands, both fans and nonfans, the drama of bloody boxing matches, the contagious excitement of champion thoroughbreds racing neck to neck, and the mounting achievements of America's first baseball teams. By pioneering the field of sports journalism in 1829 Skinner and those who followed him succeeded in transforming what began as a simple, artless task into a much more polished craft ready for national consumption.

Sports Journalism Blossoms

2

In the matter of turf and sporting news the World is without equal in daily journalism. It is the authority.

—*New York World* (1883)

On an afternoon in the fall of 1856 *New York Times* reporter Henry Chadwick was leaving a cricket match in West Hoboken, New Jersey, when he noticed two New York City teams, the Eagles and Gotham clubs, playing baseball. Impressed by the close game and the skill of the players, he found himself watching it with more interest than any baseball game that he had seen.[1] Twelve years later he recalled the moment as an epiphany:

> It was not long before I was struck with the idea that base ball [*sic*] was just the game for a national sport for Americans, and . . . it occurred to me, on my return home, that from this game of ball a powerful lever might be made by which our people could be lifted into a position of more devotion to physical exercise and healthful out-door recreation than they had hitherto . . . been noted for. At that period . . . I need not state that out-door recreation was comparatively unknown to the large mass of the American people. In fact . . . we were the regular target for the shafts of raillery and even abuse from our outdoor sport-loving cousins of England, in consequence of our national neglect of sports and pastimes, and our too great devotion to business and the "Almighty Dollar." But thanks to Base Ball . . . we have been transformed into quite another people.[2]

Sometimes, a chance event, seemingly unimportant, changes history dramatically, and that was true of the baseball game that the thirty-two-year-old Chadwick happened upon in 1856. While previously he had found the sport "juvenile and uninspiring," he suddenly was fascinated by the game's speed and ruggedness, biographer Andrew Schiff noted, and felt it was ideally "suited to the American temperament."[3] This led to Chadwick becoming a leading, lifelong champion of baseball and, as the country's first full-time sportswriter in 1857, he was in the forefront of taking sports journalism into a new era that stretched into the twentieth century. Toward the end of his life, President Theodore Roosevelt invited him to the White House to recognize his accomplishments and fittingly called him "The Father of Base Ball."[4]

From the mid-1850s until the end of World War I in 1918—as baseball flourished with Chadwick's help to become the country's first national game and college football also began gaining momentum—readers thirsted for more and more sports news, particularly in large cities, causing publishers to expand their coverage significantly. The country was well on its way to becoming sports crazy, and newspapers and magazines eagerly took advantage of this national trend.

**

Born in England, Chadwick immigrated to Brooklyn with his family in 1837 when he was almost thirteen years old and grew up playing cricket, billiards, and chess along with enjoying fishing, bird hunting, ice skating, and sledding. Meanwhile, his father, James Chadwick, feeling a knowledge of science was important, taught him astronomy, biology, botany, physiology, and physics. This education turned out to be extremely beneficial later when Henry wrote a number of articles about the scientific side of baseball, including one about the physics of the curve ball for *Scientific American*. After beginning work at sixteen as an assistant librarian, he followed in his father's footsteps two years later and began teaching piano, which he continued doing for years. But it was not his real passion. That emerged in 1843 when, despite his father's reservations for reasons that are unclear, he began writing news articles, including several on cricket, for the *Long-Island Star* in his hometown. That was followed over the years by working for the *Brooklyn Daily Eagle*, the *Brooklyn City News*, the *Times*, the *New York Herald*, the *Sun*, the *New York World*, and the *New York Daily Tribune*, and becoming more and more a part of the city's sporting community.[5]

On that day in 1856, when Chadwick stopped to watch the baseball game in West Hoboken, everything was aligned to have a historic effect on the game of baseball and the business of sports journalism; unlike in the past, conditions now were suitable in the United States for an enormous growth in sports. The Industrial Revolution had a huge impact by more clearly creating two distinct parts of a worker's life: labor time and leisure time. It also resulted in many middle-class people working in cramped offices, where they were vulnerable to disease and sickness, and being in jobs that did not promote exercise and physical activity. All of this not only cultivated an audience that was interested in sports but also encouraged people to play them. Chadwick, who was an outspoken advocate of health and exercise, wrote about the importance of a physically fit worker in 1867 in the *Ball Player's Chronicle*: "To business men we would say, that experience has proved conclusively that better work and more of it is to be got out of employees who are allowed time to recuperate their physical powers by recreation than the most slave-worked laborer can yield." He also championed baseball as "a remedy for the many evils resulting from the immoral associations [that] boys and young men of our cities are apt to become connected with."[6]

To Chadwick, baseball seemed to have the qualities to quickly become more popular than cricket, which was a major sport in England, because it was faster. "Americans do not care to dawdle over a sleep-inspiring game all through the heat of a June or July day," he proclaimed. "What they do, they want to do in a hurry. In baseball, all is lightning; every action is swift as a seabird's flight." But while baseball needed publicity in order to grow, his paper, the *New York Times*, ordered him to keep stories to the "smallest possible limit." A typical article appeared on July 10, 1856: "On Tuesday a match of

Base Ball was played between the first nine members of the 'Gotham' and nine members of the 'Baltic' Clubs, at their ground at the Red House [in Harlem]. Play commenced at 4 o'clock and ended at 5, the 'Gothams' beating easily, the 'Baltics' making but two aces."

Such stories, which were nothing more than summaries, disappointed Chadwick, who wanted to write far more about baseball because he felt the sport was important for the country, but his frustration did not last long. In 1857, he was named the baseball and cricket editor at the *New York Clipper*, a popular weekly entertainment journal, and he covered baseball for it until 1888. According to Schiff, the new, expanded exposure of baseball in the *Clipper* was beneficial because it "not only fed an audience that already was interested in sports and games, but also helped to create a following for baseball by exposing it to a new audience." And, because the journal was distributed nationally, the "new audience" was not just in New York City. Chadwick felt all of this boded well for the sport: more positive coverage would result in the game becoming better known, which would cause other metropolitan papers to increase their coverage of it, thus upping interest in the readers.[7]

Until his death in 1908 Chadwick was the leading baseball writer in the United States, doing all of his writing by hand for a number of years even after typewriters became available in the late 1860s, and his success led to many others being hired as newspaper baseball writers as the game's popularity escalated rapidly. In promoting the sport he felt from the beginning that emphasizing its social aspects would increase its popularity. For example, after an 1858 game between the Brooklyn Excelsiors and the Eagle Club of Manhattan, he wrote in the *Clipper* about the "tremendous cheering by the two parties . . . in a congratulating and jovial spirit, which invariably indicates the gentleman and gives evidence [that] our friends of the base-ball fraternity are possessors of [a] noble and generous disposition, and know as well how to bear defeat, as how to wear the laurels of victory." After the game, he noted the teams had dinner together.[8]

Chadwick's success with promoting baseball was not just because of his expanded newspaper coverage, however. More than probably any sportswriter in any sport in U.S. history, he played a major role in shaping the rules of the game, which he felt were "crude and hastily prepared" before he became interested in standardizing them. For example, he quickly became a member of the rules committee of the newly formed National Association of Base Ball Players, and then in 1860 he spread news about baseball far beyond the New York City area with the publication of baseball's first guide, *Beadle's Dime Base-Ball Player*. The annual digest for baseball fans included: lists of teams in the area; the game's rules, which he said were "appropriate to introduce" because there was no general agreement about them; the sport's equipment and how to make it; descriptions of each position defensively and how to hit the ball most effectively; and the history of the game. The latter was compiled solely by Chadwick, who had no sources to cite or people to challenge his interpretation because he was baseball's first historian.[9]

A year later the second annual *Beadle's Dime Base-Ball Player* was one of the most influential publications in the sport's history because Chadwick created a way to keep a game's statistics (now known as a box score) in a scorebook. For example, each of the players was given a number, some of which are still used today (such as 7, 8, and 9 for left field, center field, and right field respectively), and letters of the alphabet corresponded to what a batter did (such as K, HR, and F for strikeout, home run, and fly ball respectively). While the system was somewhat different, and more complicated, than the way games are recorded statistically now, it gave fans a shorthand way to keep track of what happened, which Chadwick considered a necessity if baseball was to become America's national pastime. "In order to obtain an accurate estimate of a player's skill, an analysis, both of his play at the bat and in the field, should be made, inclusive of the way in which he was put out," he wrote. Then, in his 1869 annual guide, he provided a simplified version of his scoring system, which was more similar to what is used now. Among the most significant statistics that he created, which are still at the heart of the game, were a pitcher's earned run average and batting averages. He was particularly proud of the leading role he played in the creation of these statistics and his method of scorekeeping, as well as helping to codify the rules; this turned baseball in his view from a "simple field exercise" in the 1840s into a "manly, scientific game" in the 1860s.[10]

Besides statistics Chadwick was especially interested in ridding baseball of what he called "evil influences." He expected the players to be fair and gentlemanly—in 1860, for example, he suggested players should be fined for swearing and complaining about umpires' calls—and he continually spoke out against gambling, inebriation, and rowdiness. "The two great obstacles in the way of the success of the majority of professional ball players are wine and women," he proclaimed in 1889. "The saloon and brothel are the evils of the base ball world at the present day." He also advocated crowd control to keep unruly fans in line. Writing about Chadwick's death in 1908, a newspaper noted he probably did not like the fact that at the last game he attended at Brooklyn's Washington Park "many in the field stands jumped the fences and rushed out and seated themselves on the grass a few yards behind the base lines."[11]

Chadwick sometimes became part of the game that he was constantly trying to improve and promote. In his early years as a baseball writer he occasionally umpired games that he was covering, and umpires sometimes stopped a game and had him come out of the stands to make a rules interpretation. In his defense, however, there was no national ethical code for newspapers until one was adopted by the American Society of Newspaper Editors in 1923. And there is no evidence that his contemporaries ever questioned his ethics. Two years after Chadwick's death Christy Mathewson, one of the game's all-time great pitchers, dedicated a book to him: "To the memory of Henry Chadwick, the 'Father of Baseball,' whose life was centered in the sport, and who, by his rugged honesty and his relentless opposition to everything that savored dishonesty and commercialism in connection with the game, is entitled to the credit, more than any other, of the high standing and unsullied reputation which the sport enjoys today." In 1938 his contributions to baseball were recognized when he was elected to the Baseball Hall of Fame.[12]

While Chadwick played a major role in newspapers increasingly hiring sportswriters, he was not the only reason that this occurred. Another impetus came from baseball. The Cincinnati Red Stockings became the first professional team in 1869, and two years later the National Association of Professional Base Ball Players was formed with nine teams stretching from the East Coast to as far west as Rockford, Illinois. The National Association lasted through the 1875 season, and then the National League began in 1876 with eight teams and was followed by the American Association in 1882 with six teams.[13] The two leagues had several striking differences. The American Association appealed to working-class audiences by charging 25 cents admission—compared to 50 cents in the National League, which was considered more of a game for the middle class—and by selling alcohol and playing Sunday games, neither of which the older league did at first.[14]

But whatever the social class professional baseball quickly became the national pastime because it united local residents, historian Steven Riess wrote.

> Fans became part of a community of like-minded spectators who rooted for the local club in a collective demonstration of hometown pride and boosterism. Baseball competition became a metaphor for interurban rivalries, and a victory over other towns in the league symbolized the superiority of your city. The presence of a person at a ball game, particularly on Opening Day, became a means of publicly displaying civic-mindedness. . . . Since players on professional teams were mercenaries recruited from out-of-town, the local pride exhibited in sports teams was hardly rational: a victory by the Braves over the Giants did not prove Boston's superiority over New York. . . . Nevertheless, journalists believed that if a city deficient in self-pride developed positive spirit because of baseball, then localism was good and proper.[15]

With this urban pride, which led to more attendance at baseball games, it was no surprise that newspapers began creating sports sections and hiring more sportswriters; printing the news that readers wanted meant higher circulations and bigger profits. Furthermore, the public wanted to be entertained, and papers—realizing by the 1880s that they were competing with vaudeville shows, nickelodeons, and sports events for people's entertainment dollars—found colorfully written sports stories to be essential. They frequently had a tinge of the sensational that kept readers coming back day after day.[16]

Into this atmosphere strode Joseph Pulitzer. After turning the *St. Louis Post-Dispatch* into one of the top newspapers in the Midwest, he bought New York's faltering daily, the *World,* in May 1883 and in the first month created the country's first newspaper sports department. He named H. G. Crickmore, who was an expert on horse racing, as the sports editor. The paper boasted in an editorial: "In the matter of turf and sporting news the *World* is without equal in daily journalism. It is the authority." Vigorously pushing sports coverage was a shrewd move by Pulitzer. He was publishing a paper for the masses—it cost only two cents a day—and he made no apologies for covering events that would keep them interested rather than solely printing what was important. For example, an editorial noted that seven thousand spectators had showed up for a championship boxing match at Madison Square Garden three days after the presidential election of 1884. It said this "demonstrates how easy it is to shift the popular mind from politics to fisticuffing. The people have had enough of the disturbance about the Presidency. They long for entertainment that is substantial and edifying. Let the games of the arena proceed. The Republic has been saved."[17]

While Pulitzer felt baseball and boxing were the two sports with the most appeal for the masses, that was not all that the *World* covered. He told his editors that he wanted "the foremost expert" writing regularly on every sport, including in the main Sunday paper, whether it was about fishing, golf, cycling, or rowing. And in doing so the stories sometimes were at the top of the front page instead of inside the paper, further emphasizing the importance that Pulitzer placed on sports coverage. That was abundantly clear in April and May of 1894, when two noted Irish-Americans competed in a local marathon walking race with the winner covering 610 miles on a track in six days. For eight consecutive days, this was the lead story on the front page of the *World*, and it was accompanied by thirty-two illustrations. That was the most coverage of any event during the paper's first three years, including the final days of the 1884 presidential race. The prominence of sports coverage, along with a number of other significant changes, quickly made the *World* one of the two leading newspapers in New York City as it rose from 15,000 circulation when Pulitzer bought it in 1883 to almost 1.5 million in 1898.[18]

But even though Pulitzer stressed sports coverage, he was not equally enthusiastic about all sports, no matter how much they were growing in popularity. One of those was college football, which had begun in 1869 when Princeton played Rutgers. He viewed it as a game of college elites, who were far different from his typical working-class readers, many of whom lived in tenements. Furthermore, he felt football encouraged young men to act like "hooligans." In an 1884 editorial the *World* wrote contemptuously: "The young Apaches of Yale and Princeton can come together in gangs, pit themselves against each other in phalanxes, fight, kick, punch, gouge, bite, scratch and macerate in one wild and riotous rough-and-tumble until they are covered in blood, and this will pass muster under the eyes of sensitive women and discriminating men as an unexceptional outdoor sport." As a result, the paper at first played down games, even if they were important. For example, Yale and Harvard played for the 1883 national championship near New York City before a crowd of eight thousand, and the story was buried on page 5.[19]

But other papers were not so reticent about football, and, as they wrote about it, the crowds at games grew and more colleges started playing it. Part of the reason for the increasing coverage was the fact that most of the important games were on Saturdays. Because it was normally a slow news day and many newspapers were expanding their

Sunday editions in the latter part of the 1800s, papers were looking for copy and football easily provided it.[20] As historian Michael Oriard noted:

> By the mid-1890s, both the quantity and the quality of the football coverage in the daily papers in New York, Philadelphia, and Boston were staggering: front-page, full-page, several-page accounts of the big games, accompanied by sometimes dozens of often sensationalistic illustrations. The development of college football from a campus matter to a public event was paralleled by the development of football coverage in the daily press from paragraph-length notes to multipaged features drawing on the full range of the papers' personnel and resources. It is easy in this case to identify cause and effect. The daily press in New York had an impact on college football in the 1880s and 1890s greater than television's effect on professional football in the 1950s and 1960s. It has long been a truism that television assured the survival of the upstart American Football League and raised the popularity of the professional sport to a level that rivaled baseball's. The late nineteenth-century daily newspaper "created" college football to an even greater degree, transforming an extracurricular activity into a national spectacle.[21]

Just as newspapers were increasingly covering sports toward the end of the eighteenth century so were magazines, the number of which exploded in the 1800s. From fewer than a hundred in 1825, there were about six hundred in 1850, seven hundred in 1865, twelve hundred five years later, twenty-four hundred by 1880, and thirty-three hundred in 1885.[22] This growth, which was not matched in any other country at this time, was the result of several factors: technological improvements in printing, including higher speed presses and linotype machines, which lowered production costs; a more educated audience, which liked to read; and an increase in the number of libraries.

With this growth in publications came specialization, as it seemed there was a magazine for every subject, including specific sports. For example, riding bicycles, which were called velocipedes until 1869, became a fad in 1868 and led to the first magazine for its adherents a year later. In 1876, realizing that a market existed for bicycles not only for travel and exercise but for racing, manufacturers increased their production of them, which helped create a cycling fad among the middle class by the end of the century. As the number of bicycles made in the U.S. rose to a million a year in 1899, when about one of every seven people owned a bike even though they cost about $100 (equivalent to $3,000 today), cycling magazines increased "beyond all reason," according to sports historian John Rickards Betts.[23]

No magazine covering sports was more celebrated in the latter part of the 1800s and the early 1900s than New York City's *National Police Gazette*. On the day it began in 1845, a customer in a New York saloon excitedly waved around a copy of the new publication, which carried a story about "Lives of the Felons." When the owner of the bar commented that one of the people written about, who was in jail for murdering the brother of his fifth wife, should be hanged, a bottle was thrown at him. A brawl ensued in which one person lost an ear and two fingers and another was killed. Two weeks later, the magazine bragged that the fight had helped to sell the publication: "But the editors of this weekly will not feel adequately repaid until it has irritated all of New York's vermin to public battle whereby they shall destroy themselves."[24] Thus, from the first, crime news was a staple of the publication.

The *Gazette* struggled along until 1874, when Richard Kyle Fox, a new immigrant, was hired as the business manager. An experienced Irish newspaperman, he owned the magazine by 1876 and within two years brought out his first sixteen-page issue, calling it a "new era in illustrated journalism." In particular, it featured large woodcut illustrations on the cover and self-promotions in every issue. To generate content Fox hired dozens of writers, provided them with a large amount of whiskey, and locked them in a room on weekends. They were let out on Monday, when they were paid ten dollars for their stories, and to make sure that he got what he wanted, he hired a former boxer to guard the door and stop them from leaving early.[25]

Besides playing up crime and sex, the *Gazette* made sports and games a focal point beginning in the 1870s. This was reflected in 1880 when Fox changed the *Gazette*'s slogan in the banner from "The only criminal journal in the United States" to "An Illustrated Journal of Sporting and Sensational Events." But he did not limit himself merely to the usual sports, such as baseball, boxing, football, yachting, tennis, and horse racing. He created contests for anything that he or someone else could think of, and from 1876 to 1892 alone, he provided 436 trophies, medals, belts, and other prizes for what he termed "champions." As historian Guy Reel has noted, the so-called "sports" included such things as dancers, rat catchers, egg eaters, drinkers, oyster shuckers, bridge jumpers, banjo players, dog trainers, bodybuilders, steeple climbers, barbers who gave the fastest haircuts (one person did it in thirty seconds), and two men who rowed across the Atlantic Ocean. One man even got a belt for having his head knocked through an iron block with a sledgehammer.[26] Media sociologist David B. Welky noted the contests had several purposes:

> These events seem silly today, and may have even then. It is also true that these novel contests . . . were all ploys by Fox to garner attention and increase subscriptions. . . . But crass motives aside, these events helped to address the working-class need for an escape from anonymity. The *Police Gazette* proved that anyone who had a modicum of talent in any so-called skill could be immortalized in print, and could even earn the immortal sobriquet of "champion." Were it not for the *Police Gazette*, T.F. Grant would have lived his life as a nameless cripple. Instead, in 1884, he became the *Police Gazette* champion one-legged clog dancer of the world. . . . We may consider Marquis Bibbero merely as a prime candidate for drowning, but after swimming ten miles in a river with his hands and feet tied, he became the *Police Gazette*'s champion scientific swimmer. Finally, we may

not even know what to make of George Clegg of Cleveland, but after he established a new glass-eating record for Ohio in 1889, he too became a champion.[27]

While these contests helped the *National Police Gazette*'s circulation soar to as much as five hundred thousand, it was Fox's promotion and coverage of boxing, which included his usual money, belts, and other prizes, where he left an indelible mark on American sports journalism. In 1997, when he was inducted posthumously into the International Boxing Hall of Fame, he was credited with modernizing the sport. He liked boxing, according to Reel, because it was "a perfect vehicle" to play up manliness. "[P]ictures of boxers gave Fox a good excuse to repeatedly show men shirtless, often with fisticuffs raised. Boxers were both heroes and outlaws, men of both brawn and brain—in short, boxing amounted to a decisive way to answer challenges to dominant masculinities in the late nineteenth century." Since the sport was particularly popular with men in taverns, where the *Police Gazette* was widely circulated, its coverage was an obvious way to increase circulation.[28]

Fox's drive to cover boxing apparently intensified on an April night in 1881 at Harry Hill's tavern in New York when he went there to have a few drinks, smoke a cigar, and eat roast beef. Coincidentally, Boston's John L. Sullivan, one of the best up-and-coming boxers in the country, also was there, fresh from a victory a few nights before over fighter Steve Taylor on the tavern's stage. That impromptu fight had occurred when Sullivan had offered anyone fifty dollars who could last four three-minute rounds with him; Taylor stepped forward and lost in the first round. Seeing Sullivan, Fox supposedly told Hill to have the fighter come and see him. Sullivan refused, demanding instead that Fox come to his table if he wanted to meet him. Reel noted these snubs set up a relationship that changed the face of sports journalism and altered both men's lives: "Fox was indeed, in 1881, embarking on the years of his greatest success, partly attributable to his insatiable ego and partly to his inarguable talent as a kingmaker. Somewhere over the next few years, Fox may have realized that he and Sullivan could be perfect foils. Fox, an egocentric media tycoon, helped create the first great American sports superstar; at the same time, he would owe much of his success to a man he supposedly despised."[29]

Before Sullivan's emergence in the boxing world the sport was considered low and even barbaric at times, but it began to rise in popularity after some rule changes and the emergence of groups that supported the less barbaric "sparring." By the 1880s, when Fox began to consistently cover boxing matches in the *Gazette*, the sport was, for the most part, considered acceptable. In fact, it provided the magazine a significant boost in readership. During most of the final twenty years of the nineteenth century, the *Gazette* consistently averaged around 150,000 readers, but the numbers jumped significantly when it promoted or recapped a boxing match. For example, circulation topped 400,000 in 1880 when it carried weekly coverage of a fight between Paddy Ryan and Joe Goss. This came just one year after Fox added a sports column to the *Gazette*, which was now printed on pink-tinted paper to draw attention to the magazine, and in response to the increased circulation he created a sports department and allowed people to submit information.[30]

The beginning of Sullivan's public appearances in the *Gazette* came in May 1881, when he fought John Flood on a barge in the Hudson River with the winner getting $750 of the $1,000 purse. A New York City reporter, writing with the typical exaggeration of the time, said Sullivan's first blow hit Flood so hard in the jaw that it "swelled his ankles," and he was knocked unconscious in the eighth round with blood coming out of one of his ears and his face swollen badly. A collection of $98 for Flood was taken up from the spectators, and Sullivan charitably gave $10. While Fox did not sponsor the match, the next issue of the *Police Gazette* featured a woodcut of it in what historians believe was the first art of Sullivan in action.[31]

Sullivan's victory set up a bigger match with Ryan in February 1882. Fox guaranteed half of the $5,000 purse and far outstripped all other media sources in his coverage as he added eight pages to the normal sixteen with each weekly edition including updates on the training by the two men. The fight, which the *Gazette* labeled "The Battle of the Giants," was held in Mississippi City, Mississippi, despite the state legislature banning prizefighting. So many people from New York City took the train to it that the coverage claimed, "Gotham was depleted of her fancy element almost entirely." Hitting Ryan with what the magazine called "sledgehammer blows," Sullivan knocked him out in the ninth round. Sales of the *Gazette's* special supplement on the fight more than doubled its circulation, hitting three hundred thousand.[32]

At the conclusion of the match Sullivan was presented with the *Gazette's* championship belt but refused it, sneeringly calling it a "dog collar." While Fox was insulted and had not liked Sullivan since the night that he had refused to come to his table at Harry Hill's tavern, he shrewdly recognized that the fighter and his sport could drive the circulation of the magazine upward. Thus, he substantially increased the frequency of boxing pictures. In 1880, the *Police Gazette* devoted less than a one-fourth of a page on the inside of an average issue to illustrations of boxing or bodybuilding, but by 1905, the average had risen to about three and three-fourths pages of pictures per issue. Along with the images, the magazine promoted boxing more than any other subject on its front page. Almost 30 percent of the covers' headlines involved boxing from 1879 to 1906 with the peak coming in 1889, when Sullivan retired, at about 60 percent.[33]

The coverage of boxing continued as the 1880s progressed, but while the *Gazette* included information on other boxers from time to time, Sullivan remained the main circulation draw. Twenty-five thousand people watched him in an exhibition in Boston in 1883, and a few months later he defeated Charley Mitchell, knocking him over the ropes at one point, despite the *Gazette* reporting that Sullivan had health problems. Fox also began delving into his rocky 1883 marriage to Annie Bates Bailey Sullivan. It was rumored that the two frequently fought after drinking, and he beat up both her and her sister. However, she denied the stories, telling a *Gazette* reporter that Sullivan's "great misfortune is that he has a heart too big for his body, and is so lavish in entertaining his friends that he sometimes oversteps the bounds of prudence in his sociability and then is a little morose and surly."[34] With Fox drawn to such a celebrity scandal, as well as to others, one historian called the *Gazette* the *National Enquirer* of the 1800s.[35]

As Sullivan's career advanced and his fame grew, Fox continued to change and upgrade his coverage and his promotions. For example, he began listing all of the important people at matches; he brought in foreign competitors to battle Sullivan; and in 1884 he created a $2,500 championship belt, which was fifty inches long and eight inches wide with gold, silver, and diamonds. In 1892 Sullivan came out of retirement to fight James "Gentleman Jim" Corbett but was knocked out in the twenty-first round, which ended his career.[36]

In the end it was a perfect relationship for both men, according to Reel: "[T]he fighter was the perfect hero (or antihero, depending on how much one believes in their supposed feud) for the editor. Sullivan was the giant of an era defined by defense of masculinities; Fox was there to chronicle those defenses." While boxing was not the only topic that the *Gazette* featured during the 1880s and into the 1890s, it was one of its most important ones, and the Fox-Sullivan relationship was at the forefront of the boxing coverage.[37]

In 1883, thirty-nine years before the end of Fox's career at the *Police Gazette* in 1922, the magazine made a prescient comment about his contribution to American sports coverage: "The name of Richard K. Fox is inseparably associated with American athletic sport, and justly so, for to him that line of American sport owes the healthy and prosperous life it enjoys today. It is but a few years since he found it languishing in a barren field, unpopular, only practiced in a desultory way, without encouragement or efficient championship. He took it up and made its cause his own, and gave it the vitality it now has."[38]

But that did not mean that Fox liked every sport. While football certainly had manly qualities, he chose initially not to cover many of the games in the *Gazette* because he considered it not as physical or as "scientific" as boxing. And like Pulitzer he was not impressed with the elitism of college football, particularly at colleges such as

Harvard and Yale, where he felt the students looked down on boxing as a brutal, stupid sport for lower-class men.[39] Oriard noted that this bias by the magazine may have actually made the sport more popular: "In mocking the pretensions of 'gentlemen's' sports, the *Police Gazette* voiced the class antagonism of its readers. But its representation of football as a slugfest, and of its audience as the sort of sporting crowd that also patronized prizefights, cockfights, and dogfights, probably had another, unintended effect: making the game more attractive and accessible to working-class males for whom universities were alien institutions. In its campaign against football, the *Police Gazette* may have ironically helped broaden the college sport's audience."[40]

Another reason for football growing in popularity in the late 1800s was a major difference between it and baseball. With professional baseball in a small number of cities east of the Mississippi River, this generally meant that only nearby papers sent sportswriters to the games and everyone else had to rely on wire service coverage. However, as colleges all over the country, rather than just in the northeast, started playing football, it suddenly became a local story for numerous papers of all sizes and was cheap and easy to cover, resulting in a rapid increase in the number of articles about it. For example, the *Chicago Times* ran little on football until the mid-1880s other than occasional stories about a game in the East. But in 1888, when the University of Michigan, one of the first universities outside the Northeast to have a team, played a Thanksgiving game against the Chicago Athletic Association, it was on the front page while a Yale-Princeton game was pushed back to page 2. Then, in 1892, the University of Chicago started football under famous coach Amos Alonzo Stagg, and its games against Michigan, along with the Chicago Athletic Association's contests against various teams, caused the *Times* to dramatically increase its coverage and use illustrations.[41]

As the number of college teams continued to increase sharply—a study showed there were 432 teams in 555 American cities by 1905—interest in football also was helped by the formation of conferences, which played a major role in starting to make it a national sport.

By the mid-1890s, for example, there was the Western Intercollegiate League (Chicago, Michigan, Minnesota, Northwestern, and Wisconsin), the Western Interstate University Football Association (Iowa, Kansas, Missouri, and Nebraska), and the Southern Intercollegiate Athletic Association (Alabama, Auburn, Georgia, Johns Hopkins, Sewanee, and Vanderbilt). These helped to build fan interest and spark more press coverage, as intersectional rivalries developed quickly just like they had in the Northeast where football had started.[42]

Meanwhile, baseball's popularity declined somewhat in the 1890s, which was reflected in less coverage in the top newspapers and magazines. The attendance drop, which put seven of the twelve National League teams in the red at the end of the century, was blamed by some on the "evils" of the game.[43] A Rochester, New York, newspaper wrote:

> The decline in the popularity of the game, which is now lamented by American newspapers and by lovers of clean sport, is due mainly to the lawlessness that the club owners and managers encourage in the play. The decisions of the umpire are not respected in baseball as they are in all other kinds of sports. . . . [E]ven when hundreds of women are among the spectators, language is used that is simply disgraceful. No wonder attendance at the game falls off and women dislike to go. In the cities embraced in the National League complaints of rowdyism on the field are universal and continuous. . . . There used to be a time when the owners of baseball franchises were genuine sportsmen, but now little sporting blood flows in the veins of any of them. They are in the game for money, and if they cannot win by fair means, they do not hesitate to resort to foul means. The lovers of baseball can bring them to their senses by continuing to remain away from the games. Appeals through the press are useless; they can be reached only through their pockets.[44]

The *New York Times* agreed that "rowdyism" was a cause for the decline in the game but also noted that its popularity suffered from other sports, such as football, golf, and cycling, growing rapidly in spectator interest.[45]

However, baseball rebounded at the turn of the century. The American League was formed in 1901 along with the National Association of Minor League clubs, which helped expand the game. Then, the first World Series took place two years later with the Boston Americans (now the Red Sox) defeating the Pittsburgh Pirates, five games to three. Although the media did not pay much attention to the series, and neither did the public, which was shown by small crowds at the games, that changed quickly as baseball followed the same pattern as football: numerous college teams and local teams in thousands of communities led to increased coverage.[46]

Emporia, Kansas, with a population of about ten thousand, was typical of the local prominence that the game assumed far from the centers of professional baseball. *Emporia Gazette* publisher William Allen White recalled what it was like when his hometown played teams from other towns. "[O]f a late summer afternoon, the town gathered at these games with noisy loyalty and great excitement, the women in their best big hats and high sleeves and wide skirts, the men in what then were called shirtwaists, tailless shirts gathered with a rubber string under the waist just inside and below the trouser top—quite fashionable and exciting," he wrote in 1946. "The ball game was the only public summer sport."[47]

In the last half of the nineteenth century photography played a distinct role in the increasing popularity of sports, which did not go unnoticed by the press. American newspapers had begun using illustrations, printed from woodcuts, in the early 1700s; by the Civil War, as printing technology improved, they appeared more and more in magazines because they found that using pictures could lead to higher circulations, thus increasing profits. Spurring on the public's growing fascination with illustrations was the New York City firm of Currier & Ives; it advertised itself as "Publishers of Cheap and Popular Pictures" and produced more than seven thousand different lithographs, totaling over one million hand-colored prints, from 1835 to 1907. Numerous sports, including hunting, fishing, baseball, boxing, rowing, yachting, boat racing, and trotting, appeared in the prints, which became common in homes across the country.[48]

Meanwhile, photography had started in the late 1830s, and several factors were responsible for the public developing an intense fascination with it by the end of the century. One was Civil War photos taken after some of the famous battles. Viewers, used to heroic drawings and paintings of battle scenes, were mesmerized and stunned by suddenly seeing real images of the carnage up close. Then came Eastman Kodak in Rochester, New York, which developed a burgeoning mass market for both public and commercial photography starting in 1889. Eleven years later, it brought out the famous Brownie camera, which was inexpensive and easy to use (Kodak's advertising slogan was, "You press the button, we do the rest"), and this helped establish photography as a popular public pastime.[49] Another factor was the stereoscope, a hand-held device that was invented about the same time as photography. The user looked through two lenses at a card with two identical photographs, and the result was a startling 3-D image. By the late 1800s its popularity swept the country as it became many viewers' windows on the world, noted former photographer and historian James Staebler in 2000:

> Indeed, the stereoscope was a powerful time machine that allowed viewers to travel instantaneously from their parlors to far-off corners of the world at a fraction of the price it would take them to travel to the next town. In almost every parlor, sitting room and most classrooms there was a well-used, odd-looking device. Looking like a pair of binoculars with a stick protruding from the front, it was able to visually transport someone to another time and place, with all of the reality of depth and scope allowed in three inches of a photograph. Although this may seem a small area, when viewed it encompasses all of one's vision. Much like the gigantic neo-classical paintings or panoramas, where one was forced to continuously

move one's head around to try unsuccessfully to encompass it all at once, the stereo views captured a person's senses as the gigantic paintings captured Thomas Jefferson's.[50]

Millions of stereograph cards were made over the years, using photographs from around the world on all types of subjects, and like the Currier & Ives prints, some of them showed sporting scenes.

By the late 1880s and early 1890s photos of athletes and outdoorsmen began appearing commonly in magazines, which realized that this could give them a competitive edge by setting them apart from other publications, and newspapers soon caught up, thus virtually ending the use of woodcuts. New York's *Daily Graphic* was the first daily paper to publish a photograph in 1880, but even though it was known that pictures could boost circulation, they did not become common in metropolitan papers until 1897 because of technical and reproduction problems. By that time both magazines and newspapers "exploded" with photographs, noted Staebler.[51] Some of those pictures involved sports as the American public quickly showed a penchant for wanting to see athletes and athletic competition, not just read about them, and this desire would mushroom in the media in the twentieth century.

Other new technologies also began increasing the immediacy of sports coverage. In 1898, for example, Italian Guglielmo Marconi used his wireless radiotelegraphy system to cover a sailing regatta in Ireland from a ship, sending minute-by-minute accounts of the race to Dublin's *Daily Express*. This created such excitement that the *New York Herald* invited him in the following year to come to the United States to cover an America's Cup yacht race, which he did successfully, thus joining news and radio for the first time in this country. The fact that the stories were sent in dots and dashes did not diminish the importance of the accomplishment. By 1913 sportswriters were able to send stories to their newspapers and magazines by telegraph from the site of most sports events, and three years later the Associated Press sent a play-by-play account of the World Series, between Boston and Brooklyn, to all of its U.S. subscribers. This required the use of twenty-six thousand miles of telegraph wire; inventor Thomas Edison was so impressed that he wrote one of the wire service's executives: "The Associated Press must be wonderfully well organized to be able to accomplish what was done in the ball games. Uncle Sam now has a real arterial system."[52]

Shortly before photographs became common in newspapers William Randolph Hearst purchased the *New York Journal* in 1895 and took on Pulitzer in a circulation struggle that culminated in what became known as "yellow journalism"—which was characterized by sensational and colorful, but not always true, stories. Recognizing the importance of sports coverage, Hearst began devoting immense amounts of space to it; while rival papers ran from three to seven columns of sports news daily, he had two to four times more with a special twelve-page section on Sundays. In doing this, he took some of his best cartoonists and cleverest writers and created what Betts called "the modern sports section." It included experts who specialized in such sports as baseball, boxing, and rowing, as well as one writer who ghost wrote for athletic champions, along with top athletes who wrote about their sports under their own bylines. And all of the writing was "flippant, humorous, slangy," which readers liked, press critic Will Irwin noted in 1911.[53]

But while this increased readership Irwin was not impressed: "This created an artificial demand for 'sporting stuff' far beyond the natural appetite of even an English-speaking people. That demand became so insistent that the other newspapers of all shades of opinion were forced to meet it; and now no newspaper is so conservative and intellectual as not to have a sporting page."[54] He was not surprised, however, that other newspapers followed what Hearst did because, like him, they recognized a truism of yellow journalism: write what would attract the most readers, not necessarily what was most important. Thus, while women liked to read about love and scandal, men gravitated to sports because, like politics and wealth, these subjects were about power.[55]

Irwin was not the only person critical of newspapers of the late

1800s and early 1900s. In a 1976 book about the history of American sports writer James Michener noted papers had always valued sportswriting because it kept circulation up and sometimes increased it, but he particularly attacked what had been written about baseball as unethical. "For the first hundred years of its existence, baseball had the press of this nation in its pocket," he wrote. "The true story of baseball was never told. The game received an unconscionable amount of free publicity, often written by men who were little more than paid lackeys of the owners. . . . And the public loved it." Pointing out that sportswriters sometimes were paid by both their newspapers and the teams they covered, which he labeled "scandalous," he added: "If the sanctity of the press has been the holy grail of the editorial page, it has been a cup difficult to find in the sports section."[56]

The "free publicity" issue was not ignored by the press. *Editor & Publisher*, the leading newspaper trade journal, wrote a blunt editorial in 1911 on what it termed "baseball graft"—the large amount of space devoted to the sport by metropolitan dailies, which put out sports extras on games even though they took a loss on them. Meanwhile, the club owners purchased no advertising. "Why is it the games are not advertised?" the journal asked. "Because the ball magnates see no need of it. What is the use of spending thousands of dollars in the newspapers when the latter give them hundreds, if not thousands, of columns of the best kind of advertising free of charge? . . . A business that has been made successful by the newspapers ought to be willing to pay them a fair amount for the work they have done." Until the baseball owners began advertising, *Editor & Publisher* recommended that papers should "cut down the space given to the games to a sane amount, and entirely eliminate the mass of personal data, gossip and cartoons that now fill the sporting columns."[57]

But whatever problems existed, Michener admitted that they were offset "by the brilliance of the writing." This was a reference to how sports coverage began changing in the late 1800s from virtually everything else in newspapers. The difference was clearly evident by 1920 when the *New York Times* hired a Yale University English professor to look at the paper's literary quality; he found that sports was the only place where the writing truly excelled.[58] Baseball writers, for example, had become particularly imaginative in coining new terms to liven up what otherwise would have been dull accounts of games. As one historian noted: "pitchers became 'hurlers,' outfielders were 'gardeners,' hits were 'stings' and 'wallops,' bases were 'sacks,' runners were 'nailed at the plate,' pennants were 'gonfalons.'" While readers loved this sprightly writing, and so did publishers because of the positive effect that it had on their circulations, in many cases, it was simply bad prose. "At times, the sports pages seemed to be a bad dream by Sir Walter Scott," the historian concluded.[59]

But a few exceptional writers stood out. One of the early leaders in taking sportswriting to a higher level was Ring Lardner, who from 1907 to his death in 1933 worked for seven newspapers in Chicago, Boston, and St. Louis, as well as the *Saturday Evening Post*, and had a nationally syndicated column in more than 115 newspapers. By writing more than forty-five hundred articles and columns he is credited with originating the modern American newspaper column.[60] Historian Mark Hodermarsky noted his importance: "Before Ring Lardner's appearance as a baseball writer, few members of the literati took baseball prose seriously. It was assumed by the educated class that baseball columnists only wrote for the boorish fan, the unrefined reader. Ring Lardner erased permanently the snobbery directed toward baseball writers. Winning the admiration of such noted authors as F. Scott Fitzgerald, Ernest Hemingway, H. L. Mencken, and Virginia Woolf, Lardner's work transcended the baseball world and awakened future readers and writers to the fact that baseball could be a source of serious literacy material."[61]

While Lardner stood out for having the ability to almost always turn a game into interesting reading by offering insights into the players that others missed, he became particularly famous for accurately portraying American slang. Previously, such words had been used as a comic device to make fun of the speakers, but he wanted readers to see what ballplayers were really like and how they thought, and this influenced the writing of not only future sportswriters but also some of the country's literary giants. As historian Scott Topping noted: "His practice of 'listening hard' to those around him enabled him to portray the language of uneducated baseball players."[62]

For all of his good points, however, Lardner was like Chadwick in one important way: they were too close to the game to be unbiased. Like numerous sportswriters after them, they were in love with their subject, which presented a dilemma although it did not bother readers. Baseball historian Eliot Asinof talked about this side of Lardner: "[H]e was a great baseball fan. . . . Ballplayers were heroes. He constantly thought of them as big men and himself as a kid. A major-league star was someone who used his talent to get to the very top. And when, as a result of his work, Lardner became friendly with them, . . . he could not get over his adulation."[63] Jonathan Yardley, in his 1977 biography of Lardner, noted that by the early 1900s most of the regular professional baseball writers were "an advocate rather than a critic," who wrote only "the good news" about the teams that they covered and suppressed anything negative. In fact, he labeled their relationship with the players and teams as "whorishness:"

> There were other reasons why it behooved the "scribes" to toe the line. Many of the teams, Ring wrote in "The Cost of Baseball," "'pay the freight' for newspaper correspondents." That suited the newspapers for which they worked just fine, as it enabled them to give their readers baseball coverage without having to pay anything for it except telegraph charges and their reporters' insubstantial salaries. A reporter who didn't write what a club liked could get dropped from its retinue—so he faced pressure from his employer as well as the club to write the company line. As if those pressures weren't enough, there was always the fear of physical violence at the hands of an inebriated or pathological (or both) ballplayer offended by a story criticizing his play.[64]

With writers like Lardner contributing to the growing popularity of both baseball and football in the first two decades of the twentieth century, newspapers were on the rise. Although the number of daily papers remained relatively the same from 1900 to 1920, moving only from 1,967 to 2,042 respectively, their circulation increased from 15.1 million to 27.8 million, which largely reflected the percentage growth in the country's population along with a continuing increase in literacy. All of this meant more and more people reading about sports.[65]

Another major factor in the increased interest in sports news was the United States' participation in World War I in 1917–18. As men poured into the army and the navy regimental and divisional athletic teams were formed in numerous sports, including baseball, football, boxing, volleyball, swimming, wrestling, hockey, basketball, and track, and large crowds turned out for the competitions. The soldiers and sailors found participating in sports their "greatest [off-duty] diversion," noted Betts, and all of this was played up both in military newspapers and in civilian newspapers, which sometimes collected athletic equipment to send to the army camps.[66] He pointed out the post-war impact: "What had the war done for sport? . . . [I]t returned millions of men so tired of war and so recently trained in athletic games as to comprise a tremendous core from which the gospel of sport might spread. Industrial athletics were promoted as an outlet for the workers, and volleyball became extremely popular. Newspapers acquired new readers of the sports page, gymnasiums and athletic clubs found many new converts, and those foremost in the commercialization of sports acquired a reservoir of enthusiastic spectators."[67]

***

With the nation embracing athletic competition after the war more than ever, this set the stage for what became known as the "Golden Age of Sports" in the 1920s. It became a decade of stunning superstars, who were glorified by a press consisting of more than just newspapers and magazines—radio and newsreels joined in to make major sporting events even more accessible and exciting to Americans all across the country. As Betts put it: "All the momentum of the athletic impulse was released on a generation tired of war."[68]

Newspapers and Radio Begin to Coexist 3

> There is no question that radio reporting of a prize fight,
> ball game, President's speech, is in many respects superior
> to any reporting possible on the printed page. It is
> instantaneous. You feel in actual contact with the event.
> —*Editor & Publisher*, 1924

On Sunday, October 19, 1924, about ten million people, who were subscribers to more than a hundred newspapers across the country that took the *New York Herald Tribune* wire service, awoke to find a story by Grantland Rice about the Army–Notre Dame football game on the previous afternoon in New York City. In about thirty minutes in a noisy press box,[1] he wrote a story considered by many to have the most famous sports lead in American history:

> Outlined against a blue-gray October sky, the Four Horsemen rode again. In dramatic lore they are known as Famine, Pestilence, Destruction and Death. These are only aliases. Their real names are Stuhldreher, Miller, Crowley and Layden. They formed the crest of the South Bend cyclone before which another fighting Army football team was swept over the precipice at the Polo Grounds yesterday as 55,000 spectators peered down on the bewildering panorama spread on the green plain below.
>
> A cyclone can't be snared. It may be surrounded, but somewhere it breaks through to keep on going. When the cyclone starts from South Bend, where the candle lights still gleam

through the Indiana sycamores, those in the way must take to storm cellars at top speed. Yesterday the cyclone struck again, as Notre Dame beat the Army, 13 to 7, with a set of backfield stars that ripped and crashed through a strong Army defense with more speed and power than the warring cadets could meet.[2]

Biographer Charles Fountain attributed the article's greatness to a number of factors. For example, there was the striking imagery: Notre Dame's backs had "the mixed blood of the tiger and the antelope," and the Army defensive line tried to stop them "but when a tank tears in with the speed of a motorcycle, what chance has flesh and blood to hold?" And throughout the article, Rice kept returning to the cyclone metaphor; Notre Dame "opened like a zephyr" and "struck with too much speed and power to be stopped." But no matter how literary Rice was, he never forgot that he had a story to tell, with the whats and the whys and the hows, which he did chronologically.[3] Fountain concluded:

It was not even necessary to have read, or even heard of, Vicente Blasco-Ibanez's novel, *The Four Horsemen of the Apocalypse*, to have seen the Rudolph Valentino movie of the same name, or to be versed in the Book of Revelation to comprehend and enjoy Rice's simply and clearly stated reference to the Four Horsemen. Thus, Rice the sportswriter was, in this story and in so much of his work, all things to all people. There were readers who cared not a whit for sports who enjoyed his writing; there were others who wouldn't know a poem from a point-after-touchdown who were equally avid. . . .

The story has endured because Grantland Rice fashioned a phrase that was clever, memorable, and fit precisely with the event and the times. It was not that Rice's story stopped people in their tracks—readers across America were not grasping Rice's story in wonder and telling each other that this was the greatest story in sportswriting history. . . . It was merely that the event had captured their attention, and the phrase lingered in their consciousness.[4]

Rice's story, and its everlasting fame, was in many ways an indicator of just how extraordinary the 1920s were in American sports. A group of superlative athletes in various sports had their feats glamorized to a nation that was in love with them just as much as it was with jazz and blues and ragtime, speakeasies and roadhouses, and flappers dancing the Charleston. It was a wild, exciting decade in America and sportswriters played it up breathlessly—and in ever-increasing breadth. In 1925 there was two thousand inches of sports copy in the average metropolitan newspaper each week, which was double what there had been only ten years before. And by the late 1920s, when one-fourth of all news that appeared in the *New York World* was about sports, the assistant managing editor said, "My intellect is offended, but my editorial judgment approves it." His comment reflected the fact that the post-war economic prosperity along with rising literacy had increased newspaper circulation from twenty-eight million in 1914 to thirty-six million in 1926, and his newspaper could not afford to ignore what readers wanted.[5] There was an attempt to rein in papers, to make them more ethical and responsible, but this largely was ignored in sports sections. Like Pandora's box, sportswriting was too far unleashed by the 1920s to totally control it, and readers could care less. And if they wanted even more sports excitement, radio was ready to provide it.

***

Rice, who came to be known as the "Dean of American Sportswriters," was born in 1880 in Murfreesboro, Tennessee, and moved with his family two years later to Nashville, where, on his first Christmas, he got a football, a baseball, and a bat, which he recalled became "the sounding instruments that directed my life." He grew up playing football and baseball with his friends along with competing in marbles, spinning-top wars, track-and-field events, and horseshoes. After attending a local prep school, where he was on the football, baseball, and track teams, he went to Vanderbilt and majored in Greek and Latin but took no English because the university felt that Latin prepared students better in the rudiments of English grammar. When not in class he was involved heavily in football, track, and basketball with some success, but it was in baseball that he excelled. Before graduating in the spring of 1901 he captained the Vanderbilt team and started at shortstop as it won the Southern Association championship.[6]

After playing semi-pro baseball for about a month Rice returned to Nashville to work in a dry goods store but, not liking the job, he quickly decided with the encouragement of his father to become a reporter. This would seem to have been a strange choice since he had taken no journalism classes at Vanderbilt—there were none—and had not written for the university's student newspaper or its literary magazine. "My dad figured that inasmuch as I hadn't gone in for engineering, law or medicine at college—but had done creditably well in the arts—I might try my hand at journalism," explained Rice. He immediately got a job paying five dollars a week at the *Nashville Daily News*, covering the state capitol, the courthouse, and the custom house along with writing sports.[7] After becoming sports editor, he left in 1902 to take a similar position at the *Atlanta Journal* for the next four years. That was followed by stints at the *Cleveland (OH) News* and the *Nashville Tennessean* before moving permanently to New York in 1912, where he wrote sports for forty-two years on the *Evening Mail*, the *Herald Tribune*, and the *Daily News*. During the 1920s, when he was making $100,000 a year and had his column, "The Sportlight," syndicated to more than 250 newspapers, he also did a weekly article for *Collier's* magazine and freelanced for other magazines, edited the *American Golfer* magazine, and wrote the first movie script whose star was a baseball player (Ty Cobb in *Somewhere in Georgia*).[8] Shortly before his death in 1954, when he was still writing a column six days a week that appeared in about 80 newspapers, he calculated that he had written more than 67 million words, including over 22,000 columns, 7,000 poems (which sometimes started his columns), more than 1,000 magazine articles, and 14 books. That averaged out to about 3,500 words a day over fifty-three years, making him "possibly the most productive writer in the history of the craft," according to biographer William Harper.[9]

At Rice's funeral, long-time friend Bruce Barton summed up his sportswriting philosophy:

> He was the evangelist of fun, the bringer of good news about games. He was forever seeking out young men of athletic talent, lending them a hand and building them up, and sharing them with the rest of us as our heroes. He made the playing fields respectable. Never by preaching or propaganda, but by the sheer contagion of his joy in living, he made us want to play. And in so doing he made us a people of better health and happiness in peace: of greater strength in adversity. This was his gift to his country; few men have made a greater [one].[10]

As Barton noted, Rice steadfastly wrote about "good news." That is because he felt it was better to be positive than negative. "If anything, I give the other guy a break," he said. "That's because I've been an athlete and made mistakes, too. In a 2–0 baseball game, for instance, I tend to give the pitcher credit for pitching a good game, instead of belaboring the other team for poor hitting." And on another occasion he noted he had never been accused "of being a calamity howler." Instead, he "always preferred looking on the sunny side of things" without "peering into the shadows searching for ghosts of trouble and phantoms of sorrow." As one of his colleagues said: "If he couldn't say anything nice about an athlete, he was likely to write about another athlete." While biographer Mark Inabinett noted that Rice sometimes was critical, he used the same hyperbole and lyricism as when he was glorifying something to make it go down easier not only for the readers but also for the athletes. For example, in the 1926 World Series, he called New York Yankee shortstop Mark Koenig, whose error in the seventh game led to a St. Louis Cardinal rally that won the championship, "the ill-fated son of destiny who must have killed an albatross in his youth to become an ancient mariner of woe."[11] Such obvious sympathy appeared over and over in Rice's long writing career. "A kind man, he damned no reputations," wrote Fountain, "and his culpability came in giving a man a break he might not have deserved."[12]

That attitude made Rice the leader of what became known as the "Gee-Whiz" school of sportswriting, which basically praised and glorified athletes in contrast to the "Aw Nuts" writers, who were far more skeptical about attributing greatness to anyone.[13] Furman Bisher, who grew up reading Rice and became one of the country's most famous sportswriters on the *Atlanta Journal-Constitution* in the second half of the twentieth century, recalled the dominance of the "Gee-Whiz" style in a 2009 interview with historian Amber Roessner: "We had our favorites. Take Ty Cobb, for instance. I did not choose to write about the skeletons in his closet. . . . If I liked an athlete, if anything bad came up about him, I thought, 'Damned if I'm going to write that.' . . . I may have picked a fellow and overlooked his glitches but most [sportswriters] were that way."[14]

Thus, while race, religion, politics, and financial matters might divide the country, readers could depend on Rice being upbeat and cheerful. After all, unlike many sportswriters even today, according to Inabinett, he could recognize that sports were just "children's games, full of joy and fun, and the excitement and unpredictability of youth. . . . These elements of fun and drama are why sports have fans, why sports pages have readers. Rice became a conduit through which fans, by sharing in his exuberance and knowledge, could enjoy sports."[15] Another part of his positive outlook was passionately playing up good sportsmanship, which elevated the importance of sports in American culture and increased Rice's popularity. Harper noted that he believed the ideals of sportsmanship "when genuinely cultivated could provide the necessary insurance that sport would not be trivialized into show business and its performers into entertainers."[16]

Making it easy for Rice to write about good news in the 1920s was a stunning array of individual sports stars who are still well known today even though almost a century has passed. They included: Babe Ruth, who led the New York Yankees to three World Series championships in the decade, hit sixty home runs in 1927, and in 1939 became one of the first five players elected to the Baseball Hall of Fame; Jack Dempsey, the heavyweight boxing champion from 1919 to 1926; Bobby Jones, who as an amateur won thirteen major golf championships between 1923 and 1930; and Bill Tilden, who won seven U.S. men's singles tennis titles and three Wimbledon championships between 1920 and 1930. Others were Red Grange, a three-time All-American halfback at the University of Illinois from 1923 to 1925 who then played pro football until 1934 and in 2008 was named by ESPN the greatest college player of all time; and Knute Rockne, who coached Notre Dame to five national football championships between 1919 and 1930 and had a record of 105-12-5.

To Rice, these were almost mythical heroes, and his writing continually celebrated their athletic accomplishments, "transforming them from mortals into deities," noted historian Mark Hodermarsky.[17] He had no apologies for the adulation that he heaped on them; in his view, that was simply what a good sports reporter should do. "When a sportswriter stops making heroes out of athletes," he said, "it's time to get out of the business."[18] In his autobiography, which was published after his death, Rice explained why it was important not only to him, but to the public, to have heroes: "Almost every one of these heroes of sport taught me something, gave me some insight into how to live and added to my philosophy of life. And, I think these champions and the way that they lived have something to say to all of us. . . . To reach the top in any sport—or in life—you need confidence and belief in yourself."[19]

Many people in the United States never had an opportunity to see the sports "heroes" of the 1920s in action because they did not live near where they played. As a result, the public thirsted for what Rice as well as other sportswriters wrote about them, eagerly accepting what they said because television did not exist to show it to them and movie theater newsreels were not yet common. Quite simply, sportswriters brought great athletes to life with vivid, entertaining reporting that read like literature, making the stories unlike articles anywhere else in a newspaper. For example, Rice wrote the following in 1926 when Ruth became the first player to hit three home runs in a World Series game against St. Louis:

After the manner of a human avalanche hurtling on its downward way from the blue Missouri heavens the giant form of Babe Ruth fell upon the beleaguered city of St. Louis today and flattened it into a pulp of anguish.

If another mighty planet had slipped its ancient moorings to come crashing through unlimited space against the rim of the earth it could not have left one sector in its path more dismantled or forlorn. . . .

An enraged bull in a china shop of fragile bric-a-brac would be a mere kitten playing with yarn compared to the astonishing infant who lashed the ball over the stands into Grand Avenue twice and then hammered another home run into the center field seats 430 feet away, for the first time in Missouri history. . . .

It is just a picture of a large portly form taking a wild cut at the ball and then loafing along the open highway with a stunned and startled crowd wondering who let old Doc Thor or the bolt-heaving Jupiter into the show. It was smash-smash-smash and then a steady, even unhurried trot from the plate back to the plate with the ball bounding on its way down St. Louis thoroughfares through brokenhearted crowds.[20]

Inabinett noted that Rice's writing style, which he pioneered and was the leading practitioner of in the 1920s, would be criticized now for being "quaint" and "as archaic and embarrassingly naïve as the old practice of bloodletting."[21] But to view history correctly, you must be able to put yourself back in time and view it as people at the time did, and his writing perfectly suited his readers. Red Smith, who became one of the country's top sportswriters and was awarded a Pulitzer Prize for Commentary in 1976, said of Rice in 1975: "Make no mistake about Granny: he was a giant. Some of his stuff seems like immature gushing today, but he was exactly right for his time, and if he had lived in another time he would have been right for that one."[22] What made him "exactly right" was that readers could see what he had seen and could feel the excitement and could visualize the thrills, whether this involved a rising new star, an old veteran who was attempting a comeback, or an athlete who defied long odds to find success. "Sportswriters became poets in the press box, thrill spinners rather than statisticians," said Inabinett. "With telegraph operators waiting at their elbows to transmit stories as soon as the game ended, the sportswriter wrote rapidly, weaving lush leads, and coining slogans and nicknames that telegraphed images to readers."[23] So, Ruth was called the "Bambino" and the "Sultan of Swat," Dempsey became the "Manassa Mauler," and Grange was the "Galloping Ghost."

As the most widely read sportswriter of the 1920s and clearly the most famous, Rice's significance lay in the way that he changed his craft. No longer were sports journalists merely reporters and statisticians. The best of them also were celebrated writers—and a few of them, such as Rice, became as famous as the sports stars that they covered, spending time not only with top athletes but with presidents, radio and movie stars, and well known writers.[24] Columnist Arthur Daley of the *New York Times*, who in 1956 became the first sportswriter to win a Pulitzer Prize, wrote two days after Rice's death in 1954 that it was doubtful that anyone had had a more "profound effect" on sportswriting. "He gave it fire and enthusiasm and sparkle," he said. "He could reflect the drama and the excitement as few men could. There was an era in the 1920s when every young writer tried to emulate Grantland Rice."[25] Sportswriter Jimmy Cannon of the *New York Journal-American*, writing a day after Daley, also noted that Rice's writing style had influenced all sportswriters although few could "handle the language with as much grace. Many croak because we can't sing."[26]

Forty years later, when Rice's historical significance could be more accurately assessed because of the passage of time, Inabinett agreed with Daley and Cannon that he had had a major impact on sportswriting:

The modern sportswriter who sees little but laughable purple prose in Rice's work should remember the debt owed to

Rice. You can often hear the claim that the best writing in newspapers can be found on the sports pages. Not coincidentally, sportswriters have traditionally had more editorial license and leeway than news reporters. At one time, sportswriters habitually abused this freedom, turning out copy riddled with jargon-filled gobbledy-gook understandable only to sports insiders. But as news writing became more formulaic sportswriters retained some of their freedom, no small thanks to Rice. He used his Vanderbilt education in the classics, his sense of drama, and his connections to the literary elite of his day to bring a respectability and acclaim to sports reporting that it had never had. The quality and popularity of his work gave sports writing direction and, at the same time, justified its continued editorial license.[27]

The freedom enjoyed by sportswriters was indirectly challenged in 1923. Beginning in the second half of the 1800s, and particularly increasing with the blatant sensationalism of the yellow journalism period in the 1890s and early 1900s, the press as well as the public debated the need for national journalistic standards. Then, in a 1906 speech, President Theodore Roosevelt made one of the most famous attacks on journalists when he criticized them for being "muckrakers" because of their many articles about corruption in business and politics.[28] The press also was castigated numerous times for fake stories, partisanship, suppression of news, and advertisers' control of editorial content.[29]

In 1922, when the American Society of Newspaper Editors (ASNE) was founded, its constitution stated: "Although the art of journalism has flourished in America for more than two hundred years, the editors of the greater American newspapers have not hitherto banded themselves together in association for the consideration of their common problems and the promotion of their professional ideals." A year later, at the ASNE's first annual meeting, it adopted the journalism profession's first national code of ethics, "Canons of Journalism," with the society's president noting, "public confidence is essential to effective journalism, and confidence, in a newspaper as in an individual, must be founded upon character."[30] Among the professional values mentioned in the "Canons," which particularly were germane to sportswriters because of the way they wrote although they were not specifically singled out for criticism, was the need for journalists to avoid partisanship and to be impartial. Referring to the latter, the code said: "Sound practice makes a clear distinction between news reports and expressions of opinion. News reports should be free from opinion or bias of any kind."[31]

While the push for professional ethics had little or no appreciable impact on sportswriters, a subtle change in their craft began. For the first time women made what historian Dave Kaszuba noted were "significant inroads" into sportswriting in the Roaring Twenties with about thirty-four of them working in the field from regularly to only occasionally.[32]

Maria "Midy" Morgan, who worked on the *New York Times* from 1869 until 1892, is acknowledged as the first woman sportswriter. Born on an Irish estate in 1828, she grew up riding horses and hunting and became extremely knowledgeable about farming and breeding. After her father died in 1865, she went with her mother and sister to Italy and was introduced to King Victor Emmanuel II, who was so impressed with what she knew about horses that he hired her to go to Ireland to purchase six mares. After a memorable return trip on thirty-two trains and steamers, as well as having to walk the horses over a mountain pass in the Alps, she presented them to the king, who was so pleased that he gave her a hunting watch with his initials set in diamonds. In 1869 she came to America with a letter of introduction to famed editor Horace Greeley of the *New-York Daily Tribune*, but he was not impressed with the large, six-foot-two woman. "Midy undoubtedly was a strange spectacle for any editor to take to on sight," wrote historian Ishbel Ross, who noted that she wore "rough tweeds" and "terrific" hats.[33] Undeterred, she talked the *New York World* into letting her cover horse races in Saratoga as a special correspondent, and she did so well that she then went to the *Times* to see editor in chief John Bigelow. Ross continued:

"[H]e was astonished to see a huge girl in Irish tweeds glowering down at him over his desk one day. She had a letter of introduction in her hand and she wanted a job.

"'The only vacant post we have is livestock reporter,' he told her.

"'I can fill it,' said the odd apparition. 'Why not?'

"'All right, try,' said Mr. Bigelow, after she had talked him down with a persuasive Irish tongue."[34]

Over the next twenty-three years on the *Times* Morgan was not only New York City's only woman writing about livestock but she also became one of the country's experts on horse breeding and horse racing; so much so that Ulysses S. Grant sought her opinion on horses. "Few could match her on horses," said Ross. "Midy sat on fences with the experts and brought her trained eye to bear on the animals parading past. . . . At first the breeders looked with amazement at the huge awkward girl who went about chewing straws, but after watching her work they doffed their hats to her."[35] M. L. Rayne, writing in 1893 about work open to women in the United States, called Morgan's job on the *Times* a "somewhat bizarre occupation" but praised her for believing "if she behaves herself, a woman can earn her living wherever she develops the most aptitude."[36]

Following Morgan's lead other women gradually began writing about sports, but in many cases they worked in other editorial departments on newspapers and only occasionally wrote a sports story. An early example was Elizabeth Cochran (better known as Nellie Bly) of the *New York World*. Famous for stunt reporting, particularly her trip around the world in 1889–90 in which she did it faster than the eighty days in Jules Verne's famous novel, she interviewed champion boxer John L. Sullivan at his New York training camp in 1889. She charmed him with a multitude of questions, including "Do you take cold bath showers?" and "How are you rubbed down?" Before she left he told her, "You are the first woman who ever interviewed me. And I have given you more than I ever gave any reporter in my life."[37] Five years later, she put on boxing gloves and persuaded a new boxing champion, James J. Corbett, to give her a lesson in the ring. In the midst of it, finding fighting quite exciting, she knocked him down and bloodied his mouth. She recounted the incident to the *World*'s readers:

> "'See what I did,' I said proudly to the spectators.
>
> "'Oh, that's nothing.' Mr. Corbett said. 'You hit me in the mouth with your elbow.'
>
> "'You won't confess that I drew blood with my fist,' I replied, as my pride vanished.
>
> "'Well, I bear you no ill feeling. I'm glad the championship stays in America,' he said."[38]

Another sports stunt, resulting in a newspaper story, was made in 1922 by Mary Bostwick of the *Indianapolis Star*. After being denied access for years to the press box at the Indianapolis Speedway, she decided to see if she could be the first woman to drive around the track in a racecar. So, she disguised herself as a man with khaki pants, goggles, and a cap and went to the track's infield. "[I]t was necessary to keep an eagle eye out for Speedway officials," she wrote, "and I'd have to crawl into a rain barrel, or behind a bush, or try and look like a spare tire every time one of them hove into view. It was nerve racking but I figured it would be worth it." Then, when no one was watching, she climbed into a Peugeot and completed seven laps on the two-and-a-half-mile oval, reaching 110 miles per hour. She said this "cured" her of ever wanting to do it again.[39]

Meanwhile, a small group of women began covering sports regularly. For example, Sadie Kneller Miller, an undergraduate at Western Maryland College, began writing about the Baltimore Orioles (and also taking photographs for her stories) for the *Baltimore Telegram* in 1884, making her apparently the first woman to cover major league baseball. She used the byline SKM, in order to hide the fact from readers that she was a woman, and her gender was not discovered by them until three years later when she was traveling with the team. And by 1920 other women also were covering sports, with one of them even serving as a sports editor, at newspapers in Dubuque, Iowa; San Francisco; Trinidad, Colorado; and New York City. They included Nan O'Reilly, who began a golf column at the *New York Evening Post* in 1916, and, like Miller, wrote under a fake name (Jean Sanderson) to keep readers from discovering that she was a woman. She also worked for the Associated Press with her editor mailing her checks to her home so that she did not have to come into the office and "disclose the fact to the staid A.P. that she was a baby-faced girl with rather long curls," noted Ross.[40]

As the number of women not only writing sports but also doing sports columns increased in the 1920s, other firsts kept appearing. One example was Lorena Hickok of the *Minneapolis Morning Tribune*. In 1924, when she was an award-winning reporter on the city desk, her editor became disenchanted with the paper's lackluster coverage of the University of Minnesota football team and sent her to do a color story on a home game. Her article was so entertaining that she immediately was assigned to write about every game of the Golden Gophers, making her the first woman to regularly cover Big Ten football. For several years, she traveled on the train with the team and stayed at their hotel, covering games from the stands because women were not allowed in press boxes and never attempting to interview players in the locker room after a game like her male counterparts on other papers. Her enthusiasm for the team was never more apparent than at one game when she rushed out of the stands to hug a Minnesota player who had just scored a touchdown, resulting in another player wittingly nicknaming her "Miss Goofer."[41] But it was not such antics that distinguished her work as a sportswriter. "Hickok humanized [University of Minnesota] coaches and athletes more deftly than the male writers who stressed hype and play-by-play specifics," noted Kaszuba.[42]

Another woman who distinguished herself in the male-dominated field of sportswriting was Jane Dixon of the *New York Telegram*. A gifted feature writer, whom Ross said "juggled adjectives with an experienced touch," she covered a wide variety of sports for the paper in the

1920s. These included the World Series, yacht races, football games, major horse races as far away as Kentucky, and tennis matches at the famed Forest Hills courts. "In short," continued Ross, "everything that went on around the town was graphically chronicled by Miss Dixon."[43]

But boxing coverage was where Dixon truly excelled and developed a national reputation. When she joined the *Telegram* in 1918 after working on newspapers in her hometown of Marion, Ohio, and Poughkeepsie, New York, she was restricted at first to largely reporting for the women's page although she sometimes did features on celebrities for the news section. Her writing so impressed the paper's editor, however, that he assigned her in 1919 to do preview stories on the Jess Willard–Jack Dempsey heavyweight championship fight in Toledo. While a male counterpart would provide the usual boxing camp stories, the paper told readers that her job was to write about the "lighter . . . human element" and particularly to give "a feminine twist" to her stories. It was hoped these articles would be of interest to women and increase female readership. So, she wrote about such things as Dempsey's closeness to his mother, noting that he wrote her daily and planned to send her a telegram after the fight. "She'll be waiting," he told Dixon, "and her dear old heart will be fluttering from the moment she figures I will be in the arena until she gets that message. I hope I will have good news for her." As for Willard, she explained why his wife usually did not attend his fights. "It is easy to understand," she said. "No woman could sit there and see the man she loves pounded, punched and pummeled. It would be beyond the bounds of womanly endurance." She also wrote about the fighters' physiques, describing Willard as "the man oak of the species" while Dempsey had shoulders that looked like they had been "modeled by a sculptor who loved the clay he wrought." She was struck, too, by his eyes, which she said were "deep set with something of the dreamer in [their] brown depths."[44]

The *Telegram* was so pleased with what she wrote that she covered all but one of Dempsey's championship fights over the next eight years, thus writing more about boxing than any other woman of that era.

She encouraged women to attend prizefights by always playing up the woman's angle; this meant never giving a blow-by-blow account of a fight but concentrating instead on the socialites in the crowd and the clothing fashions on display along with the boxers' personalities.[45] "She was at once a progressive feminist and yet stereotypically feminine," noted Kaszuba. "For example, she saw women's attendance at boxing matches, baseball games, and other male-dominated sporting events as both their right (a feminist view) and as a vehicle by which they could share their husbands' interests and strengthen their marriage and home (a feminine view)."[46] He said all of this made her a groundbreaker:

> [W]hile Dixon's career valuably illuminates women's entrance into the sports writing field circa the 1920s, it also sheds light on the wider struggle that women of the era faced. Fresh off World War I–related employment gains and the suffrage victory, women of that decade were realizing the results of a feminist agenda while also experiencing a cultural backlash that called on them to reprioritize marriage and family. . . . Dixon's sports writing highlighted the struggle they shared . . . [and] impressively managed to straddle the line. By writing about sports from a "woman's point of view," she found a way to have the best of both worlds: She could cover boxing and other sports that were typically off limits to female reporters, thus challenging the gender restrictions of the newspaper industry and earning a platform from which to argue for society's acceptance of female spectators at prizefights and other male-dominated sports events. Yet at the same time, she also could use her sports writing as a means to affirm traditional notions of femininity during an era when the backlash against the feminist movement demanded that marriage and motherhood reclaim priority. Melding these two objectives, she used her sports stories to remind readers that women could pursue anything from economic independence to a love of sports, all

without abandoning traditional feminine interests in matters both big (such as relationships and marriage) and small (such as beauty and fashion).[47]

The slowly increasing number of women reporters was not the only change occurring in sports journalism. Technology continued to provide new ways to increase the immediacy of newspaper coverage. In the 1890s telegraphic accounts of baseball games started to be recreated, pitch by pitch and out by out, on small diamonds around the country, and by the time of the first World Series in 1903 these recreations became more elaborate and drew larger crowds in what were annual rituals. The eagerly awaited 1919 World Series between the Chicago White Sox and the Cincinnati Reds brought "scoreboard watching" to new heights; more than a hundred thousand miles of telegraph line were used to bring the games to crowds in smoke-filled rooms in 250 U.S. cities as well as Winnipeg, Canada, and Havana, Cuba. "The reports would be read aloud, pitch by pitch, in a manner attempting to recapture the spirit of the game," wrote historian Eliot Asinof. "A diamond-shaped chart on the wall would move the players from base to base a few seconds later. Those who had seen this fascinating new procedure at work would testify to its excitement. It was almost like being there, they said." This same scene was duplicated in Times Square in New York City, where as many as five thousand people, sometimes standing in the rain, watched a reenactment of games on a large green baseball diamond with cutout figures of players. Such recreations continued through most of the 1920s before finally ending as attendance dropped off when radio made it possible for people to hear the games at home.[48]

Another threat to newspapers' stranglehold on sports coverage in the 1920s was motion-picture newsreels. The filming of sports events went back to the early 1890s, when viewers would pay to watch a peep show of a boxing match at parlors in New York City. To see the entire fight, they would have to move from one film machine to another, constantly putting in nickels to see more rounds, until they had spent

60 cents. However, this did not make as much money as expected because many people only put money in the final machine since all they wanted to see was the knockout. This was followed in 1895 by projecting a silent fight film on a screen at a Broadway theater. Historian Raymond Gamache noted this had a number of advantages over the peep-show machine: a bigger picture, the chance to view the film with others instead of alone, and the possibility of having a longer film. It also needed only one projector instead of a number of them, which reduced wear on the equipment and thus cut costs while increasing revenues. The *New York World* was enthusiastic about the screening: "It is all realistic, so realistic indeed that excitable spectators have forgot themselves and cried, 'Mix [it] up there!' 'Look out, Charlie, you'll get a punch,' 'Oh! What do you think of that Mr. Barnett?' and other expressions of like character."

More changes came quickly. Filmmakers began shooting other sports, such as horse racing, yacht races, and wrestling; the films were lengthened up to two hours; sometimes they were hand-tinted in color; band music accompanied the shows; and the films began showing in other parts of the country. And, perhaps most important, a film of a heavyweight championship fight in 1897 featured a boxing expert providing commentary for what was on the screen, making viewers feel even more like they were at the actual fight even though there were none of the sounds from it. As one historian noted, "the sports announcer had arrived."[49]

As more and more sports were filmed—college football for the first time in 1903, for example, and major league baseball three years later—the leading film companies began forming newsreel divisions in 1911, and sports unsurprisingly was a regular staple of what was shown, mostly as highlights or short clips. New newsreels were put out every week and shown throughout the country as Americans grew increasingly fascinated with films, with the number of cinemas increasing from nine thousand in 1908 to about fourteen thousand five years later. Then, in October 1927, the first *Fox Movietone News* with sound was shown at a New York City theater, and in it were scenes from an Army-Yale football game and a rodeo.[50] Gamache noted this new cinematic art evolved quickly after that: "In early sound newsreels, microphones were strategically positioned to capture the sounds of the bands and cheerleaders, and canned footage 'of cheering throngs and football pageantry were edited into the game action.' As newsreel editors became more comfortable and ambitious with the sound-on-film process, commentary was used to enhance the excitement of sports segments."[51]

Rice was involved with films as a sideline to his sportswriting. Starting in the mid-1920s and continuing for twenty-five years, he produced more than two hundred Sportlight Films, usually about ten minutes in length, on 123 sports and recreational activities. Because they were a study of sports rather than a report (like newsreels) on the latest sports news, they were designed to be shown in theaters between movies with subjects ranging from football, baseball, hunting, and fishing to alligator wrestling, horseshoes, and marbles. He said that he felt these short films were important because they introduced many moviegoers to sports and gave them "a keener appreciation [of them] in general." The quality of the films was shown by his six Academy Award nominations, two of which resulted in Oscars, for best short subject.[52]

But no technology had an impact on sports journalism in the 1920s like radio. Demonstrations of wireless telegraphy had begun in the 1880s, and the invention had advanced enough by the summer of 1898 for Italian Guglielmo Marconi to transmit the first live reports of a sporting event, the regatta of the Royal St. George Yacht Club in Dublin Bay off the Irish coast. Sensing the opportunity for a publicity stunt Dublin's *Daily Express* had its sailing correspondent cover the two days of racing from the bridge of a tug that followed the ships; he constantly passed short messages to the cabin, where Marconi transmitted them in Morse code to a wireless operator on shore. They were then telephoned to the newspaper, which posted the messages as they arrived outside of its office for an excited crowd to read and published new editions as soon as races ended. What made these wireless reports striking was how difficult it had always been to follow such races from shore, even with a telescope; the yachts were frequently either far away on the horizon or totally out of sight, and at times rain and fog obscured them from view. Now, however, no matter what the weather was or even if the ships were twenty-five miles from shore, Marconi updated the race progress almost minute to minute. Two Irish newspapers were so amazed at what wireless telegraphy had done— more than seven hundred messages had been transmitted during the regatta—that they devoted entire pages to it, including interviews with Marconi and his assistant.[53] A year later the Italian electrical engineer was paid $5,000 (worth more than $150,000 today) by the *New York Herald* to cover an America's Cup yacht race off the New Jersey coast from a boat, and the more than two thousand words that he sent enabled the paper to scoop its competition by putting out an edition with the race result before the ships returned to shore.[54]

New developments occurred rapidly as wireless telegraphy morphed into radio over the next twenty years. In 1901 Marconi was able to send a message from England to Newfoundland, and six years later he connected Europe with the United States, which caused the *New York Times* to exclaim in a headline: "Wireless Joins Two Worlds." Meanwhile, Canadian inventor Reginald Fessenden reportedly made the first public broadcast on Christmas Eve in 1906 when he told some wireless operators on United Fruit Company ships off the Atlantic Coast, along with a group of newspaper reporters in New York City, to listen on their headsets at a specific time. They first heard him broadcasting from Brant Rock, Massachusetts, in the usual Morse code, and then suddenly he read from the Bible and played a violin, which was followed by a recording of classical music before he wished them a merry Christmas. Historians Christopher Sterling and John Kittross noted why this is considered the first "public" broadcast: "Fessenden had tried to ensure a maximum audience, and, although some ship operators and a smattering of reporters in New York had to act as surrogates for the general public, this transmission was intended for a general audience; it was telephony, speech and music; it required no special knowledge for decoding; and anyone with a receiver could pick it up." In 1909 Charles David "Doc" Herrold opened the first broadcasting school, the College of Engineering and Wireless, in San Jose, California, and began a regular weekly thirty-minute news and music program that became daily a year later. Then, starting in 1916, similar broadcasts were made in New York City and Pittsburgh for those who had crystal radio sets.[55]

A new era dawned in 1920 when the U.S. Department of Commerce granted the country's first full commercial license to Pittsburgh's KDKA, which went on the air on November 2 with results from the Warren Harding-James Cox presidential election. Over the next ten years radio growth exploded in both the number of stations and the number of sets owned by the public. By 1923 there were 576 stations, and this would increase to a maximum of 733 in 1927; meanwhile, the number of sets in homes went from about 400,000 in 1922 to 6.5 million in 1927, more than 10 million a year later, and slightly over 12 million in 1930. Another indicator of how radio became a national fad was the presence of one set in every four hundred homes in 1922, but by 1930 one in three had a radio.[56]

Sports quickly became a staple on radio in 1921 although at first, instead of coming on regularly like daily or weekly music and news programs, the broadcasts were tied to sporadic events. As one historian put it: "Sports-casting had no crawling or creeping stages. It jumped down from the obstetrical table, kicked its heels in the air and started out to do a job."[57] KDKA led the way nationally. On April 11, 1921, it broadcast a ten-round boxing match from Pittsburgh's Motor Square Garden; three months later it teamed with WJY of Hoboken, New Jersey, to carry a heavyweight championship fight between Dempsey and French challenger Georges Carpentier in Jersey City, which was said to have had two hundred thousand listeners; and in August it aired Davis Cup tennis matches in Pittsburgh as well as the first broadcast of a major league baseball game between the Pittsburgh Pirates and the visiting Philadelphia Phillies. Harold Arlin, who broadcast the game, recalled he was not excited about the assignment: "Our guys at KDKA didn't even think that baseball would last on radio. I did it sort of as a one-shot project, kind of [as an] addendum to the [sports] events we'd already done." But Arlin then did play-by-play broadcasts that fall of two University of Pittsburgh football games. In the second game, with Nebraska, he yelled so loudly into the microphone after a Pitt score that he broke the equipment and listeners missed several minutes of the game while repairs were being made.[58]

In 1922 radio began subtly increasing sports' national appeal. This occurred when WEAF, a New York City station, used long-distance lines to do the first cross-country broadcast of an eagerly awaited college football game, Princeton at Chicago. Besides those with radios being able to hear the broadcast, the station blared it out on a public address system on top of a truck to thousands who jammed Manhattan's Park Row. Sports historian Ronald A. Smith noted the importance of the broadcast: "[This] was the first of a number of interregional games that were used to promote college football and bring financial rewards to radio stations and networks. . . . [R]adio had made itself an integral part of the nationalization of football by making interregional competition immediately available to masses through the airwaves."[59]

The first live World Series broadcast also occurred that fall. In the previous year, the sports editor of the *Newark (NJ) Sunday Call* had sat in a box seat and reported the games by telephone to a local radio station, WJZ, and an announcer had repeated his account to listeners. But that changed in 1922. Rice sat behind the visiting team's dugout wearing earphones, held what was called a radiophone, and announced the first two games between the New York Yankees and the New York Giants to about 1.5 million listeners within three hundred miles. Suddenly, unlike in 1921, they could hear the roar of the crowd, the crack of the bat when a ball was hit, and the calls of the peanut vendors, which brought a heightened realism to the broadcast. The live report created so much excitement that stores selling radios set up loudspeakers, with more than two thousand people jammed into one store, and many students at nearby Princeton cut classes to hear the game. At the WJZ studios, the crowd was so large that it clogged the streets, and police had to direct traffic.

For Rice, it was less than satisfying; he said having to concentrate on the broadcast left the game's details a blur to him. Never having announced a game, he would watch each play in silence and when it was over he would tell succinctly what had occurred. Broadcast officials wanted him to keep talking between the action, but Rice admitted, "I didn't know what to say." One listener commented about his pauses: "I would hear the crowd let out a terrific roar, and it would seem ages before I knew whether it was a single or a three-bagger that had been made or whether the side had been retired. Of course, it was only a matter of seconds before we got the announcement, but the interest was so intense that it seemed longer. . . . It was in a way too realistic. . . . It was a wonderfully successful broadcast." A colleague of Rice's on the *New York Herald Tribune* agreed about the broadcast's success, calling it "the most remarkable project ever undertaken in the annals of communication."[60] A year later, on WEAF, Rice was again in the announcing booth for the World Series, but in the fourth inning of the third game, he turned over the broadcast to his assistant, Graham McNamee, because it was interfering with his principal work as a sportswriter.[61]

Also in 1922 KDKA may have had the first live sports "blooper." It hired a University of Pittsburgh sophomore, who had placed a $100 bet on his team, to cover a football game by walking up and down the sideline with a microphone. Down by one point Pitt was threatening to score in the last thirty seconds of the game when the student announcer said, "Time in—they're coming out of the huddle—they're lining up—double wing-back formation, and [Jack] Hoozis will take it. Signal—here comes the play—Hoozis has his arms out for it—the ball's passed—and . . . O-o-oh! The goddamn bonehead fumbled it." He was so mortified by what he had said that he dropped the microphone and walked off, never to do another game for KDKA.[62]

Meanwhile, sports broadcasts on radio kept increasing—by 1924, college football was broadcast every week—and the audiences for major events kept steadily rising. On September 23, 1926, Dempsey fought Gene Tunney for the heavyweight title in Philadelphia, and NBC, which had formed the first network that year, broadcast the bout to its affiliated stations while a Schenectady station sent it by shortwave to South America and England, enabling about fifteen million people to hear the fight. The idea of a network was so new that the *New York Times* ran a map on the following day, showing the location of the stations that carried the broadcast. Then, on January 1, 1927, NBC used another multi-station hookup for the Rose Bowl football game between Stanford and Alabama, and that was followed on September 22 by the Dempsey-Tunney rematch in Chicago, which millions heard on an NBC broadcast on more than sixty stations. The *Times* noted that the anticipation of the fight was so high that one department store sold more than $90,000 of radio equipment in two weeks.[63]

As the listening public bought more and more radios in the 1920s, the rapidly increasing popularity of the new technology was viewed warily by newspapers. At first, editors and publishers welcomed it; they believed that advertising for radio equipment would move out of technical journals to papers and magazines because they had broader audiences. In addition, some newspaper owners were so enamored with radio that they began operating stations, and the number of such stations doubled between 1922 and 1923. As for the threat of competition that was downplayed at first. "The broadcasting station never will supplant to any material extent the daily newspaper as a source of information," the editor in chief of the *Detroit News* said in 1922. Two years later RCA's David Sarnoff noted that the importance of radio was that it "makes every listener a participant," but the radio executive added that they would still want to read a newspaper account of what they had heard because of how much more information was offered.[64]

The pros and cons of the competition issue were addressed in 1924 in *Editor & Publisher*, the major newspaper trade publication:

> The organized press has never shown excitement over any threatening aspect of radio, because no matter how much it

may be controlled and commercialized, it possesses physical difficulties which, in general terms, makes it a poor competitor for the established newspaper. These difficulties include the impossibility of exercise of the selective processes of the reader—he sits at his radio and takes what is being sent, whether he likes it or not, and he takes the full dose.

With a newspaper the eye skips around on printed pages, selecting that which it desires as food. Who will be willing to sit through a radio reading of crop reports to get a craved baseball tidbit? Will men retire when women's features are being read, and will women turn to the phonograph for relief when tomorrow's racing entries are flowing from the loud speaker? Furthermore, will transportation companies equip their cars with radio to entertain the morning and evening trippers?

Broadcast radio news service is efficient when it deals with fixed, scheduled events. There is no question that radio reporting of a prize fight, ball game, President's speech, is in many respects superior to any reporting possible on the printed page. It is instantaneous. You feel in actual contact with the event. A clever observer tells you more than a reporter could write or a newspaper print. You get color, atmosphere and a sense of miraculous presence.[65]

The last paragraph summed up the problem faced in the 1920s by newspaper sports sections. In the second half of the 1800s sports coverage had become an invaluable contributor to increasing circulation. But now, at least in terms of major sports events, would people still want to read about what they had already heard on the radio? As Rice's biographer William Harper noted, sportswriters began worrying about being put out of work by the new technology.[66]

In 1932 Jack Graney, who played baseball for fourteen years for the Cleveland Indians, was hired by the team to announce its games on the radio, and, in doing so, became the first former major leaguer to work as a broadcaster for a team.[67] This became a tradition that has grown with each subsequent generation, and athletes now work as broadcast commentators in all sports. In some cases former athletes also have transitioned successfully from playing sports to writing about it. Rick Telander, who was a cornerback and punter on the Northwestern University football team and an all-Big Ten selection in 1970, became one of the best sportswriters in America at *Sports Illustrated* and the *Chicago Sun-Times*.[68]

***

As newspapers struggled with adapting to radio another important issue arose in the 1930s and 1940s: the emergence of popular black superstars in track, boxing, and baseball. Some of the white press and white journalists were openly racist in their coverage of these athletes, others were more subtle or ignored the race question altogether, as they mirrored the culture of a country that was racially divided. As for black newspapers, which were growing larger and more powerful and influential, they were quite willing to play up their sports heroes and use them as a means to get more equality for blacks, even as their journalists struggled against oppression, segregation, and separateness.

Sportswriters and Black Athletes

4

> Dodger writers gave generous space to my play, and were scrupulously fair. However, they fell into a habit of calling me 'The Dodgers' Negro star' in their accounts of games. This was like calling Carl Furillo 'Italian' or Gene Hermanski 'Polish.' Several years were to pass before copy editors blue-penciled Negro into limbo.
>
> —Baseball star Jackie Robinson, 1964

In the high-octane atmosphere of New York City, where extraordinary events are more common than anywhere else in the U.S., excitement gripped the city on the evening of June 22, 1938. As many as eighty thousand fans jammed Yankee Stadium to watch heavyweight champion Joe Louis of Detroit, the black son of a former Alabama sharecropper, meet German challenger Max Schmeling, the only man to beat him in thirty-six professional fights.[1] But to many, far more was at stake than a boxing title. It was American democracy, goodness, and might squaring off against the Nazis' arrogant racial policies and totalitarianism, which three months before had resulted in Germany's annexation of Austria. In the spring, President Franklin D. Roosevelt had invited Louis to the White House and during a brief meeting had asked to feel his arms. He said admiringly, "Joe, we need muscles like yours to beat Germany." Then, on the day of the fight, Louis emphasized his patriotism in a nationally syndicated, ghost-written newspaper article: "Tonight I not only fight the battle of my life to revenge the lone blot on my record, but I fight for America against the challenge of a foreign invader. . . . This isn't just one man against another or Joe Louis boxing Max Schmeling; it is the good old U.S.A. versus Germany."[2]

For those not fortunate enough to see Louis's first-round knock-out of Schmeling, radio carried it live in four languages—English, German, Spanish, and Portuguese—to about sixty million American listeners and to another forty million around the world, including an estimated twenty million in Germany, where it was 3:00 a.m. when the fight began. It was the largest broadcast audience up to that time for any event, sports or otherwise.[3]

The power of radio was undeniable; when Clem McCarthy, who called the fight on NBC, announced Louis had won, celebrations erupted around the U.S. Folksinger Woody Guthrie wrote that every-one in Santa Fe was dancing and singing and laughing with shouts of "Hooray for Joe Louis" and "To hell with Max Schmeling." Actress Bette Davis jumped with joy in Hollywood after winning sixty-six dol-lars in a fight pool at Warner Bros. Studios, and black civil rights activ-ist W. E. B. Du Bois shouted happily in Atlanta because Louis "[b]eat the hell out of the damn German bastard!" In Macon, Georgia, black bandleader Jimmie Lunceford suddenly was ignored at a dance where he was playing when Louis's knockout was announced—"dusky maids in evening gowns and gay young bucks in the latest fads . . . danced spontaneous jigs without the music they had paid to hear." And Louis's wife, Marva, who did not attend the fight, was so elated that she served champagne in her home even though she did not drink. "My daddy told me," she said, "that he was fighting this fight not only for me but for his mother and the Race."[4]

In a 2001 memoir former President Jimmy Carter still remembered the radio broadcast vividly, even though it had occurred sixty-three years before, and how important Louis's victory was to the black field hands who worked for his father near Plains, Georgia. Since none of them had a radio, they asked Carter's dad Earl if he would let them listen to the broadcast on his battery-powered radio; Earl put it in a front-room window, and the blacks gathered in his yard. When the fight ended, no one made a sound, recalled Carter, who was thirteen at the time. "We heard a quiet, 'Thank you, Mr. Earl,'" he wrote, "and then our visitors walked silently out of the yard, crossed the road and the railroad tracks, entered the tenant house, and closed the door. Then all hell broke loose, and their celebration lasted all night."[5]

Nationally famous sports stars of "the Race," as Marva Louis referred to them, were covered extensively by the press in the 1930s and 1940s. They not only included Louis but also Jesse Owens, who won four gold medals at the 1936 Olympics in track and field, and the Brooklyn Dodgers' Jackie Robinson, who became the first black to play in baseball's modern major leagues in 1947. While their athletic accomplishments primarily shaped what white and black newspapers wrote about them, the country's racial realities, and the nervousness of whites that blacks might usurp their athletic dominance, also sometimes subtly affected the coverage. But although memories were still vivid of black boxer Jack Johnson and the "great white hope" controversy that riveted the country from 1908 to 1915, sportswriters and broadcasters did not return to the racially charged coverage of that era.

***

Johnson, Owens, Louis, and Robinson were far from the first U.S. blacks to achieve athletic prominence. In 1875 Oliver Lewis rode Aristides to victory in the first Kentucky Derby, when the majority of the fifteen jockeys were black like him, and other blacks won fourteen of the next twenty-seven derbies. Among them was Isaac Murphy, who was the first three-time winner of the Kentucky Derby (in 1884, 1890, and 1891) and the country's highest paid athlete at the height of his success.[6] Other black standouts at the end of the century included: Frank Hart, who set American walking records in 1880 by covering 131 miles in twenty-four hours and 565 miles in six days; William Henry Lewis, who, in 1892 and 1893 at Amherst and then Harvard, was the first black to be named to Walter Camp's All-American football teams; and Marshall "Major" Taylor, who won the world sprint cycling championship in 1899 and set seven world records from one-quarter mile to two miles.[7]

The parade of outstanding black athletes continued in the first third of the twentieth century, primarily in track and football. In 1908 John Baxter Taylor Jr. was the first black to win an Olympic gold medal as a member of the U.S. 4x400 meters relay team. Other Olympic golds went to broad jumpers William Hubbard and Edward "Ed" Gordon Jr. in the 1924 and 1932 games respectively, and Eddie Tolan, who won the 100- and 200-meter sprints in 1932, setting an Olympic record in the former and a world record in the latter.[8] Meanwhile, Fritz Pollard distinguished himself in football. An All-American running back at Brown, he was one of only two blacks in the newly formed American Professional Football League in 1920 (it was renamed the National Football League two years later) when he led Akron to the league title. Then, a year later, while continuing to play for the Akron Pros, he became the APFL's first black head coach. He went on to star for teams in Milwaukee and Hammond, Indiana, during which he was the first black quarterback in NFL history in 1923.[9] Another black star was tackle Fred "Duke" Slater, who began a ten-year career in the NFL in 1922 and was named to the All-Pro team from 1923 to 1926.[10]

But none of these blacks came close to generating the amount of national athletic fame and notoriety—as well as the overwhelming press coverage—of Johnson. Born in Galveston, Texas, in 1878 to former slaves, Johnson was transformed strikingly at an early age by his mother. Labeling him a coward because he was beaten up continually at school and came home crying, she informed him that she would give him an even worse whipping if it happened again, and he never lost another school fight. Quitting school after the fifth or sixth grade, he worked at various jobs and drifted into boxing, where he had instant success because of his quickness, slugging ability, and physical superiority over other boys. By 1897, he was making a living locally as a professional fighter and a sparring partner.[11]

He left Galveston in 1901 and drifted around the country, fighting mostly blacks and establishing himself in three years as the top black in his weight class by winning a heavyweight title created exclusively for his race. But the bigger prize was the heavyweight championship of the world, which had always been held by whites; the current champion, Jim Jeffries, refused to box him because of his color. "When there are no white men left to fight, I will quit the business," he said. "I am determined not [to] take a chance of losing the championship to a Negro." Johnson kept boxing whomever was available and in 1907 increased the pressure for a fight against the white titleholder by easily defeating former heavyweight champion Bob Fitzsimmons. Jeffries had retired undefeated in 1905, but two years later, when his white successor still refused to face Johnson, sportswriters became critical, calling it bigotry. "Jack Johnson is a colored man," wrote the *St. Louis Post-Dispatch*, "but we cannot get away from the fact that he is the greatest living exponent of the art of hit-and-getaway and, as such, is the outstanding challenger for the title." White heavyweight champion Tommy Burns, who disliked blacks and particularly Johnson, and said he felt "all coons are yellow," finally agreed to a title match on December 26, 1908, because he would make $30,000, which was the largest purse guaranteed to a boxer up to that time.[12]

The money angle greatly upset former champion John L. Sullivan, who in 1892 had said that he would fight anyone as long as they were white; as for blacks, he noted he had never fought them and never would. Thus, he was upset that Burns's greed was causing him to break the color line. "Shame on the money-mad champion!" said Sullivan. "Shame on the man who upsets good American precedents because there are Dollars, Dollars, Dollars in it."[13] Newspapers in Sydney, Australia, where the fight took place, were more direct than Sullivan about what was at stake—and they could have been speaking for many people in the U.S. "Citizens who have never prayed before are supplicating Providence to give the white man a strong right arm with which to belt the coon into oblivion," wrote London's *Illustrated Sporting and Dramatic News*. And Sydney's *Australian Star* warned that the fight might be looked upon in the future "as the first great battle of an inevitable race war. . . . There is more in this fight to be considered than the mere title of pugilistic champion of the world."[14]

Thus, the significance of the fight was obvious. In numerous ways,

America was a segregated society and blacks were second-class citizens. However, if Johnson could beat Burns and become the first black heavyweight champion of the world, it would be a sign that blacks had achieved a degree of equality with whites in a highly visible and important way. The *Star* suggested this could lead to trouble. The prevailing white view had been stated succinctly in 1897 when an irate white spectator in New Orleans stopped a boxing match between a white and a black. "The idea of niggers fighting white men," he said. "Why if that scoundrel would beat that white boy the niggers would never stop gloating over it, and as it is we have enough trouble with them."[15]

To many in both Australia and America, the fight was a stunning disaster; in front of twenty thousand spectators, Johnson beat Burns unmercifully, leaving him bloody and bruised, until the fight was humanely stopped in the fourteenth round.[16] The somber mood of the American press was summed up by a sports columnist on the *Omaha Daily News*: "Never before in the history of the prize ring has such a crisis arisen as that which faces the followers of the game tonight." A reporter on the *Omaha Sunday Bee*, meanwhile, got some solace in the fact that at least an American had won the title. While Raleigh, North Carolina's *News & Observer* ran only one paragraph on the fight, noting that a "Texas Darky" had won, the *Dallas Morning News* carried a cartoon showing Johnson holding a watermelon, with thick lips and wide eyes, and saying, "Golly, old Santy sho' was good to me."[17] Johnson biographer Randy Roberts summed up the feeling of those who were disheartened by the outcome of the fight: "The sadness . . . could only be expressed in superlatives—greatest tragedy, deepest gloom, saddest day, darkest night. The race war had been fought. Armageddon was over. The Caucasian race had lost."[18]

Making Johnson's victory even worse for whites was the reaction of some American blacks. In their elation, not only did they begin treating whites rudely but they also openly displayed enormous pride in the outcome. One wealthy black Chicagoan boasted, "Johnson's victory demonstrates the physical superiority of the black over the Caucasian.

The basis of mental superiority in most men is physical superiority. If the [N]egro can raise his mental standard to his physical eminence, some day he will be a leader among men."[19] While most of the black press did not write a lot about the fight, an exception was Virginia's *Richmond Planet*, which devoted more to it—eight columns—than any other black paper. Then, a week later, it claimed Johnson's win had given "more genuine satisfaction" to blacks than anything else in the past forty years. The *Savannah Tribune*, noting this was the first time that a black had been in a major sports event, said his victory made it "fit and proper that we doff our hats to Mr. Johnson." In the same vein the *Colored American Magazine* called it "the zenith of Negro sport." And the *Cleveland Gazette* and the *Baltimore Afro-American* felt the result was a blow against racism and prejudice; the former added the fight's outcome "left an awful sour taste in the mouths of many prejudiced Americans."[20]

Johnson's victory launched a feverish national search for a white challenger who could reclaim the heavyweight title, and the term "hope of the white race" became common in the white press. Since the early 1800s the term "white hope" had never been associated with boxing or anything racial. Instead it was used over the next hundred years to refer to purity and great expectations, and it was applied to a myriad of things from a rare rose to the name of highly regarded breeding animals to a type of hog food to a person who had claimed to be the messiah. But as historian Phillip J. Hutchison noted, the term took on a blatant, "troublesome" racial meaning in the press after Johnson won the heavyweight title, and this lasted until 1915, when he finally was defeated. The usage by journalists did "not reflect favorably" on them, said Hutchison.[21]

The genesis of the shift to a new meaning for a white hope has been attributed to novelist Jack London, who covered Johnson's rout of Burns for the *New York Herald*. He wrote: "The fight!—There was no fight! No American massacre could compare to the hopeless slaughter that took place in the Sydney Stadium. . . . A golden smile [Johnson had gold-capped teeth] tells the story and the smile was Johnson's. . . .

Burns was a toy in his hands. For Johnson it was a kindergarten romp. . . . But one thing remains. Jeffries must emerge from his alfalfa farm and remove that smile from Johnson's face. Jeff, it's up to you."[22] While he did not use the terms "hope of the white race" or "white hope" in referring to Jeffries, the implication definitely was there.

Johnson had five title fights against white boxers in 1909, but none of them were described by the press as white hopes; instead, like London, sportswriters quickly settled on Jeffries as the one man who could reestablish white supremacy. Ten days after Johnson's victory in Australia, a story in the *La Crosse (WI) Tribune* said Jeffries "is the only hope of the white race now," and that apparently was the beginning of the white hope campaign. In April public pressure convinced Jeffries, who lived in Burbank, California, to come out of retirement, and a month later the *La Crosse* paper reported crowds "lined the sidewalks and cheered the 'hope of the white race' as he passed to his hotel." The "hope" term was spread rapidly and frequently throughout the country by wire services, chains of papers (such as those owned by William Randolph Hearst), and freelancers.[23] The *Chicago Tribune*, for example, wrote that the upcoming fight was between "the white man's hope and the black peril."[24] Underlying the use of the word "hope" was a belief that lighter-skinned persons were superior to those with darker skins, noted Hutchison. For example, the *New York Times* said in October that Jeffries was "expected to regain individual physical supremacy for the white race."[25] However, the paper warned two days before the fight that if Johnson won "thousands of his ignorant brothers will interpret his victory as justifying claims to much more than physical equality with their white neighbors."[26] *Boxing* magazine said bluntly that "the thought [of a Johnson victory] is too awful to contemplate."[27]

The *Times*'s confidence in Jeffries was shattered quickly on July 4, 1910, in what was publicized as the "Fight of the Century" before twenty-two thousand excited fans in Reno, Nevada. After Johnson won easily in fifteen rounds, earning a purse of $117,000, Jeffries admitted, "I never could have whipped Johnson at my best. I couldn't have hit him. No, I couldn't have reached him in a thousand years."[28] A sportswriter for Reno's *Nevada State Journal*, who was among the five hundred journalists who covered the fight, succinctly summed up the result: "'pears to me like we will have to get another 'white hope.'" It was one of the first times, if not the first, that the press shortened the term "hope of the white race" to "white hope" in referring to the search for someone to defeat Johnson.[29]

On the day of the fight large crowds gathered excitedly in auditoriums, theaters, and baseball parks in such cities as Boston, Chicago, Cleveland, Dallas, Los Angeles, New Orleans, San Francisco, and St. Louis to learn the round-by-round results from the wire services. Big city newspapers posted telegraph bulletins during the match—more than thirty thousand gathered outside the *New York Times* building to read them and more than ten thousand were at the *Atlanta Journal-Constitution*—and the *San Francisco Examiner* set up a ring in which white and black actors recreated the fight, punch by punch, as the results of each round arrived. While local regulations in some southern cities and towns kept whites and blacks from congregating together, blacks in many places gathered by themselves to get the results, and at Alabama's Tuskegee Institute, a historically black school, a room was set aside for anyone who wanted to follow the fight.[30]

Johnson's victory quickly unleashed a wave of violence across the U.S.—not only were hundreds of blacks injured but dozens also were killed—much of it the result of blacks angering whites by showing joy and pride in the outcome. For example, a black in New York City was almost lynched when he yelled to a crowd of whites: "We blacks put one over on you whites, and we're going to do more." In St. Louis, the *Post-Dispatch* said blacks "drank freely, offered to do battle in imitation of Johnson and ran alongside street cars jeering at white passengers," which resulted in an irritated white stabbing one of the blacks. Other blacks were injured or killed in such places as Greenwood, South Carolina; Uvalda, Georgia; Houston; Little Rock, Arkansas; Roanoke and Norfolk, Virginia; Wilmington, Delaware; Pueblo, Colorado; Shreveport, Louisiana; New Orleans; Baltimore; Cincinnati; St. Joseph, Missouri; Los Angeles; and Chattanooga, Tennessee. In New

York City, white gangs set fires to tenement houses where blacks lived and tried to lock the inhabitants inside as the flames spread. And in Evansville, Indiana, a black went into a grill and ordered coffee that was "as strong as Jack Johnson and a steak beat up like Jim Jeffries." The infuriated white owner slapped him, grabbed a pistol, and shot him five times.[31]

Two days after the fight the *Los Angeles Times* spoke for many whites when it warned editorially that blacks should not think Johnson's victory changed their status: "Do not point your nose too high. Do not swell your chest too much. Do not boast too loudly. Do not be puffed up. Let not your ambition be inordinate or take a wrong direction. . . . Remember you have done nothing at all. You are just the same member of society today you were last week. . . . You are on no higher plane, deserve no new consideration, and will get none. . . . No man will think a bit higher of you because your complexion is the same as that of the victor at Reno."[32] Some black newspapers agreed. The *Advocate* in Portland, Oregon, wrote, "Racial superiority is not decided by tests of physical . . . endurance."[33]

For whites, making matters worse was that Johnson had taken on the aura of a "Sport" even before he won the heavyweight title. It was a lifestyle that white men could have if they could afford it, and few would complain about it, but it was considered highly inappropriate for blacks because it showed they did not know their place in society. Style was important for someone who desired to be a "Sport" and dressing well was a big part of it. Johnson easily made enough from boxing to have a large wardrobe—a sportswriter said he had at least twenty-one suits at one point and changed clothes three times a day—and he had a maid whose only job was to take care of what he wore. Then there was sometimes a stylish cane and the slow and graceful way that he moved on the streets. As for entertainment, he enjoyed nightclubs; drove fast, expensive cars; went to brothels; and openly traveled and lived with prostitutes, both black and white, sometimes with several at a time. All of this, combined with his success in the ring, infuriated whites. "No longer the respectful darky asking, hat in hand, for massa's permission, Johnson was seen as the prototype of the independent black who acted as he pleased and accepted no bar to his conduct. As such, Johnson was transformed into a racial symbol that threatened America's social order," wrote Roberts, his biographer.[34]

While blacks were far more accepting than whites of Johnson's lifestyle as a "Sport," some worried that his excesses might impede black progress in the country, slow though it was. Ten days after his victory over Jeffries, the black *New York Age* offered him advice in an editorial: "Mr. Jack Johnson must conduct himself in a modest manner. He can hurt the race immeasurably just now if he goes splurging and making a useless, noisy exhibition of himself. We hope that he will not be arrested on any charge. Any undue exhibition on the part of Mr. Johnson will hurt every member of the race; on the other hand, becoming modesty and self-control will win him many lasting friends."[35] As time passed historian Carrie Teresa Isard noted that black newspapers became less tolerant of him because his controversial lifestyle conflicted with black ideals: "an insistence on dignity, morality and temperance."[36] A *Baltimore Afro-American* columnist in 1912 said he did not view Johnson as "a race leader" and hoped "we will not produce any more like him," and two months later the *Washington Bee* called him a "fool" and said "his money and lack of brains cause him to do things that sensible colored men would not do."[37]

With Johnson's lifestyle remaining unchanged after the Jeffries fight, reporters, columnists, and headline writers in the white press began pushing an even stronger "white hope" campaign in late 1910. These publications frequently used the words "fizzle" and "flops" as Johnson defeated one white challenger after another. Black newspapers, meanwhile, rarely referred to the losers as white hopes. Instead, they "mocked the boxers' 'hope' status and chastised the white press for its 'nauseating' efforts to portray such mediocre boxers as legitimate contenders," noted Hutchison. In 1914 the *Chicago Defender* even went as far as accusing some sportswriters on white dailies of writing "harangues" about Johnson, which showed their "personal race-prejudices."[38]

The white hope campaign in the press continued unabated until April 5, 1915, when Johnson was knocked out in the twenty-sixth round by Jess Willard in Havana, Cuba. The *New York Times*—noting that the result "restored pugilistic superiority" to whites and not only satisfied them but also "intelligent colored people"—predicted there would not be another black heavyweight champion for "at least as long as the present generation endures."[39] In fact, it would not take that long; in twenty-two years another black would win the heavyweight title.

In putting together his 2005 television documentary on Jack Johnson, *Unforgivable Blackness*, filmmaker Ken Burns interviewed historian Geoffrey C. Ward. "I've been dealing with American history for years and years," said Ward, "and I had a sort of intellectual understanding of what racism was like at the turn of the twentieth century. I knew it was in many ways the worst period. But until I immersed myself in the newspapers and the magazines of the time, when they were dealing with Jack Johnson, I really had no idea, I think, of the depths of it."[40]

Ward's comment about racism and how it showed up in the press in the first fifteen years of the twentieth century is interesting when examining press coverage of Jesse Owens and Joe Louis in the 1930s. Although twenty years had passed since Johnson was the heavyweight champion, they enjoyed the same national and international fame that he did. And, like him, they were black. Since the stature of blacks in the U.S. had essentially not changed from the time when Johnson was champion, and because America was still very much a segregated country, it would seem the press treatment that they received would be the same as Johnson. But it was completely different.

Other than having grandparents who had been slaves, Owens had little in common with Johnson. Born in Oakville, Alabama, in 1913 as the tenth child of poor sharecroppers, he moved with his parents when he was nine years old to Cleveland, and when he was thirteen Charles Riley, a junior high school coach, noticed his long legs, which made it possible for him to outrun and outjump his classmates. As Owens described it he had inherited his father's "long, lion-spring legs." Before school each day Riley began showing him the fine points of running and the importance of technique, and he quickly came to love track.[41] Sports journalist and author Jeremy Schaap noted the significance of the moment:

> It was an odd feeling for Jesse to have someone take so much interest in him. His mother had always told him that he was special, but that was his mother. Now, having that idea reinforced by an authority figure—a white man, no less—he blossomed. With each blistering lap on the track, with each pat on the back from Riley, Jesse allowed himself to believe that there was a future for him in running, in simply doing what felt as natural to him as breathing. With Riley pushing him, he was empowered, and for a black teenager in the 1920s, that in itself was an achievement.[42]

Owens noted that Riley, the first white he had known well, "proved to me beyond all proof that a white man can understand—and love—a Negro." He said Riley made him "behave," and without his influence he "very easily" could have ended up in jail.[43]

At Cleveland's East Technical High School, where Owens' popularity was shown by his election as student council president in his senior year, he won seventy-five of seventy-nine races. The highlight came at the National Interscholastic Championship track meet in Chicago in June 1933 when he set a world record in the 220-yard dash and tied the mark in the 100.[44]

The only one of his siblings to finish high school, Owens accepted a work scholarship to Ohio State, which surprised his black friends because the university had "a notoriously bad reputation for racially prejudicial attitudes and policies," noted historian William J. Baker. The *Chicago Defender*, one of the country's two largest black newspapers, editorialized against his choice. "He will be an asset to any school," it wrote, "so why help advertise an institution that majors in prejudice?" By going there, the paper said it meant that he approved of hate and prejudice rather than fighting against them militantly.

"The day has passed for turning the other cheek," it continued. "We must either fight or perish under the iron heel of the oppressor." When Owens entered the university in October 1933, he was surrounded by prejudice; as a classmate of his recalled, Columbus was "a cracker town . . . just like Jackson, Mississippi." He was barred from living in a university dorm because of his color and had to stay at a boarding house one-fourth mile from campus with other black students, and while he could eat at the campus union none of the restaurants next to campus would serve him. As for his work scholarship, he ran a freight elevator in the rear of the State Office Building, where the public did not see him, unlike white athletes, who ran the front passenger elevator.[45]

None of the prejudice, however, affected Owens on the track. Labeled a "magnet" because of the way he attracted spectators to Ohio State meets, the height of his collegiate career was on May 25, 1935, at the Big Ten championship in what is considered the greatest single day's performance by one person in the history of track and field. Within one hour, he broke world records in the 220-yard dash, the 220-yard low hurdles, and the broad jump while tying the world record in the 100. A sportswriter for the black *Cleveland Gazette* observed, "The 12,000 spectators were alternately stunned into silence and then moved to tremendous salvos of applause when the Buckeye ace staged his almost unbelievable show."[46]

Coinciding with Owens's success in college was a renewed controversial discussion in and out of the press about whether blacks were highly successful in track because of their race. In the late 1800s, as blacks rose to athletic prominence, there was considerable speculation that this was because their physiological makeup was different from whites, and this was used by some to explain Johnson's success in boxing from 1908 to 1915. After dying down for several decades the drumbeat of racial theories arose again in the 1930s because of the Olympic success of black American track stars. Many argued that blacks had an advantage over whites because of their longer heel bones and stronger Achilles tendons, but Dean Cromwell, the University of

Southern California track coach and a U.S. assistant Olympic coach in 1936, had a different explanation: blacks were more primitive than whites. "It was not so long ago that his ability to sprint and jump was a life-and-death matter to him in the jungle," wrote Cromwell. "His muscles are pliable, and his easy-going disposition is a valuable aid to the mental and physical relaxation that a runner and jumper must have." He also said he believed almost all great sprinters "are of a nervous, high-strung type." Another notable track coach, Lawson Robertson of the University of Pennsylvania, agreed. "Nervous energy makes for great speed and explosive energy," he said. "These are racial assets of the Negro. The average [black] track and field athlete is built for speed. The legs are symmetrical, and muscles are tapering and seldom bunched."[47]

The definitive comment on this issue, however, came from Dr. W. Montague Cobb, a black associate professor of anatomy at Howard University. In an article in the *Journal of Health and Physical Education* in January 1936, he noted that a "number of recent comments in the press" attributed blacks' success in the sprints and broad jumping to specific characteristics of their race. This led to him carefully examining Owens' body for two days to determine if this was true. He concluded:

Since man has begun to measure the quality of his athletic performances with stop-watch and tape he has constantly improved. This has been due not to a betterment of human stock but to experience and better nurture.

No particular racial or national group has ever exercised a monopoly or supremacy in a particular kind of event. . . . The split-second differences in the performances of the great Negro and white sprinters of past and present are insignificant from an anthropological standpoint. So are the differences in the achievements of the two races in the broad jump.

The physiques of champion Negro and white sprinters in general and of Jesse Owens in particular reveal nothing to indicate that Negroid physical characters are anatomically concerned with the present dominance of Negro athletes in national competition in the short dashes and the broad jump.

There is not a single physical characteristic which all the Negro stars in question have in common which would definitely identify them as Negroes.[48]

Owens was already involved in another racial controversy before Cobb's article was published. In 1933, when Adolf Hitler became the German chancellor, he barred Jews from participating on German sports clubs and using public athletic facilities, which virtually made it impossible for them to be on the 1936 Olympic team. As a result, the Amateur Athletic Union (AAU) voted that American athletes should not participate in the next Olympics in Berlin unless Germany stopped discriminating against Jews. This immediately resulted in a struggle with the American Olympic Association, which was against mixing politics and sports and supported U.S. participation in the next Olympics after several of its members visited Germany and were artfully spun by the Nazis. Then, in September 1935, when Germany instituted the Nuremberg Laws, stripping Jews of their citizenship and lessening their legal rights, the outcry in the U.S. about competing in the Olympics the following summer escalated dramatically. Churches, labor unions, city councils, and the National Association for the Advancement of Colored People (NAACP) called for an American boycott.[49]

Black newspapers quickly joined the fray. Pointing out that Americans who were concerned about German minorities showed little interest in ending segregation and the lynching of blacks in America, the papers said U.S. whites supporting a boycott were hypocritical. But there was no consensus among the papers about the wisdom of a boycott. Some of them felt this was necessary because it would be a high-profile stand against racism. "Humanity demands that Hitlerism by crushed," editorialized New York City's *Amsterdam News* in encouraging black athletes to not compete, "and yours [the blacks] is the opportunity to strike a blow which may hasten the inevitable end."

But others felt it was more important for them to go to Berlin, where their expected success would be a dagger against both German and American racism. Furthermore, as well-known *Pittsburgh Courier* columnist George S. Schuyler noted in criticizing the boycott movement: "With the possible exception of the Scandinavian countries, where could the Olympic Games be held where liberty is not stamped into the mud and millions are not ruthlessly persecuted and exploited?"[50]

In December 1935, undeterred by the NAACP's position, Owens and four other U.S. black track stars wrote the American Olympic Association that they wanted to compete in the Berlin Olympics although they were not satisfied with the treatment of blacks in America. "No political situation should alter plans for the coming games in Berlin," said sprinter Ralph Metcalfe.[51] Cleveland's *Call & Post* urged Owens to reconsider his position, calling the Nazis "the world's outstanding criminal gang," and Walter White, the NAACP's executive secretary, tried unsuccessfully in a telegram on December 4 to get him to change his mind:

> I fully realize how great a sacrifice it will be for you to give up the trip to Europe and to forgo the acclaim, which your athletic prowess will unquestionably bring you. I realize equally well how hypocritical it is for certain Americans to point the finger of scorn at any other country for racial or any other kind of bigotry.
>
> On the other hand it is my first conviction that the issue of participation in the 1936 Olympics, if held in Germany under the present regime, transcends all other issues. Participation by American athletes, and especially those of our race, which has suffered more than any other from American hatred, would, I firmly believe, do irreparable harm. . . . I hope . . . that you will take the high stand that we should rise above personal benefit and help strike a blow at intolerance. I am sure that your stand will be applauded by many people in all parts of the world, as your participation under the present situation in Germany

would alienate many high-minded people who are awakening to the dangers of intolerance wherever it raises its head.[52]

But Owens, who had worked hard for years to achieve track greatness, refused to change his mind and easily won all three of his events at the U.S. Olympic trials. In fact, blacks won the 100-, 200-, 400-, and 800-meter races along with the broad jump and the high jump and also finished second in all of those events except the two longer races. Shirley Povich of the *Washington Post* attributed their dominance in track to being "one of the sports in which they are permitted to contest against the best of the white race and thus the bulk of the Negro talent is directed into that line."[53]

As the Olympics neared Fred Farrell of the *Daily Worker*, the Communist Party newspaper that was a big supporter of blacks, mirrored what many American sportswriters were writing: the Olympics were expected to be a bitter "disappointment" for Hitler. "When the time comes to present medals to Negroes and Jews his ideas of racial supremacy for the people he wants to be supreme will suffer something of a shock," he wrote. "Will he shake hands with Jesse Owens, for example?" Black newspapers particularly played up the fact that the U.S. team had eighteen blacks (sixteen of whom were men), compared to only six on the previous U.S. Olympic squad in 1932. The *Pittsburgh Courier* gushed, "On every tongue, the name of the fleet-footed sons and daughters of Ham are being bandied about."[54]

Owens was easily the Olympic leader of what sportswriter Grantland Rice called a "darktown parade." Syndicated columnist Westbrook Pegler echoed that sentiment, saying the U.S. would win the Olympics, "thanks to the Negro athletes, whose presence on the squad is proof of the democracy of sports" in America. Owens won gold medals in the 100- and 200-meter sprints, the broad jump, and the 4x100-meter relay, breaking or equaling nine Olympic records and setting three world records. Referring to his performances, as well as other American blacks, Joe Williams of the *New York World-Telegram* wrote on the third day of competition, "It begins to look as if we will have to make the 'Darktown Strutters' Ball' [a popular song] the official hymn of the American Olympiad."[55] But not all of the press was enamored with their success. In a study of the Olympic coverage of twenty-six Deep South newspapers, historian Robert Drake found: eight of the papers had no stories about the blacks while the other eighteen only had minimal coverage; few photographs of the black athletes were used; and the blacks were "consistently depicted . . . as foolish, child-like, lazy, unintelligent, and dangerous."[56]

At the end of the first week of the Olympics Owens summed up the importance of what U.S. black athletes were accomplishing in a letter to the *Pittsburgh Courier*: "I am proud that I am an American. I see the sun breaking through the clouds when I realize that millions of Americans will recognize now that what I and the boys of my race are trying to do is attempted for the glory of our country and our countrymen. Maybe more people will now realize that the Negro is trying to do his full part as an American citizen."[57]

Joe Louis's experiences, both in life and with the press, were strikingly similar to what Owens encountered. Born in Lafayette, Alabama, in 1914 to a poor sharecropper, he moved when he was twelve with his family and seven siblings to Detroit, where they were on relief. He enrolled in a vocational school two years later, and an instructor noted presciently that he "should be able to do something with his hands." In 1963 Louis recalled: "All my life my hands felt important to me. They felt big, strong, and they seemed to want to do something special." Outside of school, he developed his physique by delivering sixty-pound blocks of ice, sometimes up several flights of stairs.[58]

His boxing career began unpromisingly in 1932 when he was knocked down seven times in his first amateur match. Briefly discouraged, he soon returned to boxing and won local light heavyweight Golden Gloves titles in 1933 and '34 before also winning a national title in Chicago before twenty thousand fans. Labeled by a white newspaper "the Detroit colored lad with the frozen face" because of his implacable look in the ring, he quickly was championed by the *Chicago Tribune*, whose sports columnist gave him money for travel expenses to a tournament, and the black *Chicago Defender*. After winning an AAU light heavyweight title in the spring of 1934 and with the *Defender* calling him the best amateur boxer in the country, he wanted to turn pro that summer because he not only disliked having to work in a Ford plant between matches but also was having trouble as an amateur finding anyone who would fight him for free. Becoming a professional, however, appeared to be a prescription for failure. "Negro fighters are used merely to build up 'white hopes,'" wrote the black *Norfolk Journal and Guide* in 1934. "Their activities are confined to fake and fraudulent bouts through unscrupulous managers and promoters who are more eager to replenish their inflated purses than to make Negro champions." The *Defender* also was pessimistic, saying changes would occur only if a black fighter could guarantee attendance. "We've got to wait until somebody can produce a half-clown and half-gorilla to arouse the interest of our pale face brothers," it wrote.[59]

Nevertheless, Louis's two financial backers hired a veteran Chicago trainer, Jack Blackburn, who agreed to take him on although he was dubious of whether Louis could become a championship contender because of the color of his skin. From the first, Blackburn emphasized that he had to be "very good outside the ring and very bad inside." So, Louis began training regularly each morning at six o'clock, learning what it took to be a champion in the ring, while his backers began turning him into the opposite of Jack Johnson outside of it. Journalist David Margolick explained:

He would always be soft-spoken, understated, and polite, no matter what he accomplished. He would not preen or gloat or strut in the ring. If he needed his teeth capped, it would not be done in gold, as Johnson had done. He would always conduct himself with dignity and not, as Louis once put it, like one of those "fool nigger dolls" with wide grins and thick lips. When it came to women, he would stick to his own kind. . . . He would never fraternize with white women, let alone be photographed with them. He would not drive fast cars. . . . Anyone wishing to hold Louis back would get no help from Louis himself. The press would be saturated with stories of Louis's boyish goodness, his love for his mother, his mother's love for him, his devotion to scripture, his abstemiousness and frugality.[60]

The meticulous preparations paid off quickly. Moving up to the heavyweight division, Louis had his first professional fight in July 1934, and by the end of the year he was 12–0 with nine knockouts and only one bout lasting the full ten rounds. After cruising undefeated through another twelve fights, he was knocked out unexpectedly by Max Schmeling in the twelfth round in June 1936, but after another seven victories, he fought Jim Braddock for the world championship in Chicago on June 22, 1937.[61] In giving him the opportunity to become the first black champion since Johnson in 1915, promoter Mike Jacobs had to make a difficult choice between Louis and Schmeling. Even though many whites still thought that the heavyweight champion should only be white, Jacobs chose Louis not only because he thought he would bring in more money at the box office but also because he was aware of the growing animosity and concern about what was happening in Germany. "If Schmeling fought and defeated Braddock, he might retire to Berlin with the most prestigious title in sports," wrote historian Thomas R. Hietala. "Did Americans want the crown to pass from an Irish American to a German national, a man whose country was fast becoming synonymous with anti-Semitism, anti-Catholicism, xenophobia, and militarism?"[62]

Before the fight took place both white and black newspapermen said it was only right that Louis should be given a title shot because discrimination violated American ideals. And the *Pittsburgh Courier*, which early in his career began calling itself the "Joe Louis paper" because of its extensive coverage of him, particularly painted him in glowing terms. Writer Ira Lewis called Louis a "gentleman" and a "credit to himself, to the profession, and to his race," and journalist Chester Washington described him as "a fine, clean living fellow [who] still clings to those rules of right living instilled in him by his mother." Sid Keener of the *St. Louis Star-Times* agreed that Louis was a model black who was totally different from Johnson. Meanwhile, Ring Lardner's son John Lardner of the *New York Herald Tribune* wrote that he did not expect race riots if Louis won the title: "The Negroes of Chicago seem pretty quiet and nonchalant just now. And besides, things have changed since the time of Jack Johnson."[63]

After Louis knocked out Braddock in the eighth round Richards Vidmer of the *Herald Tribune* agreed with Lardner that, unlike when Johnson was champion, there would be no race riots because Louis was not just "a fine fighter" but also had "other characteristics that go with greatness." Those traits, which were admired by both blacks and whites, included being "quiet, unassuming, healthy, and sincere." Thus, he wrote it would not be necessary to have a search for a "white hope." After the fight, Louis encountered joyful blacks dancing in the street, and one called out, "Don't be another Jack Johnson!" In the *Chicago Defender*, Louis addressed that concern: "My conduct as champion will be the same as my conduct before I was champion."[64]

On the day after his victory, Louis told Chester Washington that one of his main goals was to face Schmeling again and beat him, and he did that easily four fights later in June 1938. Among those watching the fight was Johnson, who praised Louis. "I want to say here that I think Joe's victory has done the race a lot of good and has improved race relations in every field of endeavor," he said. "I witnessed a great fight by a great champion." The black *Philadelphia Independent* agreed with Johnson about the significance of the victory, saying it resulted in more good feelings about blacks than anything since the Civil War ended in 1865. And the white *Philadelphia Record* was amazed that a black was not only the heavyweight champion but popular with all Americans. "Grandfather wouldn't have believed that possible," it wrote. "But grandfather may have been wrong about a number of things, including the rate at which America was progressing toward tolerance." Even in the Deep South, the white *Huntsville (AL) Times* was faintly complimentary of the fight's outcome: "No intelligent person, of whatever color, is likely to claim that this proves Alabama negro stock is superior to Aryan stock, but the situation appeals to the American sense of humor and love of fair play."[65]

White newspaper coverage of Owens and Louis in the 1930s was far less blatantly racist than what was written about Johnson from 1908 to 1915. But the racism was still subtly present, as historian Pamela Laucella noted in 2002 when she examined what Grantland Rice, who was one of the leading sportswriters of the first half of the twentieth century, wrote about Owens and the other black athletes at the 1936 Olympics. She labeled his coverage "blatantly racist" in its language and its stereotypical characterization of the black athletes. Not only did Rice refer to their success as "a darktown parade," but he also wrote: "Easily, almost lazily, and minus any show of extra effort, they have turned sport's greatest spectacle into the 'Black Birds of 1936.'" Furthermore, he referred to Owens as a "noble savage," an African, an Ethiopian, and a "wild Zulu." Laucella also found Rice "clearly affirmed the idea that black athletes were genetically predisposed to excelling in sports due to their physical and emotional composition. He additionally bolstered the stereotype that black individuals are lazier than other races." She concluded that Rice's Tennessee upbringing resulted in him having a southern view of race as he "failed to criticize thoughts of the period, and either exhibited apathy or sustained stereotypes, subconsciously or consciously."[66]

The same pattern of subtle racism existed in what was written about Louis, according to biographer Chris Mead. White reporters sometimes broadly labeled him an African or specifically placed him in a particular part of the continent, calling him an Ethiopian, a Senegambian, or a Nubian.[67] As for Rice, who frequently in conversations used the term "the nigger" in referring to Owens, Louis, and Jackie Robinson, historian Charles Fountain noted in 1993 that his writing about blacks was "patently and sickeningly racist." But he cautioned against judging him by today's standards.

Rice had never signed on to be a sociologist, but the world of sport [in the 1930s] was a full two decades ahead of the rest of American society in being forced to confront the reality of blacks and whites drinking from the same cup as equals. Rice's thoughts and writing on the emerging black presence in sport—on Jesse Owens and Joe Louis in particular—give evidence of glib insensitivity and ignorance. But so too does this halting, tentative canon show evidence of confusion and uncertainty, of a man whose senses, and experiences, were shaking and challenging the ingrained prejudices he shared with most Americans of his generation, and had never thought to question before.

To measure the behavior of any figure from a past time by contemporary sensibilities is to engage in what historian William Manchester calls "generational chauvinism." We can decry our blindness as a society, but we cannot judge individuals to be ignorant or malevolent simply because they behaved in a way that was wholly appropriate and consistent with the society in which they lived. Grantland Rice's writing on blacks is shameful when viewed from a perspective of more than fifty years later. Less shameful than many; more shameful than some. But so too does it represent mainstream America, mainstream American journalism. As such, it can be served by no apologies or defenses, and deserves damnation less than it demands understanding.[68]

That leaves the question of why press coverage in Johnson's era was much more negative than what Owens and Louis encountered. Segregation existed in both time periods; and blacks were second-class citizens with virtually no more equality in the 1930s than they had at the start of the twentieth century. Historians have suggested two major reasons for the difference.

One was the way that Owens and Louis acted. Johnson angered white America by deliberately adopting the lifestyle of a "Sport," with expensive clothes, gold-capped teeth, fast cars, and a travel entourage of both black and white women, many of whom were prostitutes. That was not the way that blacks were supposed to act—in other words, Johnson did not know his place. Owens and Louis, however, were careful to not draw any unnecessary attention to themselves, or be controversial, and as a result the white newspapers did not write about them negatively. As Laucella noted: "While Rice failed to change or challenge the status quo [of U.S. race attitudes], he still praised Owens' athletic prowess and achievements, thereby reinforcing and sustaining the racial opinions and prejudices of American society during the 1930s. This suggests that black individuals, who did not challenge the white man's system, could gain respect on some levels. However, it chiefly included athletic skills and certain personality characteristics, rather than intelligence or mental capacities."[69]

The other major reason cited for the positive press coverage of Owens and Louis is that they defeated athletes from Germany, a country that increasingly concerned the U.S. by the mid-1930s because of its ruthless ambitions. As Fountain explained, this forced Americans to make an "uncomfortable choice" between their "longstanding racial bias" and their negative feelings about the Germans, and nationalism won out. "Even those Americans who suffered from a less-virulent strain of his [Hitler's] poisonous notion of Aryan superiority found themselves in the unlikely position of cheering for a black man," he wrote. Hutchison agreed. As German fascism rose alarmingly in the 1930s "white America modified racial barriers and created the 'good Negro athlete' persona to exploit the talents of Louis and Jesse Owens."[70] Nationalism also was a major factor in Louis's enormous popularity among blacks (although probably not whites) even before he defeated Schmeling in 1938. In June 1935, with tensions growing rapidly between Italy and Ethiopia, Louis knocked out Italian Primo Carnera in the sixth round at Yankee Stadium. The black *Pittsburgh Courier*, whose readers were intensively interested in what happened to blacks in Ethiopia, wrote extensively of his victory, using its largest headline of the year on the main story. Reporter William Nunn Sr. called Louis "the answer to our prayers, the prayers of a race of people who are struggling to break through dense clouds of prejudice and misunderstanding, a race of people who, though bowed by oppression, will never be broken in spirit."[71] Thus, Owens and Louis were national heroes to both whites and blacks, an image that was importantly enhanced, historian David K. Wiggins noted, by them continually saying how much "they loved their country and owed America."[72]

Although the lifestyles of Owens and Louis, and their triumphs over German athletes, unquestionably contributed to their positive press coverage, historians have overlooked another factor that may have played a major role: the American Society of Newspaper Editors' adoption in 1923 of the first national code of ethics, "Canons of Journalism." Noting journalists should avoid partisanship and be impartial, the code said: "Sound practice makes a clear distinction between news reports and expressions of opinion. News reports should be free from opinion or bias of any kind."[73] While the push for professional ethics had little or no appreciable impact on sportswriters, who continued to openly express opinions in news stories, the code very well may have helped rein in their racism and cause them to be more subtle when writing about Owens and Louis in the 1930s.[74]

While Jackie Robinson enjoyed basically the same positive press coverage as Owens and Louis, the path to him becoming the first black in baseball's modern major leagues in 1947 had similar roadblocks to what Johnson experienced in boxing. In 1872, only three years after professional baseball began with the founding of the Cincinnati Red Stockings, Bud Fowler became the first black in organized baseball, playing for fifteen years and establishing himself as an outstanding second baseman. But, because of his skin color, it was a continual struggle to make a living as he moved from team to team. In 1885, when the Keokuk, Iowa, team disbanded, he was out of work for a month before joining a club in Pueblo, Colorado. This caused a weekly newspaper, *Sporting Life*, to write bluntly, "He is one of the best general players in the country, and if he had a white face would be playing with the best of them." Other blacks slowly trickled into baseball, with Moses Fleetwood Walker becoming the first black in the major leagues when he played one season with Toledo of the American Association in 1884; and between 1883 and 1898 fifty-five blacks played professionally.[75]

But even as blacks continued to play baseball in limited numbers, a "gentleman's agreement" slowly evolved to exclude them from rosters. Team owners justified this on the grounds that it made the game more professional and respectable. "The national pastime would be, at least in the public eye, wholesome, free from the taint of gamblers, and the exclusive preserve of white athletes," explained historian Jules Tygiel. "By designating some people as unworthy of admission, the baseball community elevated the status of those accepted into the profession."[76] Thus, after 1898, no blacks played again in the major or minor leagues for almost fifty years. Sam Lacy, sports editor of the *Baltimore Afro-American*, noted in 1945 the blatant unfairness of what had occurred: "Baseball has given employment to known epileptics, kleptomaniacs, and a generous scattering of saints and sinners. A man who is totally lacking in character has turned out to be a star in baseball. A man whose skin is white or red or yellow has been acceptable. But a man whose character may be of the highest and whose ability may be Ruthian has been barred completely from the sport because he is colored."[77]

Organized baseball's boycott of blacks did not mean, however, that they could no longer play. Black independent teams began springing up around the country in the early 1880s, and by the end of the century more than two hundred teams had been formed. Meanwhile, the Argyle Hotel in Babylon on Long Island fielded the first professional black team in 1885. Its players, whom the hotel claimed were Cubans and not blacks and who spoke gibberish on the field because it sounded like Spanish, played mainly white teams from the New York City area. They received weekly salaries ranging from twelve to eighteen dollars, which "helped establish baseball as a legitimate, respectable occupation within the black community, though the players worked other jobs, as well, to make ends meet," noted historian Brian Carroll. While white newspapers extensively covered white semi-professional teams they carried little about black baseball and frequently made derogatory remarks about the teams and the players.[78] By the early twentieth century strong black teams existed in such northern cities as Chicago, Indianapolis, New York City, and Homestead, Pennsylvania, as well as Birmingham and Nashville in the South. With black baseball becoming the top entertainment attraction for urban blacks by the end of World War I, the Negro National League was started with eight teams in 1920. Because of the Great Depression, it was dissolved in 1931, but a second National League began two years later, and it was followed by the Negro American League in 1937. The former lasted through 1948 while the American League did not close until 1962.[79]

In covering the Negro leagues extensively the black newspapers continually—but unsuccessfully—urged the white owners of big league teams to sign black baseball stars, because it would make their teams stronger and increase attendance. Then, in 1933, as the press kept up the drumbeat for racial equality in all areas of black life, the two largest black papers, the *Pittsburgh Courier* and the *Chicago Defender*, along with some others began pushing harder for the integration of major league baseball in a campaign that lasted twelve years. "In black America, if there could be racial equality in baseball," this book's coauthor Chris Lamb wrote in 2012, noting the significance of the campaign, "there could be racial equality elsewhere in U.S. society."[80] While this kept the subject of major league integration alive for readers, they saw no changes. It appeared promising in April 1945 when Lacy met with the major league owners, who agreed to his plan to form a committee to study "the possibilities and [find] the best way of ironing out the many ramifications" of having blacks on their teams. However, the committee never accomplished anything because it never met.[81]

In contrast, white sportswriters largely supported segregation in the major leagues by rarely writing about it. "The color line could not have existed as long as it did without the participation of the nation's sportswriters," pointed out Lamb, agreeing with a black sportswriter who labeled what occurred a "conspiracy of silence." Lamb noted they subtly defended segregation by not writing about blacks getting tryouts with major league teams and not asking why tryouts were sometimes cancelled without any explanations. They also claimed there were no blacks good enough to play in the majors and predicted riots would occur if baseball was integrated. As such, the sportswriters supported the views of baseball management "and served as its apologists and defenders," he concluded. "They were willful conspirators in the perpetration of the color line."[82]

But there were a few notable exceptions in the white press, particularly the Communist Party's *Daily Worker*. Both Lamb and Carroll agree that the newspaper has not received the credit it deserves for pushing for the integration of baseball. It covered blacks heavily in all areas of the news in an attempt to lure them to the party, and from 1936 to 1946 it ran more stories than all of the other daily newspapers combined about the need to desegregate the national pastime, calling this dramatically "The Crime of the Big Leagues!" Its criticism was so stinging that baseball management angrily labeled its writers "agitators" and "social-minded drum beaters," which the paper unapologetically admitted was true. As the *Worker*'s Lester Rodney claimed, "We were the conscience of journalism."[83] While black sportswriters welcomed the support of the paper, they were wary of it because of the political ramifications. The *Baltimore Afro-American*'s Lacy feared the *Daily Worker*'s involvement could hurt the campaign to end segregation as well as him personally. "It upset me that I might be considered a Communist," he recalled in 1999.[84] There was no hesitation, however, in accepting the help of sports columnist Jimmy Powers of New York's *Daily News*, the largest circulation daily newspaper in the country. He criticized baseball segregation more than any other mainstream sportswriter in the country, which Lamb noted was important because it was a message to black sportswriters that they were not alone in their campaign.[85]

The campaign to end segregation in baseball became one of the most important stories involving racial equality in the 1930s and 1940s. To black newspapers, if there could be racial equality in baseball, there could be racial equality elsewhere in society. To black sportswriters—

including Lacy and the *Pittsburgh Courier*'s Wendell Smith, who would later be inducted into the writers' wing of the Baseball Hall of Fame for their contributions to ending the color line in the national pastime—the campaign was a personal one because they, too, faced racial discrimination in their profession. The Baseball Writers' Association had its own color line. Black sportswriters were barred from press boxes, dugouts, and locker rooms at big league ballparks,[86] and they were barred from working for mainstream newspapers, where they would have been paid more and their articles would have been seen by more readers. Instead, most black sportswriters spent their careers telling stories ignored in the white press and toiling for understaffed and underfunded weeklies that had a fraction of the circulation of metropolitan dailies. But the writing of Smith and Lacy and other black sportswriters was as influential with their readers as the columns of Grantland Rice, Red Smith, and Arthur Daley were with their readers. "[They] actively accompanied black players to tryouts with major league teams, making their case face to face with white owners," author Jim Reisler wrote in *Black Writers/Black Baseball*. "Arguably, their campaign was what finally pushed big league owners to question and finally end the color ban."[87]

The "gentleman's agreement" abruptly collapsed in 1945, when Branch Rickey, the president and general manager of the Brooklyn Dodgers, stunned the baseball world by signing Jackie Robinson to a minor league contract. On orders from Rickey, scout Clyde Sukeforth had watched Robinson play for the black Kansas City Monarchs and was impressed in talking to him. He recalled: "There was something about that man that just gripped you. He was tough, he was intelligent, and he was proud."[88] He took Robinson to New York to meet Rickey, who immediately said, "Jack, all my life I've been looking for a great colored ballplayer and I have reason to believe you might be that man." He added, however, that being an outstanding player was not enough—he was going to constantly be the target of racial abuse, and he had to have the "courage" to not retaliate. "[I]f you want to take this gamble," Robinson assured him, "I promise you there will be no incidents." Although the contract was signed on August 28, 1945, Rickey requested that no announcement of it be made at that time. So, the signing remained a secret until Rickey revealed it at a press conference on October 23.[89]

Robinson, who was a gifted athlete (he was a four-sport letterman at UCLA and an All-American in football), did not disappoint Rickey. The first test came in spring training in segregated Florida in 1946, when Robinson had to endure blatant racism—he could not eat with his white teammates in many restaurants or stay with them in hotels, and sometimes he could not play in games because city ordinances made it illegal for blacks and whites to play baseball together.[90] He spent the season with the Montreal Royals, the Dodgers' top minor league team, and led the International League with a .349 batting average and forty stolen bases as well as being the best fielding second baseman.[91] With that success, it was no surprise when he joined the Dodgers for the 1947 season. Historian Roger Kahn captured what it was like for fans to see him in a game:

> Robinson was the cynosure of all eyes. For a long time he shocked people seeing him for the first time simply by the fact of his color: uncompromising ebony. All the baseball heroes had been white men. . . . Every coach, every manager, every umpire, every batting practice pitcher, every human being one had ever seen in uniform on a major league field was white. Without realizing it, one had become conditioned. The grass was green, the dirt was brown and the ball players were white. Suddenly in Ebbets Field, under a white home uniform, two muscled arms extended like black hawsers. *Black*. Like the arms of a janitor. The new color jolted the consciousness, in a profound and not quite definable way.[92]

Robinson recalled that the Dodgers' beat writers for the white newspapers were not only "generous" in how much they wrote about him but also "scrupulously fair." His only complaint was "they fell into a habit of calling me 'The Dodgers' Negro star' in their accounts of games. This was like calling Carl Furillo 'Italian' or Gene Hermanski 'Polish.' Several years were to pass before copy editors blue-penciled Negro into limbo."[93] A 1980 study of the coverage in his first season by three of the main New York City papers—the *Times*, the *Herald Tribune*, and the *Daily News*—basically bore out Robinson's recollections. This book's coauthor Patrick S. Washburn found that while there was "subtle bias" in what was written, it gradually changed until he was covered no differently than white stars by the end of the season instead of as a racial barrier breaker. This included a large decline in the use of adjectives referring to his race. A possible reason for the fairness of the coverage was the issuance of the famous Hutchins Commission report, *A Free and Responsible Press*, a month before the major league season began in 1947. It called upon the press to give a "representative picture of constituent groups in society" and to avoid stereotyping. Since the report received wide coverage, sportswriters would have been aware of it and presumably affected by it.[94]

But fair coverage was not objective coverage, according to Carroll and Lamb. Both criticized the white press heavily for basically writing about Robinson in 1947 as just another athlete while generally ignoring the racial issues. "In short, mainstream media sports coverage for the most part did not change as a result of Robinson's presence in major league baseball," wrote Carroll. "The big metros continued to treat Dodger games as athletic contests devoid of social or political consequences, and their writers saw Robinson merely as one of nine Dodgers on the field." As Lamb bluntly put it, many sportswriters "missed the biggest baseball story in history."[95]

In contrast, historians Lamb and Glen Beske noted black newspapers were far more aware than the white press of the historical significance of the desegregation of baseball, and their stories contained more emotion and had more personal insights about Robinson as well as other black prospects.[96] The coverage whetted the appetite of blacks to see Robinson play in 1947, and large numbers of them began going to every Dodgers game, home or away. The papers actively encouraged the attendance phenomenon. The *Baltimore Afro-American* had a sports quiz with the winner getting a free trip to Brooklyn to see Robinson play; the *Birmingham World* chartered a train to take fans from Memphis to his first game in St. Louis; and the *Amsterdam News* in New York City announced a booster club had been formed in Harlem with the five hundred members agreeing to purchase two tickets to all of the Dodgers home games. But in encouraging the increased attendance, the papers were aware this could be damaging because of how white fans might view the influx of blacks. The *Pittsburgh Courier* challenged readers to be on their best behavior at games:

> The challenge to keep our mouths closed and give Jackie the chance to PROVE he's major league caliber! The challenge to conduct ourselves at these ball games in the recognized American way! The challenge to NOT recognize the appearance of Jackie Robinson as the signal for a Roman holiday, with the Bacchanalian orgy complex! The challenge to leave whiskey bottles at home or on the shelves of the liquor store . . . and to leave our loud talking, obscene language and indecent dress on the outside of the ball parks. The challenge to learn something about the game . . . in order that we will know what's going on out on the ball field, and won't humiliate Jackie by our lack of knowledge.

The *Chicago Defender* followed suit, telling blacks to not hold up a game in order to "present him with a box of southern fried chicken," and the *St. Louis Argus* told readers to "act like human beings and not like a tribe of cannibals" at games. It added that blacks should not say anything to whites who made "IGNORANT" remarks about Robinson.[97]

Overall, the black newspaper coverage of Robinson in his first major league season stressed what was positive and generally ignored the negatives, such as the fact that he received a large amount of hate mail, some of which contained death threats. Playing a major role in shaping the coverage positively was Wendell Smith, the sports editor of the *Pittsburgh Courier*. A longtime, strong advocate of ending segregation in the major leagues, he began working for Rickey in 1946 for fifty dollars a week, which equaled his *Courier* salary. His duties included serving as a companion for Robinson on the road, finding places where he could stay and eat, alerting Rickey to other players in the Negro leagues who had the ability to possibly play in the majors, and being a public relations practitioner of sorts for Rickey and a press agent for Robinson.[98] Carroll said the *Courier* was unconcerned about the ethics of Smith working for both the paper and the Brooklyn Dodgers because it gave him "THE front-row seat for what the [black] papers called 'The Jackie Robinson Beat.' Smith had the best access of anyone. Because Robinson's signing was so significant for the black community, these benefits far outweighed any potential problems ethically, though there was no mention of any ethical concerns by anyone at the time, only much, much later. And black papers never swore allegiance to the sort of journalistic objectivity that mainstream presses valued, because these black papers had a mission, an agenda, a purpose."[99]

In his PR role, Smith not only used his weekly column to promote the further integration of baseball but also helped Robinson ghostwrite twenty-five columns—"Jackie Robinson Says:"—that ran in the *Courier* from March through September in the 1947 season. Robinson's columns were notable, said Carroll, because they "cropped out racism" and never considered the possibility that he might fail. Instead, they portrayed a season "largely devoid of racial strife and characterized by harmony among his teammates, financial support from the team's fans, and interactions with opponents that he almost uniformly described as 'nice' or 'swell.'" This mythical view of what the season was like, which Carroll noted "essentially deceived *Courier* readers," had a powerful impact because it appeared in the largest and most influential black paper in the country with a weekly circulation of more than 350,000.[100]

Following Robinson's success in 1947, when he was named the National League Rookie of the Year, baseball finally was fully integrated in 1959, when the Boston Red Sox became the last major league team to use a black player in a game.[101]

**

Beginning in the 1950s newspaper sportswriters would face new challenges. While they had learned to coexist with radio, a new magazine suddenly appeared with classic photographs and well written, in-depth articles that quickly captivated sports fans. And as if that was not enough, television, with its technological advantages, exploded on the sports scene and gave viewers a ringside seat like they had never had before. Sports journalism was on a dizzying rush forward that no one could foresee in the 1940s.

Sports Illustrated and ABC Television

5

> Part of the problem [with television sports coverage]
> is the fan. We must confess our own guilt. We have,
> for some fifteen years or so, simply seen too much.
> If there was a network greed which was matched by
> an owner's greed, then it was also matched by a fan
> greed. Football was there every Sunday, it was free,
> or almost free, and so we watched it. One game
> was not enough, so we watched two.
>
> —Historian David Halberstam, 1974

On October 18, 1954, a stunning new invention came on the market: the world's first commercially available transistor radio. Like many new products whose initial price is high, the Regency TR-1 was extravagantly priced at $49.95 (the equivalent of nearly $500 today), but its striking features offset the cost. It was lightweight (only 11 ounces with circuit-board transistors instead of vacuum tubes), it came in a rugged plastic case that protected it if it was dropped, it could run more than twenty hours before a new battery was needed, and it was small (three inches wide, five inches tall, and one and a quarter inches thick). More than one hundred thousand TR-1s were sold in the first year, causing a popular consumer magazine to note, "If you owned one, you were the coolest thing on two legs."[1]

Considered by *Fortune* as "arguably the most important invention of the 20th century," transistors made possible a myriad of "Personal Electronic Devices" common today, such as iPods and iPhones.[2] Their effect on sports journalism was dramatic. Vin Scully, the longtime baseball announcer for the Dodgers in Brooklyn and Los Angeles, recalled what it was like listening to games when he was growing up in New York City in the pre-transistor days. "We had that big four-legged radio with a cross piece underneath to give support for the legs," he said in 2014, "and I was about eight and I'd take a pillow and I would crawl under the radio so the speaker was right over my face, and the roar of the crowd came out of the speaker like water from a showerhead. I would get goose bumps from head to toe."[3] But with transistor radios came freedom. No longer was it necessary to be at home or in a car or in an office to listen to sportscasts; listeners could be anywhere—a picnic in the country, a boat on a lake, or a playground in a park—as long as they could receive a signal. And one place where transistor radios particularly showed up was at sports events. For the first time, spectators could watch a game live while having it described to them at the same time, which many felt made the event better because of the immediate oral information that they received. Scully recalled a 1960 Dodgers' game that demonstrated how many people in the stands were listening to his radio broadcast. Discovering it was umpire Frank Secory's birthday, he announced he was going to count to three, at which point listeners should scream, "Happy Birthday, Frank!" On his signal, it seemed like all 27,626 spectators followed his instructions, which startled the umpire.[4]

Thus, as a consequence of transistors, even more people could hear live sports broadcasts on radio, which gave it a big advantage over newspaper coverage of the events on the following day. But transistor radios were only one of many advances in sports coverage in the 1950s, '60s and '70s that transformed the field. In magazines, *Sports Illustrated* instituted a new type of print coverage that still resonates with readers today, and television suddenly blossomed nationally with a notable array of technological advances as well as new ways to showcase sports. No longer were newspapers and radio the only main purveyors of sports news.

***

On August 12, 1954, a new weekly sports magazine appeared on news-stands around the country. The cover of this first issue of *Sports Illustrated*, which had $1.25 million in advertising, showed the Milwaukee Braves' star third baseman, Eddie Mathews, swinging at a pitch against the New York Giants as thousands in the stands watched a recent night game. The *Wall Street Journal* had reported on August 2 that the magazine already had three hundred thousand subscribers, but over the next ten days, another fifty thousand people were added, giving it the highest pre-paid circulation for a magazine's first issue in U.S. history. Inside the "book," as it was known in magazine parlance, readers found what author Michael MacCambridge called a mixture of "stories, pictures, and departments that was . . . trying to be all things to all people."[5] The 144 pages included stories on a mile race between two sub-four-minute runners, the art of throwing a boomer-ang, baseball card collecting with color reproductions of Topps cards, why the 1950s was the "greatest sports era in history," getting dogs in shape for the winter hunting season, trout fishing near Yellowstone Park, and a famous sports artist. And besides football, baseball, golf, tennis, and horseracing, there were photographs of a title fight between heavyweight champion Rocky Marciano and Ezzard Charles, a short sports quiz, and six sports cartoons.[6]

In welcoming readers to the first issue publisher H. H. S. Phillips Jr. explained why Time Inc., which already had such well-respected and highly successful magazines as *Time*, *Life*, and *Fortune*, decided to publish *Sports Illustrated*.

Our intentions—so far as we understand them—have been quite simple [in the magazines we publish]. We never went in for 'me too' publishing. We always tried to invent new jour-nalistic forms to fill not just a vacuum but a surging need. . . .

[I]n SPORTS ILLUSTRATED *you will see something of* TIME's *nose for news and the full, coherent weekly recital of that fasci-nating world in itself, the Wonderful World of Sport.* . . .

[*I*]*n* SPORTS ILLUSTRATED *you will see that sport has emerged from the era of isolated contest into a new era of tremendous size, of national and international importance; . . . a new phenomenon, needing and deserving its stimulating but wise chronicler. . . .*

[*I*]*n* SPORTS ILLUSTRATED *today's miraculous cameras will have a weekly field day in a field that is peculiarly theirs, to capture the instants of dramatic excitement, of human and animal grace, of victory and defeat, that are what sport is made of. . . .*

It is our hope and our promise that in some tomorrow you will no longer think of SPORTS ILLUSTRATED *as Time Inc.'s newest baby, but as the accepted and essential weekly reporter of the World of Sport.*[7]

Phillips's optimism about the possible future success of *Sports Illustrated* was not borne out by the past performance of general interest sports magazines. In December 1935, two former Time Inc. employees published the first such magazine, titled *Sports Illustrated*; beset by money problems, they sold it in several months, and it only lasted until March 1938 because the new owner lost most of his money in the stock market. That was followed in August 1946 by Macfadden Publications' *Sport* and Dell's *Sports Album* two years later, but the latter quickly folded when *Sport* threatened to sue because its rival had copied it. Finally, Dell brought out another *Sports Illustrated* in February 1949. However, it lasted only five months before closing because of low circulation and high overhead costs.[8]

Thus, *Sport*, which came out monthly, was the only competition when Time Inc. began considering having some type of general interest publication in 1947 with an important caveat: it must have significantly different content from already existing Time Inc. publications so that it did not detract from their advertising revenues. But the project languished over the years. As MacCambridge noted, "None of the ideas seemed like quite the *right* one; none seemed big enough to seize the imagination of a company that was respected in Washington DC, trusted across America, and known throughout the world."[9]

Meanwhile, Henry Luce, the co-founder of Time Inc., began noticing how often sports came up in conversations at dinner parties, and he asked Emmet Hughes, the articles editor of *Life*, why this occurred. "Well, Harry," he explained, "because sports, like music, is a universal language. Everyone speaks it." With several others encouraging him to start a sports magazine, Luce had a two-hour meeting in June 1953 with some of his top executives to discuss such a publication. Everyone immediately liked the idea, but there were two reservations: not enough advertising could be found for a sports weekly and Time Inc. staffers were generally not knowledgeable about sports, necessitating the hiring of a number of new people to put out the magazine. Both points were ignored although the latter was a correct assessment. MacCambridge pointed out: "Although Time Inc. spoke to the American middle class, its staff did not closely reflect its readers' middle-class pastimes. Knowledge of sports within the company, from Luce on down, was shockingly low, owing less to the company's supposed Ivy League predominance than an overarching, serious-minded gentility. Time Inc. people didn't sweat; their sports were rich men's pursuits— yachting, golf, croquet." But Luce liked the idea, and a week later he formally proposed a new sports weekly magazine to the group with a newsstand price of fifteen cents and 1.5 million circulation.[10]

On July 9, 1953, a seven-man committee began working on what was labeled Project X. It did not go smoothly, and no one was more pessimistic than Ernest Havemann, one of *Life*'s major writers. On July 26 he dropped off the project, telling John Shaw Billings, the editorial executive overseeing the committee, that he had concluded a sports weekly could not succeed. "I naturally feel that we should abandon the project, that any time or money we spend on it will be wasted and that if we should ever actually publish the magazine it would be a costly failure," he wrote. Then, on the next day, he delivered an eleven-page analysis to Billings that argued each sports fan was only interested in a narrow number of sports, and covering a large number of different ones in each issue of a magazine would produce "a hodge-podge that pleases nobody." After mentioning a number of other problems that he saw with a sports magazine, he wondered how he "could have ever been enthusiastic about the idea." Billings felt the memo ended any chance of Time Inc. putting out a magazine devoted solely to sports.[11]

But the project continued. Despite increasing fears that television's coverage of sports would negatively impact the magazine, Luce liked the rough page layouts and staff hiring began with his approval in September 1953. He remained cautiously optimistic in December, writing one of the project's members: "Fingers must always be crossed about futures, but it does indeed look as if we have a good magazine coming up."[12] Warning signs of possible problems kept appearing, however, as pre-publication preparations escalated in 1954. In the spring, a group of advertising executives saw a dummy issue of the magazine and, when surveyed by an advertising journal, less than half of them said they would place ads in it. "It covers too much ground," complained one person. "It's a hybrid. Do baseball and boxing fans mingle with fox hunters in pink coats?" Less than a week before the first issue went on sale, *Business Week* took an in-depth look at *Sports Illustrated*, noting that the publishing industry at first thought it was "doomed." It was argued there was not enough sports news to fill a weekly magazine and newspapers already did a better than adequate job of covering sports. But *Business Week* pointed out that the skepticism had mostly vanished because of the large number of charter subscribers and the amount of advertising purchased in *Sports Illustrated* before the first issue came out. Calling its launch "a major event in the publishing world" and stressing the advantage it had because of Time Inc.'s successful thirty-year track record and hefty financial resources, *Business Week* said its performance would be watched closely by magazine executives.[13]

Compliments rolled in for the first issue of *si*, as it became known, and so did new subscriptions. Luce sent a copy to President Dwight Eisenhower, who replied that he expected to "find much of interest in it, perhaps too much for my own peace of mind."[14] But despite the promising start, it lost more than $30 million over ten years before making its first profit in 1964.[15] "[Luce] stayed with it when it was a very expensive loser and most of his associates wanted to junk it," said historian David Halberstam, "because his instincts told him the audience was there and growing. . . . Luce knew somehow that sports was about to become big business in America, that others were interested in it."[16]

A nagging problem from the first was that the magazine did not have a clear identity. As historian Ted Geltner put it: "Was it a general interest sports rag geared toward the everyday beer-and-a-hot-dog bleacher bum? Or was it a highbrow literary sports journal for Ivy Leaguers to read over tea in the smoking room at the country club?"[17] In some readers' minds, there was no question what it was. Scully recalled seeing the first issue and considering it a "rich man's magazine" rather than a sports publication: "I thought, Wow. Why aren't these guys [at *SI*] doing sports?"[18]

A "Sporting Look" section, which appeared on two pages of *Sports Illustrated*'s first issue, was the type of quasi-sports content that probably surprised Scully. Six colorful photographs showed what sports car drivers and their pit crew members, including the drivers' wives, wore at races. Basically, it was a print fashion show.[19] Three months later Phillips, the magazine's publisher, explained on page 1 why running fashion news was justified in a sports publication. "*The Sporting Look* is far more than a fashion section (although that is certainly one of the things it is)," he wrote. "It is also a vital part of the story and history of sport itself, telling each week in pictures and a few words what sports do for clothes and what clothes do for sports." He noted that Fred Smith, the editor of the section, had recently emphasized the same point in a talk to the Clothing Manufacturers Association: "When a photographer brings in a take of a field trial, the event has a flavor about it that is more than guns and dogs. It shows up in the brush pants and Loden coats and corduroy shooting jackets. And when a writer describes the U.S. Open, he discovers that Jimmy Demaret's mauve linen pants and the brilliant colors of his golf club mitts are almost as much a part of the story as birdies and bogies." Phillips mentioned that future "Sporting Look" sections would show appropriate dress for the Riviera, ski slopes in the Swiss Alps, beaches in Southern California, and cold weather sailing. He also said there would be a section on winter wear for "well-dressed" dogs, but he did not indicate if he was referring only to those used for hunting.[20]

Although the section lasted for twenty years, its height was from 1954 to 1958, when an average of twenty issues each year had a "Sporting Look" article that emphasized what upper-middle-class white, married couples wore, frequently at country clubs and resorts. And not all of the sites were in the U.S.; the backdrops included Europe's fashion capitals, such as London, Rome, and Paris. "The prevailing theme of the column was one of self-satisfied leisure and success," wrote Chris Ohmer, who studied the section. In 1956 *SI* even began annual sportswear design awards with the winners usually having their work pictured in the magazine and being invited to design exclusive clothing from swimsuits to golf apparel for *Sports Illustrated*. The awards were discontinued after 1963 because the magazine was spending as much as $100,000 a year to produce fashion extravaganzas in New York City as well as around the country.[21]

In the final decade of the "Sporting Look" section, subtle changes occurred in the photographs. Models were younger, fewer married couples were shown, and, in 1968, in the midst of the civil rights movement, the first black model finally appeared in a piece on college fashions. Jule Campbell, a writer for the section, said in 1987 that "there was never any intent to include or exclude black models or upperclass couples. Our goal [was] to represent real people in real settings." As Ohmer pointed out, however, concentrating on "real people" kept blacks out of the section for fourteen years; many were not yet in the "leisure/country club class" and few participated in the sports, such as skiing, golf, tennis, and sailing, that appeared frequently in the "Sporting Look."[22]

Changes over the years in *Sports Illustrated* resulted in the section vanishing after 1974. Fred Smith, who was in charge of it for fifteen of its twenty years, said it primarily was eliminated because television forced the magazine to shift generally from soft sports features to hard news. As people watched more football, basketball, and baseball on TV, they wanted to read about sports stars rather than what to wear to games. So the magazine gradually began targeting a different audience. "The new reader was likely to be male and less likely to belong to a country club," wrote Ohmer. "SI sought an audience who participated in sports, but more importantly, the magazine wanted readers who attended football games and watched televised sports events. . . . Fashion reports just didn't blend with this hard-news image of linebackers and technical fouls."[23]

But adjusting the content to appeal to more readers was only part of the reason that *Sports Illustrated* became a huge success; the way that content was written was equally important, and that was problematic at first. Some of the early stories were not only dry but also were little more than play-by-play accounts of games. What was missing was a perspective presented in an interesting way. As Geltner noted, a few of the top reporters "began . . . to go beyond the plays and the outcome and discuss the scene around the event. The better articles gave a larger context to the events and offered readers analysis not found in daily newspapers."[24] André Laguerre, who was managing editor from 1960 to 1974, cared deeply about outstanding writing, and he continued hiring reporters who could produce it. He also added a long article toward the end of every issue, which he called the "bonus piece," that was designed to suck in readers and keep them coming back week after week. Its hallmark was superlative writing.[25]

Sports team executive Arn Tellem, who grew up in the 1960s, still recalled fifty years later the excitement that the magazine engendered:

Every Friday night when SI came, there was this special moment when I would get into bed with my magazine and read it cover-to-end. The magazine fueled my dreams. It was such a powerful thing, to finally read SI after wondering all week who would be on the cover. My grandparents and my mother had always encouraged me to read, and I became absorbed in biographies of historical figures, but I had total immersion in the world of sports. For me, reading about sports became more enjoyable than watching them. The writers were so terrific that when I finished reading the magazine, I would fall asleep dreaming of a life in sports.[26]

Another reason for the magazine's success, according to writer James Michener, was "deal[ing] openly with those topics which men in saloons talk about in whispers."[27] An example was deciding what to write about race in sports. As MacCambridge noted, *Sports Illustrated* wrestled with the question of how to cover "political issues of the day" in the late 1960s in the midst of the civil rights movement; Laguerre worried that putting too many black sports stars on the magazine's covers might jeopardize readership because most of the readers were white. Nevertheless, in 1967, he told Jack Olsen, one of his best reporters, to investigate the current state of black athletes. Despite the belief by whites that sports had been good for blacks, he found enormous black resentment and racism and wrote a five-part series that showed how blacks were exploited in both collegiate and professional sports. Realizing that the series might not be approved for publication by Time Inc.'s management because it went against what many people thought, Laguerre did not tell them about it. Instead, he and the others who worked on it took vacations when the first story appeared on July 1, 1968, so they would not be around to face the expected ire of the top executives.[28]

Publisher Garry Volk introduced the series: "On page 12 of this week's issue, we begin a series of articles that seem certain to rank as the most socially significant this magazine has ever published. *The Black Athlete—a Shameful Story* is an investigation into the lives of Negro participants in sport—both amateur and professional—in present-day America. The revelations contained in the series will bring the reader a new appreciation of the problems and attitudes of the black athletes whose performances all of us as sports fans cheer so enthusiastically but about whom we know so little."[29]

MacCambridge called the series the "the single most important piece in *si*'s history, clearly changing the terms of the debate about the black athlete."[30] It resulted in more than a thousand letters, which is the most the magazine ever received in response to an article or series, and *Sports Illustrated* continued publishing them for a month after the stories ended. Most, but not all, were positive. One reader wrote: "I'm white. The message in . . . Jack Olsen's series was a long time coming from any national medium, sports or otherwise. Better late than anticlimactic." And the president of the United Negro College Fund said the magazine "deserves the highest commendation and a Pulitzer Prize for having the insight to research the problem, the wisdom to assign a talented reporter to the job and the courage to report the story as it is." At the other end of the spectrum was this: "[Blacks] should be damn glad their ancestors were brought over as slaves. . . . Instead of suffering through football at Kansas . . . they could be enjoying life in . . . the Congo or some other equally progressive, dignified African location."[31]

In assessing the value of the *Sports Illustrated* series in 2016, forty-eight years after it appeared, historian Reed Smith applauded the magazine for the awareness that it brought to whites of the problems that black athletes faced, making the magazine the "sports world's conscience." Other media also discussed the problems, which helped bring about changes although they were sometimes slow. "African Americans could begin to attain a level playing field both in and outside of the athletic arena," wrote Smith. "At the same time, sports journalists gained license to more aggressively pursue other issues that held sociological implications." As one historian noted, Olsen had "trod boldly where few other sportswriters had dared."[32]

But publishing boldly did not always end successfully for Time Inc. In 1997 *Sports Illustrated* president Donald Elliman felt the time might be right for a new type of sports magazine. "We have continued to define new markets and media for the *si* brand," he said. "The biggest market that we don't speak to directly is women. We would like to change that."[33] To determine if a market existed for a women's sports magazine, Time Inc. published two test issues, sending it to 450,000 female subscribers of *si*, who were between the ages of eighteen and thirty-four, and another 50,000 women from a Time Warner database as well as putting 150,000 copies on newsstands. The content was targeted at readers who were spectators of sports rather than participants, which was a formula that had worked well at *Sports Illustrated*.[34]

When the test issues were a success, a year was spent in research, and an immediate problem arose in focus groups that resulted in the magazine having a split identity. Time Inc. discovered that women wanted content that was not only directed at readers who watched sports but also those who participated in them and were interested in such things as nutrition, fitness, and lifestyle choices. As a result, it was decided to target sixteen- to twenty-four-year-old female high school and college athletes along with women interested in sports who were no older than thirty-four.[35]

In the first issue of *Sports Illustrated for Women* in March 1999, editor Sandy Bailey told readers: "We're thrilled that you, and so many girls and women like you, fell in love with our two 1997 test issues. We're sorry we've been on the sidelines so long, but we think you'll find, as you read this issue, that we never stopped thinking about you. . . . [Y]ou said you want the inside information and authority of SPORTS ILLUSTRATED. Turn the page. That's everywhere [*in Sports Illustrated for Women*]."[36]

The magazine, whose title was shortened to *Sports Illustrated Women* in 2001, was published twenty-seven times until it ended with the December/January issue of 2002–3. Historian Ashley Furrow noted that it continually wrestled with the spectator-participant split, "slowly . . . transforming into a sports lifestyle magazine [as it] began including more service journalism with articles featuring beauty and fitness products and clothing."[37] It just was never quite sure who its audience was. In the end, Time Inc. closed the magazine, which had lost advertising and therefore had fewer pages, because of the economy. The losses were too much. Dimity McDowell, who as an associate editor helped launch the magazine, concluded in 2011: "It's something about women's sports that's hard to wrap your hand around. It's like holding Jell-O. You can't quite figure it out. You know because there are plenty of women's sports and fans out there, but how to get them into a magazine just hasn't been done successfully yet."[38]

But despite occasional struggles, *Sports Illustrated*'s overall success was perhaps most notable because it blossomed in the age of television. A 1956 article in *Journalism Quarterly* by Leo Bogart, the associate director of research for a large New York City advertising firm, indicated how steep the odds were against *SI* when it began in 1954. He noted studies had shown that the amount of magazine reading decreased when people bought TVs, which were viewed an average of five hours daily in a household, and one-fourth of TV owners totally stopped reading. Of those who continued to do so, they still spent 25 percent less time with magazines than people who did not own a television. Finally, and certainly important to Time Inc., as the amount of advertising rose in television, the ad lineage in sports and outdoor magazines declined 12 percent from 1946 through 1954.[39]

Television was still a relatively new communications medium when *Sports Illustrated* began. Although there had been TV experiments and demonstrations around the world since the mid-1920s, including CBS operating an experimental television station from 1931 to 1933, the Radio Corporation of America (RCA) claimed it ushered television into the U.S. on April 20, 1939. Speaking to a television camera near its pavilion at the upcoming New York World's Fair while the press watched, RCA president David Sarnoff said grandiosely: "It is with this feeling of humbleness that I come to this moment of announcing the birth in this country of a new art so important in its implications that it is bound to affect all society. It is an art that shines like a torch in a troubled world. It is a creative force which we must learn to utilize for the benefit of all mankind. This miracle of engineering skill which will one day bring the world to the home also brings a new American industry to serve man's material welfare. Television will become an important factor in American economic life."[40]

About a hundred guests also viewed the speech eight miles away at NBC headquarters on black-and-white TV receivers with eight-by-nine-inch screens. Meanwhile, on the sixty-second floor of the RCA Building, dealers were invited to inspect the new television receivers for the first time. They ranged in price from a receiver with a four-by-five-inch screen, which cost $199.50, to a set with a screen slightly larger than seven by ten inches for $1,000. It was announced that the sets would go on sale on May 1, which was when NBC would start telecasting from 8:00 to 9:00 p.m. each Wednesday and Friday.[41]

Meanwhile, presaging the prominence that sports would assume on television, NBC followed Sarnoff's speech with a telecast of a three-round boxing match between a Golden Gloves champion and a Police Athletic League star. It took place in an arena set up in an NBC studio with former heavyweight champion Max Baer serving as the referee and veteran radio sportscaster Bill Stern doing the announcing.[42]

This was not the first sports coverage on television; CBS's experimental station, W2XAB, had already televised a form of college football in the early 1930s. When the Columbia radio network broadcast games, listeners who had a television receiver could simultaneously follow each play by watching tin footballs with teams' names on them move on a board painted like a football field. The station also had boxing matches in its small studio, which was not an ideal location. Because the room was cramped and the camera could only cover an area about five feet square, the boxers could not be shown below the waist and had little room to move or they disappeared off screen. As for the fight announcer, he was so close to the ring that he sometimes was hit by a wild punch. In addition, there were limitations in the early TV images. "Now and then there'd be a clear picture; then [the] pugilists would appear to be groping in a fog or chastising each other in a tank of milk," wrote humorist James Thurber. "Face and arms dilate and contract and look crazy, like images in those trick mirrors at amusement parks."[43]

The first televised sports event outside of a network studio was a ten-inning college baseball game between Columbia and Princeton on May 17, 1939, a month after Sarnoff's speech. The audience for the NBC broadcast was not large—only about four hundred TV sets existed in the New York City area—and what they saw was a television learning experience. The lone camera, which was on a twelve-foot wooden platform along the third base line, had no zoom capabilities, resulting in a distant picture that made it impossible to see the ball when it was pitched or hit. Furthermore, the *New York Times* described the players as looking like "little white flies" while *Variety* magazine suggested that the telecast resembled "a 42nd street flea circus" with the only difference being Stern's commentary. Without a monitor showing what was being televised, he had no choice but to announce the game like it was on radio, which resulted in him sometimes describing things that were not on the screen. His assessment of the broadcast was blunt: "[I]n that one game, we learned a complete lesson about how not to televise a sports event." One helpful suggestion came from the *Times*, which noted four cameras were needed for baseball instead of trying to swivel one camera around to cover everything.[44]

Within three months major league baseball games began being televised, and by 1947 the World Series appeared for the first time on nine stations in New York City, Schenectady, Philadelphia, and Washington, drawing an audience of up to seven hundred thousand. Baseball viewership continued to rise rapidly as the number of television stations and TV sets expanded. In 1950, the fall classic had an estimated thirty-eight million viewers, who watched on seventy-six stations in forty-nine cities that stretched as far west as Omaha and to Jacksonville in the South. Then, a year later, the World Series was available to eighty-five million viewers for the first time from coast to coast with NBC beginning a twenty-seven-year run as the only network broadcasting the games.[45]

Baseball was not the only sport that quickly showed up on TV. In 1939 college and pro football, boxing, track, tennis, bicycle racing, diving, hockey, basketball, wrestling, soccer, and fencing also appeared as sports programming became common on the new medium.[46] Then, just as new television stations started to appear, which meant increased sports coverage, the Federal Communications Commission (FCC) halted the expansion of them in 1942 because the building materials were needed for the war effort. At that point ten TV stations and some experimental transmitters existed, but in three years the number of stations dwindled to six with each broadcasting only several hours a day. After World War II ended in 1945 TV station construction began again but proceeded slowly until the spring of 1952, when 108 stations were on the air. Two reasons for the stunted growth were because station construction was expensive and the FCC did not grant any new building permits for almost four years. The commission also slowly and carefully adopted technological standards for television; it was leery of the mistakes that had been made in the 1920s, when the rapid issuance of a large number of radio licenses had resulted in chaos among the stations' signals. When the FCC's "freeze" ended in April 1952, the number of TV stations exploded, growing to 422 in 1955 and 559 in 1960.[47] And while there had been only seven thousand TV sets in the country in 1946, the number swelled to 50 million by the end of the 1950s with a record 2.8 million being sold in the first six months of 1954.[48]

Suddenly, much of the country could watch sports on television, not just those viewers in or near large cities, and the growth in it quickly became staggering, as *Sports Illustrated* pointed out in the fall of 1954. "One of the problems of television is that it is so much with us," said Budd Schulberg, the magazine's first boxing editor, who complained about too many bad fights on TV that should never have been telecast. "It is not only a hungry giant but a Gargantua with an oversized tapeworm of an appetite."[49] Twenty years later, writer David Halberstam made the same criticism in *New York* magazine, partially blaming TV viewers for the amount of sports that appeared on TV. "Part of the problem [with television sports coverage] is the fan," he wrote. "We must confess our own guilt. We have, for some fifteen years or so, simply seen too much. If there was a network greed which was matched by an owner's greed, then it was also matched by a fan greed. Football was there every Sunday, it was free, or almost free, and so we watched it. One game was not enough, so we watched two."

Writer James Michener agreed with Halberstam in 1976 that sport was overexposed by the media. As an example, he noted seventy-five and a half hours of sports had been broadcast by the three major T V networks in one weekend in May.[50] However, they did not realize that the amount of sports coverage would explode in the 1980s and beyond because of cable T V.

The extraordinary growth of television into the 1970s was tied unquestionably to technological developments that made the medium more attractive to buyers of television sets as well as viewers—and sometimes had a direct impact on sports broadcasts. One of the most important developments was in June 1951. CBS made the first hour-long broadcast in color, but because almost everyone had sets that could only show pictures in black and white, most of the viewers were in the network's studios. Then, on New Year's Day of 1954, NBC made the first national color broadcast of the Rose Bowl Parade in Pasadena, California, which was carried live by twenty-two stations to a small audience. The sale of color sets, which initially cost $1,000 or more, took off slowly, and it was not until the fall of 1966 that all of the prime-time programming on the three networks was in color. That led to more color sets being sold than black-and-white ones by the end of the year.[51]

Five and a half years later the first telecommunications satellite, Telstar, was launched by NASA and showed live pictures, which ranged from the Niagara Falls to the World's Fair in Seattle to a press conference of President John F. Kennedy, on all three U.S. TV networks as well as television stations in Canada and in Europe. The short segment that was most popular with the more than a hundred million Europeans who saw the broadcast showed two batters in a Chicago Cubs game. Most had never seen baseball, and a London television critic commented drolly that he "preferred to watch Americans play games than talk politics."[52] Thus, satellites made it possible to broadcast sports live, such as the Olympic Games, from anywhere in the world.

On December 7, 1963, another important piece of technology was used for the first time on the CBS telecast of the Army-Navy football game. When Army quarterback Rollie Stichweh ran for a touchdown, the play was immediately shown again on tape; it was so startling that the play-by-play announcer exclaimed, "This is not live! Ladies and gentlemen, Army did not score again!" The birth of instant replay was credited to Tony Verna, the director of the broadcast. While videotape was not new, it took time to cue it up, and therefore replays in the first half of televised football games were not shown until halftime, but Verna figured out prior to the Army-Navy game how to reshow the action almost instantly. Even so, the thousand pounds of equipment had been jostled when it was moved from New York City to Philadelphia, where the game was played, and it took him about thirty plays before he got it to work properly on Stichweh's fourth quarter TD. In 2013 the president of the Directors Guild of America praised Verna's invention, noting that instant replay "changed the future of televised sports, and sports direction, forever."[53]

Blimps also became a new way to augment televised sports events. After the Goodyear airship *Enterprise* provided aerial coverage of the 1955 Rose Bowl parade for NBC, as well as other televised events in the following years, CBS was the first to utilize a blimp at a sports event: the 1960 Orange Bowl football game between Georgia and Missouri. The pilot recalled it was difficult loading a studio camera on the airship and finding space for the cameraman and technician. In addition, the added weight made it necessary to throw off ballast in order to lift into the air. Blimps quickly became commonplace at televised events such as America's Cup yacht races, pro football games, golf tournaments, and car races. Besides offering unique television shots, blimps had many advantages: they offered good camera platforms, they could remain above the scene no matter how long an event lasted, and they were free to TV networks in exchange for a minimum number of TV shots and references to them by announcers during a sports event. It was a public relations dream for Goodyear, which had the only commercial airship in the U.S. when the networks began using it in sports coverage in the 1960s.[54]

In 1969 a *Sports Illustrated* writer did a nine-page article on the

Goodyear blimps, calling them "a friendly giant seemingly fascinated by the [sports] contest waged by Lilliputians in the arena below." He then addressed what blimps meant to spectators as well as Goodyear: "By its very shape and easy manner in the sky the blimp suggests contentment to people who in this frantic day have almost forgotten how good it is simply to loiter and linger. As long as there is a blimp in the sky, people will be waving up at it, photographing it and wanting to ride in it. On the losing side of football stadiums, gloomy spectators will glance up to the blimp for solace and reassurance. Winners will see it as a serene omen. And as long as people feel that way, the name Goodyear will be unforgettable."[55]

As TV sports coverage expanded into the 1960s Roone Arledge arrived on the scene and quickly had a huge impact, with a historian labeling him "the dominant figure in sports television" by the mid-1970s.[56]

At Columbia University Arledge was a student leader, serving as class president, head of his fraternity, and editor of the yearbook before graduating in 1952. His first job was at the DuMont Television Network as an assistant to the assistant program director, which basically involved filling out forms and being a "gofer." He quickly became mesmerized by TV. "There was something magical about television: the immediacy; the drama of the countdown to air; the beaming live to an audience that, by then, counted in the millions; the technology; the bright lights; the studio hush," he recalled in 2003. "I discovered what a television producer did, and I yearned for the chance to do it myself." After serving in the army during the Korean War, he began producing shows for an NBC station in New York City and won an Emmy in 1959 for a children's show, "Hi Mom." Then, when ABC submitted the highest bid to the NCAA for the right to broadcast college football games in the 1960–61 seasons, he was named the producer.[57]

Arledge's appointment came after he spent two hours writing his boss a long memorandum that suggested changing how college football was telecast. It began: "Henceforth, television has done a remarkable job of bringing the game to the viewer—now we are going to take the viewer to the game!" He mentioned numerous ways of bringing the "excitement and color" of football to viewers, which he pointed out had never been done with sports on television but was common in broadcasts of variety shows, political conventions, and travel and adventure shows to make viewers feel like they were present. As he put it, "WE ARE GOING TO ADD SHOW BUSINESS TO SPORTS!" He concluded with a notable, prescient comment: "We will be setting the standards that everyone will be talking about and that others in the industry will spend years trying to equal."[58]

The changes that Arledge made in football telecasts were remarkable and still are common today in sports broadcasts. He wanted to get viewers involved "emotionally. If they didn't give a damn about the game, they still might enjoy the program." Historian Benjamin G. Rader noted what Arledge did to "capture the full ambience of the game setting":

> He used cranes, blimps, and helicopters to furnish better views of the stadium, the campus, and the town; hand-held cameras and close-up shots of cheerleaders, pretty coeds, band members, eccentric spectators, and nervous coaches; the rifle-type microphones to pick up the roar of the crowd, the thud of a punt, or the crunch of a hard tackle.
>
> Arledge made the spectators and even the referees a part of the performance. Coin-tossing ceremonies, once reserved for the locker rooms, now took place in the center of the field before the ever-present television cameras. The referee instructed the players to speak up so they could be heard on the microphones. The officials themselves began to give signals with artful flourishes. Melvin Durslag in *TV Guide* even suggested that the officials, since they had become actors, ought to join the American Federation of Television and Radio Artists.
>
> Once the fans perceived themselves as potential performers, they began to carry banners, run onto the playing field, and engage in unseemly antics to grab the attention of the television

cameras. Arledge exercised few restraints. During one game in the first season of ABC's college coverage, the cameras repeatedly turned to a young couple in the stands who embraced and kissed passionately each time Texas A&M gained more than three yards.[59]

Not content with merely revolutionizing the televising of college football, Arledge came up with a new type of TV sports show in 1961: he said he wanted to offer viewers "the unexpected, the thrilling, and the new in faraway, exotic places." It involved traveling around the world to televise sports events, some of which Americans did not know existed and most of which had never been televised in the U.S. ABC founder Leonard Goldenson later admitted, "I thought it was the screwiest idea I'd ever heard." However, by the time ABC's Wide World of Sports ended in 1998, it had broadcast from fifty-three countries and forty-six states, winning thirty-six Emmy awards for its excellence, and Jim McKay, who hosted the show for its entire run over four decades, had become the first sports broadcaster to receive a coveted Peabody Award.[60]

In the show's first season Arledge obtained the rights to televise two top track meets (the Penn Relays in Philadelphia and the Drake Relays in Des Moines, Iowa); a soccer championship in London; a twenty-four-hour sports car race at Le Mans, France; a Russia versus U.S. track meet in Moscow; and an American Football League pre-season exhibition game between the San Diego Chargers and the Buffalo Bills. The latter was notable technologically because Arledge was allowed to have a camera in the huddles—the cameraman would sprint to the sidelines when the huddle broke—and to put a small microphone on Buffalo quarterback Jack Kemp so viewers could hear what plays he called and what he said at the line. The live mike presented a problem, however, when a lineman came back to the huddle, complaining that officials had ignored an illegal block on him, and said loudly and clearly, "Shee-it!"[61]

Over the years ABC's Wide World of Sports had numerous groundbreaking telecasts. These included the first American network sports show to broadcast from Havana (a U.S.-Cuba volleyball match) and North Korea (the world table tennis championships); cover the British Open golf tournament; carry the Indianapolis and Daytona 500-mile car races; and have the World Cup final in soccer.[62] But Arledge never gave up his idea of showing a large number of sports from all over the world, which were introduced at the start of every broadcast with the words: "The thrill of victory and the agony of defeat, the human drama of athletic competition." Among the more than a hundred sports showcased by ABC were cliff diving, wrist wrestling, surfing, sky flying, karate, rodeos, water skiing, tobogganing, skateboarding, hurling, Australian surf lifesaving, target diving, roller skating, firemen running up ladders, lumberjacking, barrel jumping on ice skates, ski jumping, ironman triathlons, motorcycle jumping, the Little League World Series, and demolition derbies.[63]

No matter what the sport was Arledge demanded that "emotion" be a central part of the broadcast. "If you can get that across to people," he said, "make it possible for them to recognize how difficult it is, give them a sense of where it is happening and a reason to want the person to succeed—or fail—then the viewer can become involved."[64] With this mandate, ABC's *Wide World of Sports* gave the show's directors the freedom "to produce original creations of sports events," said Rader. He continued:

> In this new form of televised sports drama, the director sought above all else to avoid lapses in excitement, for he strove to keep the viewer glued to the television set. Thus the director broadened and intensified the visual and aural range of the event. He employed controversial announcers, catchy music, and graphics. By telling viewers of past heroes and past records, and of how the event related to the past, the announcers established the historical context of the drama. . . . They often attempted to convince the viewer that the contest was an exciting game even though the viewer might, on his own, have found it otherwise.[65]

In 2011, on the fiftieth anniversary of the show's first broadcast,

Sports Illustrated noted Arledge's push to be interesting and exciting had become standard practice for television sports programming. Without that, it said, "There'd be no Thrill of Victory or Agony of Defeat." And it praised the show for the dignity and respect that the announcers accorded to all of the sports instead of downplaying some of them because they were strange or unknown. As a result, ABC gradually built up an audience for all sports, not just the major ones.[66]

As ABC's *Wide World of Sports* was growing in prestige Arledge began producing another new show, *Monday Night Football*. After CBS and NBC turned down the chance to do it because this would disrupt their program schedules, particularly if a game went into overtime, Arledge welcomed the opportunity to telecast the first regularly scheduled National Football League games in prime time. The initial broadcast was on September 21, 1970, a game between the Cleveland Browns and the New York Jets; critics predicted it would get no more than 24 percent of the viewers, but it surprised them by drawing 31 percent. By the end of the second season, the show had an audience of thirty million, and as that grew over time, 40 percent of the viewers were women.[67]

What made *Monday Night Football* successful was the fact that it offered the same excitement viewers had come to expect in college football games. As ABC noted in 2003 it became "a pulsating show combining outspoken journalism with abundant dashes of entertainment. [Arledge's] first decision was to create a visual and technical tour de force." Unlike regular weekend broadcasts of NFL games, which had four or five cameras, he utilized nine, including two on the sidelines and two handheld. More innovations came later, such as an electronic first-down line that showed on TV screens, super-slow-motion cameras, graphics and statistics provided quickly by computers, and reverse-angle replays. Occasionally, however, the technology provided too much entertainment. In the early 1970s cameras began showing women in the stands taking off everything except their bras and panties, usually because they were strippers and liked the publicity. Protests caused ABC to stop showing such scenes.[68]

But the most notable part of the show was what ABC called the "outspoken journalism." Announcers were selected by Arledge because they would create controversy and, before the first season was over, he admitted that he was pleased because two of his announcers had made the broadcasts "bigger than the game."[69]

This was not the first time that television sports announcers were controversial. A good example was Jay Hanna "Dizzy" Dean. A former star pitcher for the St. Louis Cardinals in the 1930s, he began announcing CBS television's baseball "Game of the Week" in the 1950s and became beloved for his down-home demeanor and southern drawl. He claimed to have attended a one-room school in Oklahoma, never progressing past the "Second Reader," and told viewers about growing up hunting opossums and eating black-eyed peas. And sometimes he would suddenly launch into the song, "Wabash Cannonball." But what caused controversy was his misuse of the language. At one point, schoolteachers in St. Louis complained about his on-air syntax because he said things such as a runner "slud" into third base. Dean fired back, "Sin Tax. Are them jokers in Washington puttin' a tax on that too?"[70] And he defended his choice of words: "Slud is something more than slid. It means sliding with great effort."[71]

Arledge chose Keith Jackson, who was replaced on *Monday Night Football* after the first season by Frank Gifford, for his play-by-play announcer. Their job was straightforward and non-controversial. But then Arledge diverged from what was the norm for past television sports shows—instead of the play-by-play announcer being joined by one additional commentator, he named two, with one being cast as the "good" guy while the other was the "bad" guy. He hoped the verbal sparks between them would turn "a popular sport into a prime-time event."[72]

For the "good" guy, Arledge hired likeable Don Meredith, a former All-American quarterback at SMU who played nine seasons in the NFL with the Dallas Cowboys and was twice voted to the All-Pro team. He called him "a Texas version of Huckleberry Finn crossed with Mark Twain." His foil was Howard Cosell, a highly opinionated New Yorker, whom Rader described as "[c]austic, unctuous, polysyllabic, given to making even the most trivial observation sound like something profound." But that was fine with Arledge. "I was convinced Howard was the key missing ingredient," he wrote. "You could hate him, at times want to strangle him, but he wouldn't let you ignore him. He forced you to watch. . . . Handsome Don and Nasty Howard. I realized the chemistry between them could be incredible."[73]

While the critics loved the first show, they hated Cosell. He was labeled the "master of the verbal cheap shot" who had "[w]retched prattle" and a [t]owering ignorance of football." Sacks of critical mail also came in from viewers, but when a reporter asked Arledge if the controversy worried him, he replied that was what he wanted. As the fall went on a *TV Guide* poll found Cosell to be both the most hated and the most loved sportscaster in the country. At a southern bar, when he came on the screen during a game, a lucky patron got to blast a TV with a shotgun, and a Texas hotel had a "Why I Hate Howie" lunch with so many people showing up that it had to open a second ballroom. There also were death threats, which sometimes resulted in FBI agents showing up at the announcers' booth during broadcasts.[74]

But the success of *Monday Night Football* was undeniable. Some Monday bowling leagues started switching to Tuesdays because of the show, and the same was true of PTA meetings. Restaurants started closing on Monday nights, with those that stayed open reporting their business went down 25 percent, and the New York City police reported crime dropped 16 percent on Mondays because criminals stayed home to watch the show. Movie theater chains began cutting prices and offering free snacks on Monday nights, a Seattle hospital attempted unsuccessfully to ban births in the hours when the show was on the air, and a Miami community college offered a course aimed at women: "Understanding and Enjoying Monday Night Football." And wherever the show traveled, mayors and governors had parades for the announcers with Cosell being mobbed by fans who had grown to like him.[75]

Arledge had now taken ABC from last among the three television networks in sports ratings to number one. And as ABC soared so did

Sports Illustrated, which had been worried about whether it could survive with the ever-growing popularity of TV. But, in fact, television had greatly increased the interest in America in sports and leisure life, and *SI* profited from that. By 1997 it was second only to *People* magazine as the most popular consumer magazine in the world with a circulation of three million and a weekly readership of twenty-four million adults.[76]

*** *

As the 1980s loomed a new all-sports cable television channel began and unquestionably changed sports journalism forever. Suddenly, viewers were inundated with sports news as never before and could literally watch it twenty-four hours a day. At the same time the field of sports journalism was subtly changing as more and more women started entering the field. They faced huge challenges in their desire to be treated the same as their male counterparts, but they were not about to give up. It was just another sign that, as in the past, the winds of change continued blowing through sports journalism.

ESPN and Women Sportswriters and Broadcasters 6

> I don't know a reporter, male or female, who likes to go
> into a locker room. [They are] unsexy, smelly, sweaty, and
> awful . . . not a place you'd really want to go . . . but it's
> part of the job; it's where the stories are.
> —Sportswriter Betty Cuniberti, 2013

Lee Leonard began the first broadcast of ESPN's *SportsCenter* on September 7, 1979, by introducing himself and his co-anchor, George Grande. "If you're a fan, *if* you're a fan, what you'll see in the next minutes, hours, and days to follow may convince you, you've gone to sports heaven," he said.[1] So began the first all-sports television network and a new era in sports journalism.

ESPN became, by its own characterization, "the worldwide leader in sports."[2] By any objective measure, it became the most significant source of sports journalism in history, providing news, play-by-play coverage, interviews, and studio analysis twenty-four hours a day. ESPN made athletes international figures, and it made celebrities out of anchors such as Chris Berman, Keith Olbermann, and Dan Patrick. Its six-note theme ("DaDaDa, DaDaDa") came to be identified not just with the network but also with televised sports. Decades after that first broadcast, the influence of a sport or a sports event can be measured, in part, by how much airtime it receives on ESPN. It forever changed sports and how they were watched. Bob Verdi, a longtime sportswriter on the *Chicago Tribune*, said in a 2001 book that he barely remembered what civilization was like before ESPN. "But," he added, "I don't care to relive it."[3]

ESPN profoundly influenced how sports were televised, covered, and discussed. Since it premiered in 1979, *SportsCenter* has exceeded fifty thousand unique episodes, far more than any other program in the history of American television.[4] ESPN popularized sports talk radio with ESPN Radio; it took on serious issues with programs such as *Outside the Lines*; it aired sports documentaries with its *30 for 30* series; it created new sports with the X Games; it published a sports magazine, *ESPN: The Magazine*; and it produced the ESPY Awards to honor those in sports just as the Oscars do with those in the motion picture industry and the Emmys do in television. ESPN has been the subject of numerous books, including *ESPN: The Uncensored History* and *Those Guys Have All the Fun: Inside the World of ESPN*.[5] *SportsCenter* also led to a prime-time television series, and its anchors inspired a generation of wannabes.[6]

Meanwhile, as ESPN rapidly established itself as the leader in sports broadcasting, women sportswriters and broadcasters were entering the sports field in rapidly growing numbers and quite literally going places (such as men's locker rooms) where no women had gone before. It was a struggle, but they proved that it was a struggle worth winning as they began to change sports journalism then and continue to do so today.

***

Given the significance and pervasiveness of ESPN today, it is perhaps difficult to believe that considerable skepticism existed about whether enough interest existed to sustain an all-sports network. In the late 1970s cable was "a vast, untamed unregulated jungle," Michael Freeman wrote in *ESPN: The Uncensored History*, "and no single conqueror had emerged with the vision to maximize its potential." Cable companies wanted nothing to do with a sports network. When Bill Rasmussen pitched the idea to sportswriters and sportscasters at a press conference a year before the first program, they laughed at him. "This is the stupidest idea I've ever heard," one of them said.[7]

Rasmussen, who then was an unemployed sports broadcaster, came up with the idea for a national cable sports network while stuck in traffic. His partners were his son, Scott, who was in his early twenties and working part-time as an announcer for a minor league hockey team; Ed Eagan, an insurance salesman who had a part-time job with a cable company; and Bill Beyus, who owned a video production company.[8] Rasmussen convinced Stuart Evey, who was vice president of Getty Oil's nonoil operations, to finance the network. The NCAA agreed to allow ESPN to broadcast college sports on tape delay, and Chet Simmons, the highly respected producer of NBC Sports, was hired to run the new network.[9]

When ESPN went on the air, Rasmussen stood about twenty feet from Leonard and Grande, watching and believing, though hardly comprehending, what was happening. Through determination and perhaps fate, he had willed the idea for ESPN into existence. But in doing so he had surrendered control and ultimately ESPN to Evey (because Getty owned 85 percent of the network) and Simmons (who demanded editorial control in return for leaving NBC). As Rasmussen watched the first broadcast of *SportsCenter*, he knew he would not be at the network much longer. He left the next year. Simmons quit in 1982 to become commissioner of the United States Football League, which competed briefly with the National Football League, and Evey was forced out when Texaco bought Getty in 1984.[10] That same year, Texaco sold ESPN to ABC for $202 million.

Even if someone had had the idea for a cable sports network before Rasmussen did, the technology would not have allowed it. Therefore, ESPN was not merely the result of the right people coming together at the right time, it was also the result of the right idea coinciding with the right technology. Time Inc. established Home Box Office (HBO), the first cable network in 1972, for the company's local cable system in New York City. It used a microwave link to show movies and then sports, but the service was neither successful nor profitable. In 1975, however, shortly after domestic satellites became available, HBO transmitted the Muhammad Ali-Joe Frazier heavyweight championship title fight from the Philippines, and millions watched it on closed-circuit television.[11]

HBO won a lawsuit two years later against the Federal Communications Commission to drop restrictions against the cable industry. The growth of cable television in the late 1960s raised concerns that pay cable television could outbid conventional television for rights to popular programs, which could then be "siphoned" from broadcast television and no longer be available free to viewers. The FCC responded by adopting anti-siphoning regulations.[12] In 1977 the U.S. Court of Appeals, DC Circuit, vacated the FCC's anti-siphoning regulations.[13] This gave cable stations greater access to programming, which triggered tremendous growth in the industry. The use of satellite transmission was cheaper and easier than using terrestrial signals, but the cost remained high and few cable stations could afford the technology required to receive satellite signals. Ted Turner, who owned the cable channel WTBS in Atlanta, used a satellite to deliver programming, including television reruns and Atlanta Braves baseball games, to cable stations throughout the country.[14] It became the country's first so-called superstation, allowing subscribers of the cable station to watch the Braves far beyond the state of Georgia.[15]

ESPN initially could not broadcast football, basketball, baseball, or any other popular sport in real time because it had neither the resources nor the staff, nor the rights to do so. It filled its broadcasts with video of obscure sports, such as Australian Rules football, high school lacrosse, tractor pulls, rodeos, ping-pong tournaments, and female mud wrestling. One ESPN staffer stuck a photograph of a Trident submarine on the wall and wrote: "Coming to ESPN: submarine racing." The photo and caption was an inside joke. "ESPN was willing to put almost anything on the air to fill air time," Freeman wrote, "and with the military's permission, even submarine races might make it."[16]

ESPN executives had to rely on their wits to keep the network on the air because it could not provide live broadcasts of high-profile sports. The network's need to fill so many hours of airtime inspired the creation of programming, such as the National Football League draft, that continues to profit the network. When NFL Commissioner Pete Rozelle learned that ESPN wanted to broadcast the league's draft he was dumbfounded, because he could not understand why the network wanted to cover something where little seemed to be happening. "Why would you do that?" he asked Simmons, who thought football fans would want to see it.[17] He was right. ESPN broadcast its first draft in 1980 and, in 2019, 47.5 million viewers watched the draft.[18]

ESPN also hired Steve Sabol of NFL Films, a football video library, to show the league's footage during the network's program that preceded ABC's *Monday Night Football*. Freeman noted that Sabol's films became "one of the most recognizable pieces of programming in ESPN history." In addition, none of the established networks were interested in broadcasting the early rounds of the NCAA men's basketball tournament; but, in March 1980, ESPN aired more than 450 hours of college basketball or related programming. Its coverage of the tournament introduced such innovations as the "cut-in," in which the network would quickly cut from one game to another.[19] ESPN eventually became synonymous with the annual tournament, broadcasting the selection of brackets, introducing words such as "bracketology," and changing the tournament into something that transformed sports.[20]

Even after ESPN began broadcasting twenty-four hours a day on September 1, 1980, the network continued to make history but lost considerable money year after year. Freeman chronicled how the pressures of working for a fledgling twenty-four-hour, all-sports network in the relatively isolated city of Bristol, Connecticut, took its toll on the staff members, who worked long days and longer weeks, month after month. Employees dealt with the stress by gambling, drinking, and abusing drugs, often while on the job.[21] Stephen Bogart, an ESPN producer, remembered the culture: "ESPN was a party. The idea was a party. The whole sports thing was a party. But we did a great job. We worked hard, we played hard, we were visionaries, we were doing something special. Above everything else, we wanted to succeed."[22]

But one issue—sexual harassment—jeopardized the network's existence. Hooters restaurant posters hung on office walls and male staffers watched pornography with the volume turned up loudly. Women staffers complained they were fondled, groped, and told they would lose their jobs if they did not sleep with supervisors. Most of the women had little recourse but to complain to one another because no females worked in management. Finally, Karie Ross, one of the few female anchors, had seen enough and heard enough from other women working for the network, and at a 1989 meeting of more than two hundred staffers she confronted the men in the room. "I stood up and said, 'Look, this behavior has got to stop. This is crazy. You guys can't be doing this. Guys, you must stop sexually harassing these women. Don't be trading edit time for a date. Quit making all the lewd comments. Just let us work in peace.' And then I said, 'I know it's illegal.' My voice was shaking as I spoke. After I finished, you could hear a pin drop."[23]

Management took little action until it suspended anchor Mike Tirico in 1992 after repeated complaints of sexual harassment. But most complaints were ignored. ESPN human resources director Ricardo Correia criticized the company for not doing more to address the issue and ultimately left the company in 1995 when he felt meaningful change was not possible.[24] A female production assistant said women addressed the harassment in one of three ways: they used their feminine attributes to advance their career; they downplayed their feminine attributes in hopes of making themselves less attractive to potential harassers; or they refused to compromise and confronted their harassers.[25]

Sexual harassment remains an issue at ESPN, although it has taken action—clumsily at times—to punish those who have acted inappropriately. In 2006 it fired baseball analyst Harold Reynolds after he hugged an intern at a restaurant; he filed a wrongful termination lawsuit and was awarded a settlement from the network.[26] ESPN also settled a sexual harassment suit in 2015 against Chris Berman, who was accused by a makeup artist of making sexual comments to her in person as well as in text messages.[27] In 2009 the network fired baseball analyst Steve Phillips for an inappropriate relationship with a female production assistant. When she told her female supervisor that he had invited her to his hotel room, she was told, "Get used to it, kid. If I had a dollar for every time I was sexually harassed at ESPN, I would be a millionaire."[28]

ESPN, however, also established a reputation for providing opportunities for women to work in sports broadcast journalism that had long been limited to them in newspapers, television, and radio.[29] The network not only hired women to work off camera as producers and production assistants but also gave them on-camera positions as reporters and anchors. Until the 1980s few women had high-profile jobs such as columnists, anchors, or beat reporters in sports. ESPN hired Gayle Gardner in 1983 from a Boston television station to anchor *SportsCenter*, making her the first female sports anchor to regularly appear on a major network. She realized the significance of her position. "There was a generation of [female] sportscasters before me . . . trying to move up," she said. "And most of that generation gave up. The battle was too big. It was too stressful to keep trying to make something happen with people who really didn't want to hire you. At a point, you say, 'Why am I doing this?'"[30]

In the early 1970s Jeannie Morris, who was at the beginning of a quarter-century-long career as a sports reporter for newspapers and radio, was not allowed in the press box while covering a Chicago Bears-Minnesota Vikings pro football game at Metropolitan Stadium in Minneapolis. So, she was forced to report the game while standing on top of the press box. She once tried to interview Ted Williams, the Hall of Fame baseball player who was managing the Texas Rangers, in a dugout before a game. He ordered her out of the dugout, saying, "What's this shrimp female doing in here. Get the hell out!"[31]

Lesley Visser, who began working for the *Boston Globe* in 1974 when she was twenty-one, recalled that her first press pass said: "No women or children allowed in the press box."[32] Two years after she joined the *Globe*, she was assigned to cover the New England Patriots, making her the first female beat reporter to cover an NFL team. After a game between the Patriots and the Pittsburgh Steelers, she approached Steelers' quarterback Terry Bradshaw for an interview. Thinking she was a fan and not a sportswriter, he snatched her notebook, signed his autograph, and handed it back to her. "Are you kidding me?" she said. "I'm a reporter."[33]

Women working in sports journalism in the 1970s were often the first to do so at a newspaper, magazine, or television station. In 1974, when Robin Herman became the first female sportswriter for the *New York Times*, she said she was hired partly because the newspaper was facing a gender discrimination lawsuit as a result of having so few women on staff.[34] A year later she made news when the National Hockey League allowed women to conduct locker-room interviews after the All-Star Game. Then twenty-three, she suddenly found herself in the middle of the story. "I kept saying, 'I'm not the story; the game is the story,'" she recalled, reflecting on the night. "But of course that wasn't the case. The game was boring. A girl in the locker room was a story."[35]

NHL and NBA teams opened up their locker rooms to female sportswriters; Major League Baseball did not. While press credentials gave male journalists access to locker rooms to interview players and coaches before and after games, women were denied the same access and forced to wait outside, hoping a player would talk to them after giving interviews to all the male sportswriters. Female sportswriters remember asking team officials if they could interview a specific player and then, when a player was finally brought to them, it was invariably not the one they had requested.[36]

In 1977 Melissa Ludtke, a reporter for *Sports Illustrated,* expressed her frustration to New York Yankees' public relations director Mickey Morabito about her lack of access to the players and manager Billy Martin. Morabito began ushering Ludtke after games from a side door of the clubhouse to Martin's office. This continued through the rest of the season.[37] The Yankees played the Los Angeles Dodgers in the World Series. Ludtke asked Dodger pitcher Tommy John, the team's player representative, if she could have access to the team's clubhouse during the series. John took a vote of the players and they agreed that since Ludtke had press credentials, she should be allowed in the clubhouse.[38]

During the middle of Game 1, Ludtke learned that Baseball Commissioner Bowie Kuhn said she would not be allowed in the clubhouse because, he said, the players' wives had not been consulted; and he thought the players' children would be ridiculed if female journalists were allowed in the locker rooms.[39] Ludtke and Time Inc. filed a civil rights lawsuit based on the Equal Protection Clause of the Fourteenth Amendment. On September 25, 1978, federal judge Constance Baker Motley ruled that all reporters, regardless of their gender, should have equal access to athletes, even if that included the locker room.[40] Motley left it up to teams to decide how they would do that. For instance, they could impose time restrictions on clubhouse visits by all journalists, they could close the clubhouse to all sportswriters and broadcasters, or they could open up locker rooms to all media.[41] Ludtke said the judge's decision was a vindication for female sportswriters who wanted nothing less—and nothing more—than the same privileges accorded their male colleagues.[42]

Male sportswriters and sportscasters often were not merely unsympathetic to female sportswriters in the locker room but also openly critical of them. Ludtke, for instance, was ridiculed by other sports journalists; her motives for bringing the lawsuit were questioned as was her ability and her appearance.[43] Male sportswriters not only disparaged female sportswriters in private but also did in public. *New York Post* sportswriter Maury Allen said the presence of female sportswriters in the locker room would have a negative impact on sports and how they were covered: "My feelings are that women don't belong in the locker rooms where athletes are. It's not a fair thing for players. They are in an area where they are dressing. It's an area where they are entitled to some degree of privacy. We don't think it's fair to the rest of the press and we don't think it's fair to the fans who have great reservations about this. What I'm afraid of is that the impact of women in sports will diminish the joy of sport, diminish the joy of athletes and athletics."[44]

Allen wasn't alone. Jerome Holtzman of the *Chicago Sun-Times*, who served as the official historian for Major League Baseball, was equally offended. "I suppose the fact that this was an all-male world was what made it so exciting to me at first. And now that it's being invaded and eroded it's much less attractive," he told the *New Yorker*. "The press box used to be a male preserve—that was its charm. I'd rather not have a woman as a seatmate at a World Series game. It wouldn't be as much fun." Leigh Montville of the *Boston Globe* huffed: "Is she serious? . . . Did she ever spit in a baseball glove? . . . Was her life absolutely dominated by sports when she was a kid?"[45]

In addition, women wanting to enter locker rooms were accused of being voyeurs who wanted to gawk at naked athletes. Paola Boivin, who at twenty-five was covering sports for a small newspaper in Southern California, went into the St. Louis Cardinals clubhouse after a 1985 game with the Los Angeles Dodgers. As she made her way through the mass of bodies, a Cardinals player blocked her path, menacingly stared at her, and asked if she wanted to interview players or stare at their penises. Before she could respond a sweat-soaked jockstrap hit her in the head. She remembered looking down and thinking, "Oh my God!" and fled the locker room. "That incident came close to ending my career," she recalled.[46]

Female sportswriters believed that if they could not win over their critics with logic or common sense, they had to do so with the quality of their writing and with their knowledge of sports. Ludtke said: "What I learned, as one of the only women covering baseball at the time, was that I better know damn well what I'm talking about when I open my mouth, because there are going to be a lot of people watching me, a lot of people ready to say that I don't know what I'm talking about. . . . That might have meant me doing a lot more reading and research and knowing things a lot better than maybe a lot of people around me did when they went up to ask questions. But it always gave me a feeling that at least I belonged."[47]

Ludtke remembered a conversation with Frank Gifford, the Hall of Fame halfback who broadcast ABC's *Monday Night Football*. He was impressed with her knowledge. "You know a lot about sports for a girl," he told her, inviting her to ABC, where she interviewed for a job but was not hired.[48] While Ludtke was at ABC she met tennis player

Billie Jean King, who had defeated hustler Bobby Riggs, a fifty-five-year-old former Wimbledon champion, before a prime-time television audience of more than ninety million viewers on September 23, 1973.[49] The so-called "Battle of the Sexes," which is widely considered one of the most important sports events in history, inspired Ludtke and a generation of girls and young women to not only play sports but also enter professions, such as sportscasting and sportswriting, that previously had been closed to them.[50]

Lesley Visser, who was a junior in college when King played Riggs, wanted to be a sportswriter but knew there were few females in the field because it was considered a male profession. "Billie Jean didn't just give me a chance," she said, "she gave every woman in this country a chance."[51] Mary Carillo, who was then sixteen, said the King-Riggs match changed the direction of her life, too. "My start in sports television happened because I watched, rapt, as Billie Jean King took out Bobby Riggs in the fall of 1973," she said. After a professional tennis career, she became a sports journalist, winning an Emmy as a reporter for HBO's *Real Sports*.[52]

"The Battle of the Sexes" provided a jolt to the Women's Rights Movement when women confronted their second-class status in much of society and demanded equality in the workplace. In 1964 Congress passed the Civil Rights Act, which prohibited discrimination in race. Then, in 1972, Congress approved Title IX, which prohibited discrimination based on sex in educational programs or anything else that received federal financial assistance. Title IX said: "No person in the United States shall, on the basis of sex, be excluded from participation in, be denied the benefits of, or be subjected to discrimination under any education program or activity receiving federal financial assistance."[53]

Title IX guaranteed women equal funding in high school and college sports and resulted in an unprecedented increase in women competing in athletics and writing about athletics. But equality or diversity could not be achieved until they had access to the same press boxes, dugouts, and locker rooms as their male colleagues. Judge Motley's decision in

Ludtke v. Kuhn was a legal victory, but it meant little if Major League Baseball, its commissioner, and its teams did not obey the decision.

Claire Smith, who worked for the *Hartford Courant*, became one of the first female major league beat writers in 1983, and the *New York Times* hired her in the following year. She entered the San Diego clubhouse after the first game of the 1984 National League Championship Series between the Chicago Cubs and the Padres in Wrigley Field and experienced perhaps the low point of what would be a long and successful career. Dave Dravecky, a Padres pitcher, angrily ordered her to leave, and she was physically removed from the clubhouse despite a rule that gave all properly accredited journalists access to the dressing room during the playoffs. When San Diego first baseman Steve Garvey learned what had happened, he left the clubhouse and sat down with her. "He told me he would stay out there as long as I wanted," she recalled, "and I was able to get my job done."[54]

Peter Ueberroth, who succeeded Kuhn as baseball commissioner in 1984, learned what had happened in the San Diego clubhouse and announced the next day that female journalists would have the same access as their male counterparts. "There are some things that are issues, but this one's a nonissue," he said bluntly. "It won't happen again."[55] Claire Smith worked for the *Times* for several years as a writer and columnist before moving to the *Philadelphia Inquirer* and then ESPN. In 2017 she became the first woman to receive the J. G. Taylor Spink Award from the Baseball Writers' Association of America "for meritorious contributions to baseball writing."[56] In her acceptance speech, she acknowledged the long fight for equality and access for female sports journalists and thanked "the women who walked the walk and fought the battles and got all of us to this point." Smith added, "No one does this by themselves."[57]

By the mid-1980s professional baseball, football, basketball, and hockey required their locker rooms to be open to female sportswriters. When players and managers complained about having women among the naked athletes, female sportswriters responded, "let them wear towels." The words inspired a documentary by that name that aired on ESPN as part of the network's documentary series about women in athletics marking the fortieth anniversary of Title IX. It included interviews with female sports journalists, who remembered the discrimination that they faced in being banned from locker rooms and the physical confrontations and assaults after they finally were allowed inside. Jane Gross of the *New York Times* recalled being physically thrown out of a locker room by a National Hockey League player. In addition, New York Mets outfielder Dave Kingman dumped ice water on Gross's head in the team's dressing room.[58] When Kingman was with the Oakland A's, he once sent a box with a live rat in a pink box to *Sacramento Bee* sportswriter Susan Fornoff in the press box.[59]

Thus, female sports journalists regularly—and often painfully—learned to enter locker rooms at their own risk. Joan Ryan of the *Orlando Sentinel* remembered being surrounded by players in the locker room of the United States Football League's Birmingham Stallions while one of them stroked her leg with a long-handled razor.[60] Jackie MacMullan of the *Boston Globe* was thrown across a hallway and into a wall when she tried to enter a college basketball team's locker room, and Shelley Smith of the *San Francisco Examiner* was physically grabbed in the locker room by 49ers offensive lineman Bubba Paris and marched into the shower room.[61]

Lesley Visser was in the University of Houston's locker room after a Cotton Bowl game when head coach Bill Yeoman saw her and screamed, "I don't give a damn about the Equal Rights Amendment. I'm not having her in my locker room!" He then marched her out the door. After another sportswriter finished his interviews, he shared his notes with her. "There are moments you have to rely on the kindness of strangers," she said. Upon entering the New York Jets locker room in 1989, Visser was stopped by the voice of tight end Mickey Shuler, who yelled, "Hey, no women in the locker room!" She laughed, thinking he was kidding, but he repeated himself, louder and with an obscenity. When he learned that she was allowed in the locker room, he wrote a letter of apology to her.[62]

During the 1990 NFL season *Boston Herald* sportswriter Lisa Olson was sexually harassed by members of the New England Patriots in the team's locker room. During an interview with cornerback Maurice Hurst, she said, tight end Zeke Mowatt "stood [naked] in front of me and said, 'This is what you want. This is what you're in here for. Do you want to take a bite out of this?'" Two or three other naked players crowded around her making lewd gestures. "I didn't know whether to scream or break down and cry. It was a premeditated mind rape," she said.[63]

Patriots owner Victor Kiam II responded to what had happened to Olson by blaming the newspaper for assigning a female reporter to cover his team and reportedly calling her "a classic bitch."[64] The NFL fined the Patriots and the players involved, but this did little to mitigate her distress. She was subjected to harassment by fans of the Patriots, receiving hundreds of pieces of hate mail and death threats while the tires on her car were slashed and her apartment was burglarized. A note left in her apartment said: "[L]eave Boston or die." The *Herald*'s owner, News Corporation, enabled her to transfer to Sydney, Australia, where she worked for six years before returning to the United States.[65]

Shortly after the incident in the Patriots' locker room, Cincinnati Bengals head coach Sam Wyche ordered a female sportswriter out of his team's locker room, and NFL Commissioner Paul Tagliabue fined him for violating the league's equal-access rule.[66] In a sign that times were perhaps changing, Wyche found himself with few coaches or writers who publicly supported him. Sportswriter George Vecsey of the *New York Times* ridiculed him as a bully and a bad loser, who was "acting out his antagonisms toward women who don't know their place."[67] Ludtke said she had hoped that the issue of whether women should be allowed in locker rooms had been settled: "Women in the locker rooms should not be the issue in 1990. Rather, the finger ought to be pointed at the infantile and repugnant behavior of some ballplayers and their inability to adjust to changing times, when gender equality should be assumed."[68]

By the early 1990s other issues of equality remained. *Sports Illus-*

trated pointed out that Gayle Gardner, who left ESPN to anchor sports coverage for NBC sports, was the highest-paid female sports broadcaster, but her salary was nearly ten times less than what the highest-paid male anchors earned. In addition, women had fewer than 20 percent of the on-camera sports jobs at ABC, CBS, NBC, and ESPN, and that figure was exaggerated because many females only worked every four years to comment on the events in which they had competed in the Olympics. Only one woman, CBS and ESPN tennis analyst Mary Carillo, regularly did commentary from the booth at a men's event during a top tournament or playoff game. Women who were fortunate enough to work for networks were hired as sideline reporters, and none did play-by-play for a television network, which was long considered the marquee assignment in sportscasting.[69]

Female sports journalists continued to be banned from locker rooms and dressing rooms. Tara Sullivan of the *Record* of Hackensack, New Jersey, was denied access to the locker room at Augusta National Golf Club after the final round of the 2011 Masters tournament. "Bad enough no women members at Augusta," she responded on Twitter. "But not allowing me to join writers in the locker room interview is just wrong."[70] Augusta National had already been criticized for not allowing its first black golfer, Lee Elder, to play in the Masters until 1975 and not admitting its first black member until 1991.[71] But a decade later it still had no female members. In 2002 Christine Brennan wrote a column in *USA Today* criticizing Augusta National for its discriminatory practices. The column acted as a call to action for woman's rights activist Martha Burk, who began a protest against the club that resulted in it finally accepting its first two female members in 2012. "This story really showed the struggles of women in sports media as well as women in sports," Brennan said.[72]

By the 2010s there were more women working in sports journalism than ever before, but they continued to lag behind in the more prestigious jobs. The Institute for Diversity and Ethics in Sports at the University of Central Florida gave the media, including print and broadcast, an "F" grade for gender representation among columnists and editors. It reported that 94 percent of sports editors were white and so were 88 percent of sports columnists, and 93 percent of columnists were male. The majority of female columnists and editors worked for ESPN, which the report noted had made a concerted effort to diversify its newsroom.[73] In 2015, ESPN hired Jessica Mendoza as an analyst in the broadcast booth during *Sunday Night Baseball*, making her reportedly the first woman to have that position during a network broadcast of a game.[74]

In May 2017 ESPN announced that Beth Mowins would become the first woman in thirty years to call the play-by-play of an NFL game during the upcoming season.[75] Only two other women had broadcast NFL games. On December 27, 1987, Gayle Sierens broadcast a game between the Seattle Seahawks and the Kansas City Chiefs in the final weekend of the regular season on NBC. The network offered her six games in the following season, but the Tampa station where she worked did not want her to split her time between the jobs. In 2009, Visser, while working for CBS Radio, became the first woman to do color commentary for an NFL game during a preseason game.[76]

As women have been promoted to higher profile jobs in sports journalism in the U.S., stories of unfair treatment against them, which were once ignored, are now far more likely to be reported. The 2018 World Cup in soccer was an example. CNN, National Public Radio, and the *Washington Post* reported on a number of sexual harassment incidents involving women journalists, who made up only 14 percent of the sixteen thousand accredited journalists covering the matches.[77]

On the first day of the World Cup Colombian journalist Juleith González Therán was reporting in Moscow for a Spanish TV channel when a male spectator grabbed her breast and kissed her on the cheek. She continued broadcasting and said later, "We do not deserve this treatment." The channel reran the video and supported her strongly: "Sexual harassment is not okay. It needs to stop, in football, and elsewhere." When a twitter user wrote that the incident occurred because "people are simply overfilled with joy," the channel responded, "Sorry, but no. Kissing someone against their will is sexual harassment. Groping a woman's breast while she's busy doing her job is sexual harassment."[78]

Júlia Guimarães, a Brazilian journalist, had a similar experience in Russia. While she was broadcasting outside a stadium where a game was being played, she successfully dodged a man trying to kiss her and then lectured him on air about what he had done. "Don't do this," she said. "Never do this again. Don't do this. I don't allow you to do this, never, OK? This is not polite, this is not right. Never do this to a woman, OK? Respect." The man, who was off screen, apologized. She wrote afterward this was the second time that such an incident had happened to her in Russia while she was broadcasting, adding: "Luckily, I've never experienced this in Brazil!"[79]

Another incident involved BBC commentator Vicki Sparks, the first woman to broadcast a live World Cup game on British TV. After the match Jason Cundy, a former English Premier League player, said on the TV show, *Good Morning Britain*, "I prefer to have a male voice when watching football. Ninety minutes of hearing a high-pitched tone isn't really what I like to hear. And when there's a moment of drama, as there often is in football, that moment needs to be done with a slightly lower voice." Piers Morgan, the co-host of the show, quickly fired back at Cundy: "Your annoyance appears to be because they have too pitchy voices though yours is just as pitchy, which seems to make you a sexist pig." After running a side-by-side comparison that showed Sparks's voice was no more high pitched than Cundy's, Morgan said to him, "This is not a fight to pick. This is not a hill to die on."[80]

Ludtke, who was interviewed on September 25, 2018, the fortieth anniversary of the court decision that ordered Major League Baseball to open its clubhouse to female journalists, expressed disappointment that sexism remained so common in sports. "I cringe every time I hear somebody criticize Jessica Mendoza for sitting in the ESPN baseball booth, using the same misogynistic phrase I heard forty years ago: 'She doesn't belong,'" she said. "Sorry, guys. You couldn't stop us then. You can't stop us now."[81] Amazon Prime Video announced on the same day that Andrea Kremer and Hannah Storm would become the first all-female broadcasting team to call an NFL game on September 27 between the Los Angeles Rams and the Minnesota Vikings.[82]

Meanwhile, ESPN was still going through changes of its own. About a quarter-century after ESPN went on the air in 1979 the network achieved a level of dominance in sports that had never existed in television. It had not merely transformed how sports journalism was covered, produced, and marketed but it had also changed how fans watched sports, followed sports, and probably thought about sports. Fans no longer waited to read or watch sports. Now, "sports junkies"—as Scott Rasmussen referred to the potential audience for ESPN when the network first aired—could watch sports or highlights any minute of any day.[83] In 2011 ESPN reached an estimated hundred million homes.[84] The ESPN franchise also includes ESPN2, ESPNEWS, ESPNU, ESPN Classic, ESPN *Deportes*, ESPN+, and the regional college football networks, the Longhorn Network of the University of Texas and the Southeastern Conference Network.

In addition, ESPN owns the country's largest sports radio network, ESPN Radio; a website that focuses on female athletes and women's issues, espnW; and a website, The Undefeated, which was created in 2016 to examine race, sports, and culture.[85] ESPN's popularity—at least for a time—did not just make the network profitable, it made everything around it profitable. The Walt Disney Corporation purchased ABC and its properties, including ESPN, in 1996. Within several years ESPN generated more money for the Disney Corporation than all of its other properties combined.[86]

ESPN and Yahoo Sports began hiring columnists and reporters by offering them salaries that neither newspapers nor magazines could equal. Rick Reilly, for instance, was paid a reported $3 million annually to go from *Sports Illustrated* to ESPN. For a few sportswriters, this meant that when they interviewed an athlete in a locker room they were the higher-paid person.[87] Many newspaper columnists continued to write for their newspapers but also hosted their own radio or television programs, where their exposure and salaries increased. For instance, the *Washington Post*'s Tony Kornheiser began hosting a radio program in 1992 and, in 2001, ESPN hired him and another *Post* columnist, Michael Wilbon, to host *Pardon the Interruption*. Neither works for the *Post* anymore.

As it succeeded ESPN faced an increase in competition, primarily from Fox Sports, but also from other radio and television networks or their websites as well as from independent websites such as Bleacher Report, Deadspin, and SBNation. In 2007 Dan Patrick announced he was leaving ESPN to host a syndicated radio program. In the 1990s, Patrick and Olbermann had transformed *SportsCenter* and sports television with their intelligence, writing, reporting, and wit. In doing so, they inspired copycats, who aspired to be them without imitating their work ethic. Aspiring sports broadcasters practiced self-conscious smirks and pithy phrases, emphasizing glibness over substance and hoping that would be enough to get them a job as an anchor on *SportsCenter*. As this was going on ESPN anchors and reporters jeopardized their objectivity by palling around with athletes, dropping names of athletes with whom they had socialized, and forgetting or not caring that they were supposed to be reporters and not publicists for an athlete or a team. Berman notably criticized press reports of drug use in the NFL, saying, "Who cares? Who cares? Who cares?" Chris Fowler, the host of *College GameDay*, a program that precedes the network's coverage of NCAA football games, attacked ESPN for revealing abuses in college athletics. According to one critic, he was "aligning himself more with the colleges than his own network."[88]

ESPN also has often been criticized for its editorial judgment, such as when it hired controversial radio talk show host Rush Limbaugh in 2003 to join *Sunday NFL Countdown* as a commentator. The network said he would provide the "voice of the fan" and would provoke debate as he did on his radio program. But his radio commentary was often singed with racism, such as praising the benefits of slavery, offering a medal to the assassin of Martin Luther King Jr., and telling a black caller "to remove the bone from his nose."[89] If it was ESPN's intent to provoke debate by hiring him, the network accomplished it. On September 28, during one of the first weeks of the season, he criticized

Philadelphia Eagles quarterback Donovan McNabb, who had struggled in the early part of the season. To Limbaugh, sports journalists had been too easy on McNabb because it was important for the NFL to have a successful black quarterback in a league that was dominated by black players. "Sorry to say this, I don't think he's been that good from the get-go," said Limbaugh. "What we have here is a little social concern in the NFL. The media has been very desirous that a black quarterback can do well—black coaches and black quarterbacks doing well. . . . There's a little hope invested in McNabb, and he got credit for the performance of his team that he didn't deserve. The defense [has] carried this team."[90]

Limbaugh was not asked to support his opinion by the announcers working with him. McNabb had indeed been ineffective during the first two games of the season, but he had been to three straight Pro Bowls and had been a runner-up for the most valuable player award during his first full season in the NFL in 2000. When informed of what Limbaugh had said, McNabb responded: "It's sad that you've got to go to skin color. I thought we were through with that whole deal." He later said he worried that Limbaugh's comment might discourage young blacks from wanting to play quarterback on the grounds of how they might "be looked upon because of the color of [their] skin." His comment intensified the controversy, prompting many to recall Limbaugh's history of incendiary and often racist comments and to demand his firing.[91] One NFL executive released a statement that criticized both Limbaugh and ESPN. "Donovan's stature as a top quarterback reflects his performance on the field, not the desire of the media," the executive said. "ESPN knew what they were getting when they hired Rush Limbaugh. ESPN selected its on-air talent, not the NFL."[92]

Limbaugh said he had not meant to criticize McNabb but had intended to criticize journalists for praising an overrated quarterback because the media and the league wanted him to succeed. He resigned from ESPN on October 1 and posted a statement on his website on the next day, saying the outrage over his McNabb comment was because those in the media had believed there was truth in what he said. "If I wasn't right there wouldn't be this cacophony of outrage that has sprung up in the sportswriter community," he said.[93]

In an essay on the response to Limbaugh's comments, sociologist Douglas Hartmann wrote that the controversial talk show host had offended sports journalists because he had violated the unspoken and unwritten rule that race and politics should be kept out of sports.[94] Instead, sportswriters and sportscasters had long denied the undeniable that race and politics were part of sports and always had been. Most sportswriters and columnists remained reluctant to mention politics unless they were quoting athletes who were doing so. In the 1960s and '70s black athletes such as Muhammad Ali, Jim Brown, Kareem Abdul-Jabbar, and Arthur Ashe confronted racial inequality in society.[95]

By the 1990s, however, the most famous athletes—Michael Jordan in basketball and Tiger Woods in golf—said little or nothing about politics or social issues because they did not want to risk their lucrative endorsement deals with corporations.[96] Both athletes insisted on—and generally received—favorable coverage from journalists, who did not want to jeopardize the opportunity to socialize with Jordan or Woods and then drop their names on *SportsCenter* or on their talk radio programs to demonstrate to their listeners or viewers that they had special access to one or both of the great athletes. In return for this access, sports journalists wrote or said nothing about either of their flaws or they could be denied future interviews.[97]

In 1997 Woods, who was then twenty-one, won the Masters by twelve strokes and soon established himself as not only the world's best golfer but also a player apparently destined to break Jack Nicklaus's record of winning eighteen times in the sport's four major tournaments. People who had never before cared about golf began watching and playing it, and viewers turned on their televisions in record numbers on Sundays to watch Woods play and often win in the final round of a tournament. The so-called "Tiger Woods effect" resulted in a spike in television advertising revenue, which translated into record prize money for golfers.[98] But on Thanksgiving night 2013 Woods's wife, Elin Nordegren, chased him out of their house with a golf club after learning of an extramarital affair. In the weeks and months that followed one woman after another went on social media claiming to have had an affair with him. Both his personal and professional lives were left in shambles, and he never returned to his former glory.[99] Thus, Woods became the latest in a string of athletes to see their triumphs in sports overshadowed by personal failings.

Meanwhile, in an important shift in what was covered, sports journalists began reporting not just from baseball fields and basketball courts and boxing rings but also from courtrooms and crime scenes. In 1989 Pete Rose, who had more career hits than any player in major league history, was suspended from baseball for betting on games while serving as manager of the Cincinnati Reds. Then, Lance Armstrong, who won international praise for overcoming cancer to win seven Tour de France cycling titles, was discovered in the 2000s to have used illegal performance-enhancing drugs. In addition, several of the most reported stories about athletes occurred off the playing field, such as the conviction of Rose for income tax evasion in 1992; the rape conviction of heavyweight boxing champion Mike Tyson in the same year; the conviction of figure-skating champion Tonya Harding for her involvement in the assault of her rival, Nancy Kerrigan, in 1994; the murder trial of Heisman Trophy winner and Hall of Fame NFL player O. J. Simpson in 1995; the conviction of NFL quarterback Michael Vick for running a dog-fighting ring in 2007; and the conviction of New England Patriots' tight end Aaron Hernandez for murder in 2015.

Before these events sports largely had been perceived as something apart from the rest of society—and newspapers' sports sections were different from news sections. Sports sections touted the triumphs, successes, and glories of athletes, ignoring their weaknesses and failures. But those myths were shattered as more and more athletes were arrested for committing crimes; more and more colleges and universities cheated to make themselves more competitive in sports; and television revenues played a bigger and bigger part in the economics of both professional and amateur sports. Journalists recognized that sports should not be restricted to the sports sections and saw that sports—for better or worse—reflected the world in which we lived. In 2011 former Penn State University assistant football coach Jerry Sandusky was charged with, and later convicted, of the rape and the sexual assault of dozens of young boys. The investigation led to the firing of Joe Paterno, then the winningest head coach in college football, and convictions for the university's president and other administrators because they concealed allegations of sexual abuse to protect the image of the university and its football team.[100] The *Patriot-News* in Harrisburg won a Pulitzer Prize in 2012 for its investigation of the Sandusky story.[101]

The journalist who won the Pulitzer, Sara Ganim, was a news reporter, reinforcing a suspicion that sportswriting was ignored by the Pulitzer committee. Such criticism is not without merit. Only four sports columnists—Arthur Daley, Red Smith, and Dave Anderson of the *New York Times* and Jim Murray of the *Los Angeles Times*—have won the Pulitzer Prize for Commentary, and none of those have come in the last three decades. In 2001, sportswriter and columnist Ira Berkow of the *New York Times* shared a Pulitzer for his part in a series on race in America, but the prize was in the National Reporting category. Frank Deford suggested that a separate category of the Pulitzer Prizes should be created for sports journalists. George Solomon, the former sports editor of the *Washington Post* and now director of the Shirley Povich Center for Sports Journalism at the University of Maryland, said the Pulitzer committee did not give sportswriting the respect it deserved. "Sports have been underrepresented by the Pulitzer committee," Solomon said. "There have been many terrific investigative stories coming from sports, such as on concussions and college sports. You have great narratives and profiles about people and institutions. I don't think [the committee respects] sports as much as other subject matters in journalism."[102]

While it is true that the sports sections of metro dailies produce some of the best columns, feature writing, and beat coverage in newspapers, they have lagged behind the news side of papers and news magazines in investigative journalism. A major reason is that sportswriters have long been criticized for their reluctance to report the bad behavior and criminal acts of athletes; they spend so much time with athletes and coaches in the course of a season that they are reluctant to criticize anything related to the team because of the possibility of reprisal. Such criticism is particularly apparent in college towns where the crimes of athletes are underreported, or not reported, to protect the image of the athletic teams, especially when they are nationally ranked and have a strong, if not fanatical, local fan base that strongly reacts to any negativity about a team. This explains in part why editors sometimes assign news reporters to investigate wrongdoings so sportswriters can continue covering a team while pleading ignorance of what those on the news side are reporting.

Some of the hardest-hitting sports reporting comes from journalists working independently of the sports desk, whether in newspapers or in broadcasting. This includes *Outside the Lines*, ESPN's Emmy Award-winning weekly investigative program, which has been anchored by Bob Ley since 1990, and a monthly program, *Real Sports with Bryant Gumbel*, which began on HBO in 1995. According to Gumbel, the program was "spawned by the fact that sports have changed dramatically, that it's no longer just fun and games, and that what happens off the field, beyond the scores, is worthy of some serious reporting."[103] *Real Sports* has won critical praise for its reporting and commentary, including awards from the Overseas Press Club, which recognizes the best in international reporting. In 2017, it was honored for its investigation of corruption within the International Olympic Committee.[104]

Sports journalists have been reluctant to criticize widespread or systemic problems in sports because such stories are often harder to report but, more importantly, they can jeopardize the popularity of a sport that is highly profitable to television networks. This almost surely played a part in why journalists were slow to report the widespread use of steroids in baseball and the connection of football to concussions.

On August 11, 1994, Major League Baseball players went on strike, ending the season and canceling the World Series for the first time. This resulted in the longest work stoppage in the history of American professional sports; and it angered fans, including many who did not return to the ballparks when a new season began in 1995. Attendance dropped by 28 percent from the last full season in 1993.[105] However, during the 1996 season, attendance increased, as did television viewership, when more home runs were hit than in any previous season in baseball history. Mark McGwire of the St. Louis Cardinals led the majors with fifty-two, which was nine fewer than Roger Maris's record for a single season and, in 1998, McGwire hit seventy and Sammy Sosa of the Chicago Cubs had sixty-six. The chase for the single-season home-run record was widely credited with restoring baseball among its fan base—and steroid use was unquestionably responsible for many of those home runs.[106]

Baseball had banned steroids in the early 1990s but did not enforce the ban with mandatory drug testing until 2003. With no drug testing, players used steroids and other performance-enhancing drugs with little fear of getting caught.[107] The players union fought testing, and baseball owner and commissioner Allan H. "Bud" Selig acquiesced in part because more home runs meant higher television ratings and an increase of $1 billion in revenue for the television networks, including ESPN and Fox, which aired baseball games.[108] The networks, which had reporters in every major league city and analysts and commentators in their studios, gushed about the home runs of McGwire, Sosa, and Barry Bonds and the pitching of Roger Clemens without questioning whether there was something suspicious behind their achievements other than a good work ethic.

Tom Verducci, an award-winning writer for *Sports Illustrated* and a commentator for ESPN, told his editors at *SI* that the next big story would be about steroids in baseball. He said that clean players were telling him: "It's an unfair game. There are so many guys using steroids that now I'm at a competitive disadvantage." He recalled: "In spring training of 2002 we at *SI*, the baseball writers and editors, had either a conference call or a meeting to talk about story ideas for the season. At that time I said, 'The story of the season will be how much steroid use is going on in baseball. And we better be the ones to write this story.'"

In a June 3, 2002, *si* article, Verducci interviewed Ken Caminiti, a former National League Most Valuable Player who was retired. He admitted to using steroids and said that the use of performance-enhancing drugs was widespread among major league players.[109] Then, in 2005, José Canseco, a former American League MVP, wrote *Juiced*, a book that detailed his steroid use and identified other players who used drugs. That was followed in late 2007 by the Mitchell Report, an investigation that found scores of major league players used steroids and human-growth hormones.[110]

Baseball became tainted by the steroid scandal, and sportswriters and fans blamed ballplayers for taking steroids. But it also is fair to blame the media, especially ESPN and Fox Sports, for not doing a better job of investigating steroid use. Why did journalists fail to do so? Home runs made good copy, and networks had an overriding interest in good ratings. Second, good reporting takes time, and steroid use is difficult to prove. And, finally, sportswriters believed that it was in their best interests not to ask certain questions. They knew if they began inquiring about steroid use, they would find few players willing to talk to them about steroids or anything else. "Over the course of a 162-game season, beat writers and columnists work their tails off to develop relationships with players," said sportswriter Jeff Pearlman. "You grovel. You whimper. You plead. You tiptoe up to a first baseman, hoping he has five minutes to talk about that swollen toe. You share jokes and—embarrassingly—fist pounds. Wanna kill all that hard work in five or six seconds? Ask the following question: Are you juiced?"[111]

ESPN baseball writer Jayson Stark went further, writing that sportswriters had no responsibility to investigate steroid use. "And you know why? Because I'm not a cop," he wrote. "I'm just a guy who covers baseball for a living. So it's not my job to police the sport. It's the sport's job to police itself." Rick Reilly of *Sports Illustrated* disagreed. He reminded Stark that he was a reporter who was paid to report, whether it was who won the game or whether someone was cheating to win the game.[112]

Sportswriters Mark Fainaru-Wada and Lance Williams of the *San Francisco Chronicle* conducted a two-year investigation of performance-enhancing drugs in sports, revealing that athletes such as Olympic gold medal sprinter Marion Jones had received illegal drugs from the supplier BALCO. In 2006, Fainaru-Wada and Williams wrote *Game of Shadows: Barry Bonds, BALCO, and the Steroids Scandal that Rocked Professional Sports.*[113] The book included leaked grand jury testimony that reported Bonds, who hit a record seventy-three home runs in 2002, had received drugs from BALCO. He sued to stop publication of the book because it used secret grand jury testimony, and Williams and Fainaru-Wada were subpoenaed to testify before a federal grand jury about how they had received the information. They refused to reveal the source of the testimony and were held in contempt of court, but the charges were dropped after a BALCO attorney admitted leaking it to them.[114]

In 2013 Fainaru-Wada and his brother, Steve Fainaru, an investigative reporter who had won the 2008 Pulitzer Prize for International Reporting with the *Washington Post*, wrote *League of Denial: The NFL, Concussions, and the Battle for Truth*, which reported how the National Football League had covered up scientific findings that demonstrated a link between concussions and football and brain damage.[115] The book also chronicled how the NFL made a concerted effort to ruin the reputation of Dr. Bennet Omalu, a Nigerian-born neuropathologist who discovered signs of chronic traumatic encephalopathy (CTE) in the brains of former NFL players while he was working at a coroner's office in Pittsburgh. Omalu recalled a discussion with an NFL doctor while reviewing the case of former Pittsburgh Steelers center Mike Webster. He said the NFL doctor told him, "Bennet, do you know the implications of what you're doing? If 10 percent of mothers in this country would begin to perceive football as a dangerous sport, that is the end of football."[116]

League of Denial was initially broadcast in 2013 as a documentary film, *League of Denial: The NFL's Concussion Crisis*, on the PBS program *Frontline*.[117] ESPN had originally been a partner in the documentary but backed out, raising speculation that it had been pressured to do so by the NFL.[118] ESPN's close relationship with the NFL also would be questioned in 2009 after it failed to report on television, radio, or its website that Steelers' quarterback Ben Roethlisberger had been accused of sexual assault. The *New York Times* wondered if ESPN did so to protect Roethlisberger, one of the league's stars, and the network's broadcast partner, the NFL.[119] The NFL forced HBO to cancel its 2003 fictional television series, *Playmakers*, because the league found the story lines, which included drug use, sexual promiscuity, homosexuality, and domestic abuse, too realistic.[120] While television networks benefit from partnerships with the NFL, they also are vulnerable to league demands if they want those partnerships to continue.

***

In his 2000 book, *ESPN: The Uncensored History*, Michael Freeman wrote that ESPN had to acknowledge that its self-created moniker, "the worldwide leader in sports," was not guaranteed. He wondered if the network had become too complacent or arrogant. "The network has become grossly smug in its dominance. ESPN's position is that it answers to no one," he said, adding, "This bold arrogance has also led to the watering down of the network's journalistic standards."[121]

On July 8, 2010, ESPN received the exclusive rights to air the decision by Cleveland Cavaliers basketball star LeBron James to leave Cleveland to play for the Miami Heat.[122] James selected the interviewer for the program, set the guidelines for it, including the advertisers and sponsors, and controlled the profits from the broadcast.[123] Leonard Shapiro of the *Washington Post* was among those who criticized the network's integrity. "The most troubling aspect of the whole ill-conceived mess was ESPN's willingness to hand over an hour of prime-time television to an egomaniacal athlete the network should be covering as a news story," he said.[124] Then, in 2015, Deadspin criticized ESPN for accepting advertising from DraftKings, a daily fantasy sports site, and using the

DraftKings network's football coverage. Critics questioned ESPN's ethics because the network had breached the wall between journalism and advertising.[125]

But the greatest threat to ESPN—and to traditional sports journalism—was something that few people, if any, could have predicted when Freeman wrote his book. ESPN could not have existed without the technology that created cable television. But then came digital technology, and cable television became vulnerable as sports journalism entered a new era. Gone were the days when sports fans had to wait until the following morning for the newspaper or the next episode of *SportsCenter*. Readers went to their computers—and eventually their smartphones—for news. Newspapers and magazines lost advertisers, revenue fell, and staffs were cut, and sportswriters were forced to find other jobs. And yet, more people than ever became sports journalists, and more people than ever consumed sports. Nobody quite knew what the future of sports would be, only that sports journalists would be there to report and talk about what had happened, wherever and however it happened.

The State of Sports Journalism

7

ESPN is arguably one of the greatest success stories in the history of television. But now even it can't escape some of the harsh realities of the ever-changing technological landscape.

—James Andrew Miller, coauthor of a book about ESPN, 2017

In late April 2017 ESPN laid off a hundred on-air and online journalists in response to the network's loss of millions of cable subscribers, increased competition, and the spiraling cost of broadcasting live sports.[1] The layoffs reflected not only the state of the "worldwide leader in sports" but also the state of sports journalism. ESPN was forced to confront the realities of changing technologies and the changing ways that viewers watched live sports. In 2011 one hundred million homes received ESPN, and the network made business decisions based on projections that the number would continue to increase. But that did not happen. The network lost ten million subscribers in the next several years, making it necessary to cut costs to compensate for losses in subscriber fees and advertising revenue. In addition, ESPN probably spent too much on television contracts to fend off its chief rival, Fox Sports. For instance, ESPN committed to an eight-year, $15.2 billion extension with the National Football League in 2011; a nine-year, $12 billion deal with the National Basketball Association; and a $7.3 billion deal to televise the NCAA football playoffs.[2] In addition, it spent $175 million to build a studio in Los Angeles to provide *SportsCenter* with state-of-the-art graphics and animation.[3]

Digital technology became the latest iteration in the evolution of sports journalism. Newspapers had once monopolized content but then had to adapt to emerging media such as radio, television, and cable television. Digital television enabled consumers to exchange expensive cable TV bundles to stream live sports and video highlights from their personal computers, tablets, or smartphones. In 2017 Amazon paid $50 million for streaming rights to ten of the NFL's Thursday night games for the upcoming season, which was five times more than Twitter had paid in the previous year.[4]

Never before had there had been such profound changes in communication and sports, and broadcast networks were deeply affected by those changes because of the intensely maniacal fan base. In 2015 Americans spent 31 billion hours watching sports on television, an increase of 40 percent over the previous decade.[5] The *International Business Times* noted:

> Twenty years ago, sports fans were more or less dependent on a copy of their local newspaper for the latest updates on their favorite sports teams. With the advent of the Internet, the last decade has seen an explosion in sports news, analysis, and chatter, with dedicated fans continuing to devour as much as they can get. There have never been more sources providing that information. Of course, there are journalists from traditional newspapers, websites and television; however independent bloggers, fans, and the athletes themselves are breaking their own news via sports related websites, and through social networks like Twitter and Facebook.[6]

ESPN's layoffs, however, were not only a direct response to the changing dynamics of technology; they also reflected a decision by the network's management that it wanted to emphasize graphics and commentary over reporting and analysis. *New York Times* reporters Joe Drape and Brooks Barnes wrote: "ESPN was wrapped in Teflon for many years, but big payouts for rights fees plus significant losses in their subscriber base were like punches to the gut and head, and now the company is trying to make sure they are strong enough to fight in the future. They've decided to change their approach to content and rely more heavily on digital; this has enabled them to let go of a big chunk of their talent base."[7]

ESPN and its parent company, Disney, continued to make a lot of money, but they were not making as much as they wanted—or as much as they had in the previous decade or two. The layoffs of so many journalists raised concerns about ESPN's priorities and the state of sports journalism. It discharged reporters, who would call several sources to confirm a single fact that was essential to a story, but retained talk show personalities, who were prone to expressing provocative opinions regardless of whether they were based on facts.

Dave Zirin, sports editor of the *Nation*, said the loss of so many reporters was not just a loss for ESPN; it was a loss for those who depended on the network to stay informed on issues related to sports. "This hurts, because for all ESPN's faults, its journalism has been critical to expanding the conversation on issues ranging from domestic violence in sports to concussions in the NFL," he wrote. "When ESPN covers these topics, they are more likely to become part of a national conversation."[8]

Neil Best of *Newsday* noted that instead of giving up on sports journalism, ESPN was staking out another position: "Information is expensive to gather and has been commoditized in an era when scoops last 10 seconds before becoming fodder for the next Twitter reply or TV chat, and when people rely on their smartphones for highlights. Sports talk radio caught on to this trick decades ago, with hosts perusing newspaper sports sections, then fashioning careers on discussing what they read."[9]

ESPN has adjusted to the changing realities of the marketplace by expanding beyond the shrinking markets of the United States and creating networks in dozens of countries and territories. For ESPN, the so-called "worldwide leader in sports," this has meant partnering with countries throughout the world, whether it is airing soccer or cricket in the United States or American-based sports to international audiences, such as professional baseball in Australia, football in Brazil, or basketball in China.[10]

✳✳✳

Print sports journalism had been in decline for two decades. Beginning in the 1990s, layoffs and early retirements became common at most newspapers as readership stagnated. The emergence of the internet led many readers to abandon papers, and the loss in circulation meant less advertising revenue, which was accelerated by the loss of classified advertising to Craigslist and other such companies.[11] Meanwhile, the gutting of staffs translated into a decrease in newspaper quality as the number of pages decreased. Many papers began publishing only a few times a week instead of every day, others published an online-only edition, and some quit publishing entirely. In 2010 the number of people who said they read a print newspaper in the previous twenty-four hours reached the lowest mark ever recorded by the Pew Research Center.[12]

By the end of 2011 fewer people were working for papers than at any time since the American Society of News Editors began collecting such information in 1978.[13] Data from the Bureau of Labor Statistics showed U.S. newspaper employment fell from 412,000 in January 2001 to 174,000 in September 2016. These losses were offset somewhat by the increase in jobs on websites.[14] One survey of sportswriters who left print jobs for online jobs found the majority of them said they were highly satisfied with their new positions, although they expressed sadness for the demise of print journalism and insecurity about the future of sports journalism.[15]

The layoffs at ESPN, the shredding of newspaper jobs, and the gnashing of teeth over what would become of sports journalism coincided with the 2017 death of Frank Deford, the most important sports journalist of the previous several decades. He began his career with *Sports Illustrated* in the early 1960s and became the leading voice on the country's best sports magazine. Michael MacCambridge, the author of *The Franchise: The History of Sports Illustrated Magazine*, described

Deford as "the anchor of the magazine, the writer around whom the rest of the issue was built." To Matt Schudel of the *Washington Post*, Deford "sought to grasp how sports were an inescapable part of the American soul, an emblem of loyalty, aspiration and, all too often, heartbreak." Like Gary Smith, another superbly talented *Sports Illustrated* writer, Deford recognized that good writing required a prolonged engagement with a player or coach to capture his or her inner drive. Deford's prose, MacCambridge said, "was a graceful mixture of storytelling and subtle (sometimes not so subtle) psychoanalysis."[16]

Deford, who was named sportswriter of the year by the National Association of Sportswriters and Sportscasters six times, left SI in 1989 to become editor of the *National*, a daily sports newspaper that folded after a year and a half. His debonair style and eloquence made him a frequent commentator on NBC, ESPN, and HBO's *Real Sports*.[17] But it was his weekly essays on National Public Radio's *Morning Edition* that began in 1980 and continued for thirty-seven years—his last one came a week or so before his death—that transcended sports and made him popular among listeners who had previously paid little attention to sports. He convinced many of them that sports mattered by connecting sports to history, culture, politics, and racism and by portraying athletes not as caricatures but as flawed and even noble human beings. In 2013 President Barack Obama presented him with the National Humanities Medal, making him the first sportswriter to receive the honor. The citation said: "A dedicated writer and storyteller, Mr. Deford has offered a consistent, compelling voice in print and on radio, reaching beyond scores and statistics to reveal the humanity woven into the games we love."[18]

He began his career when fans depended on newspapers to keep up with sports and lived long enough for fans to reject newspapers for the internet and Twitter. Sportswriting remained popular, but sports stories "were disappearing," he said in a 2010 speech accepting the Red Smith Award for Journalism from the Associated Press Sports Editors. In his speech, Deford said the way fans received their information would continue to change, but sports journalism would never be replaced because sports was one of the few pursuits that allowed so many people to personally observe the most talented in a profession. "When you go to see a baseball game at Wrigley Field or an NFL game at the Superdome or an NBA or NHL game at Madison Square Garden, the crowd may be rude and raucous, even vulgar, but what you're watching is the best, and that best you are watching is what most people care about. And that matters," he observed.[19]

While author, podcaster, and sports analyst Bill Simmons lacked Deford's skills as a journalist, he seized upon technological innovations to become perhaps the most influential sports journalist of the beginning of the twenty-first century. He had little interest in assuming the role of the traditional sportswriter, who informed fans of what was happening from the position of a reporter who interviewed players and coaches. Instead, he wanted to capture the game from the fan's perspective. He abandoned the tradition of sportswriters relying on box scores and interviews and popularized a style of reporting that drew from popular culture. In one column he might reference a description by tennis announcer Bud Collins and NBC's "Breakfast at Wimbledon" theme music; the screwball movie *Caddyshack*; the 1980s television program *Miami Vice*; basketball player Isaiah Thomas's exclusion from the 1992 U.S. Olympic basketball team; and the *E! True Hollywood Story* or the 1990s television program *Beverly Hills 90210*. One writer described Simmons as follows: "The result was writing that mimicked the sound of scraping barstools and sniping across the beer pong table—raw, opinionated, and funny (in a fratty way). At a time when people talked about whether they'd have a beer with one or another presidential candidate, Simmons was the famous guy who most guys I knew *actually* wanted to have a beer with."[20]

Simmons did not achieve influence in sports journalism by working for daily newspapers in metropolitan cities, which had been the path for most sportswriters in the twentieth century. He discovered that you no longer needed to work for an editor on a newspaper or magazine to become a sports journalist. He also realized that the internet did not mean the end of sports journalism, as so many feared, but rather was an opportunity to present content in a way that had never before existed. He had the vision and guts of an entrepreneur and wrote in a way that imitated the authoritative voice of a traditional sports columnist with the egocentric abrasiveness of a talk-radio program host. In doing so, he helped change the definition of what it meant to be a sports journalist and, more importantly, he changed how sports content was communicated to an audience, whether through his website, his podcasts, film, or on Twitter.

Unable to find a newspaper job after receiving his master's degree in journalism from Boston University, Simmons worked as a bartender at nights and spent his days writing content for his website, BostonSportsGuy.com. The popularity of the website led to a job writing for ESPN.com and for *ESPN: The Magazine*. By 2005 his columns received five hundred thousand unique visitors a month, making him one of the country's most-read sportswriters. The success of his columns led to his podcast, *Eye of the Sportsguy*, which was changed to the *B.S. Report* in 2007. In 2013 the *B.S. Report* was downloaded thirty-two million times.[21]

The *B.S. Report* coincided with the creation by Simmons and Connor Schell of *30 for 30*, which premiered in 2009. The series began as thirty television films, each directed by a different documentarian, to celebrate stories about the first thirty years of ESPN, but it has become something unparalleled in sports, according to Deadspin, because it takes "sports out of their day-to-day minutiae and examine[s] them with insight and a sense of perspective and history."[22] In 2011 Simmons created and edited the ESPN blog Grantland, named for the iconic sportswriter Grantland Rice, which recognized that digital journalism did not face the same space restrictions found in print journalism. Grantland and other websites published longer articles but also included hyperlinks allowing readers to access related articles, interviews, videos, and photographs. This enhanced the tradition of long-form journalism for writers and readers. Grantland published pieces about sports and culture, earning it praise and making it popular among readers as it received six million unique visitors in early 2015.[23]

Grantland, however, became a casualty of Simmons's deteriorating relationship with ESPN. In 2014, ESPN suspended him after he called NFL commissioner Roger Goodell "a liar" and then delivered a series of obscenities about the commissioner on a podcast.[24] ESPN did not renew its contract with him in the following year and then ceased publication of Grantland in late 2015, partly because of expenses related to maintaining its staff of writers and technology support staff, who became expendable when the network faced a decline in cable subscribers. "In an era ruled by bite-sized content and dumbed-down click-bait journalism," Justin Block wrote in the Huffington Post, "Grantland's defining characteristic came at odds with sustainable finances."[25]

After leaving ESPN Simmons signed a multi-year contract in 2015 for several million dollars a year with HBO.[26] However, HBO canceled Simmons' interview program, *Any Given Wednesday*, after four months and other projects failed. His digital venture, the Ringer, which revived the concept behind Grantland by publishing pieces on sports and culture, went on line in July 2016. The Ringer had a fraction of Grantland's traffic because it did not have ESPN directing readers to it. His podcasts continue to be popular.[27]

In 2016 ESPN created the Undefeated, a website on race, sports, and culture, which was edited by Kevin Merida, who formerly worked at the *Washington Post*. Inspired by Grantland, it advanced the tradition of long-form journalism. Furthermore, since 1991, some of the best long-form pieces have been published in an anthology, *The Best American Sports Writing*. As the book's table of contents demonstrates, long-form journalism exists not only in such traditional publications as *Sports Illustrated*, ESPN: *The Magazine*, the *New Yorker*, *Esquire*, and *Harper's* but also on websites that did not exist until relatively recently, such as SBNation Longform.[28]

But regardless of how readers received sports news, technology affected how—and how often—readers received it. During the last half of the twentieth century, fans could only learn what was happening in sports when they read it in their newspapers, saw it in a magazine such as *Sports Illustrated*, or heard it on television or radio. But the internet meant that those interested in sports could receive updates in real time from websites, blogs, and social media networks, where journalists expressed their opinions and interacted with fans, athletes, and other reporters. Yet, amid these revolutionary advances in technology, little changed in the way games were covered. Reporters watched from press boxes and then crowded around players and coaches after the games. Stories consisted of the final score and a game summary; sidebars that focused on a specific play or players; and columns in which writers tried to put a game into a larger context.[29] Bill Simmons asked: "Do we really need 25 people crammed in baseball locker rooms fighting for the same mundane quotes? What's our game plan for the fact that—thanks to the Internet and 24-hours sports stations—a city like Boston suddenly has four times as many sports media members as it once had? Why are we covering teams the same way we covered them in 1981, just with more people and better equipment?"[30]

Sports writing—like news writing—was highly routinized; the structure of game stories, sidebars, and columns remained frozen in time, hardly changing as one generation of sportswriters replaced another. Conventions associated with traditional journalism became outdated in digital journalism as sports journalists no longer finished their story or stories and then said nothing else until the next day. Sportswriters were expected to write more stories a week than before, including blog posts and keeping a constant, active presence on Twitter and other social media, post links and video clips, and respond to readers' questions and comments.[31] When Jemele Hill of ESPN was a sportswriter for the *Orlando Sentinel*, she said she might receive as many as sixty emails after a particularly provocative story or column. Once she started working for ESPN.com in late 2006 and had a national audience, she said, a story or column might generate two thousand emails.[32]

In addition, sportswriters used to be on deadline after a game. Now, they are always on deadline and expected to produce a lot more content than they did a decade before, noted historian Brian Moritz in 2015: "This might include in-game updates, a running game story posted immediately after the final buzzer, a rapid recap, a short post on key players, statistics, an interactive report card in which fans are asked to grade the team's plays, a story using advanced statistics to break down the game, shot charts, a write-through on the game story, a sidebar, a column, [an] updated recap, and a postgame video featuring the report, and social media updates during and after the game."[33]

Thus, anyone with a computer could find out quickly what was happening in sports—and anyone with a computer and a blog could become a sportswriter or at least claim to be a sportswriter. Sports websites were created that published commentary from people who had little or no training in journalism, and many of them were not interested in learning what it took to be a journalist. This alarmed sportswriters, who had learned their trade by working for newspapers or magazines, where their work had to meet or exceed certain standards before it would be published. Sportswriters "expressed significant concerns regarding what they perceived as an overall decline in the quality, accuracy, and integrity of sports journalism" that appeared on the internet.[34] In 2012 a sportswriter labeled what was happening to sports journalism "the TMZ effect," which was a reference to the celebrity gossip website: "The biggest problem with sports journalists shifting mostly to the Internet is that it has become like talk radio; some people are writing gossip and have no integrity. When I moved online, a friend told me I would become the TMZ of the NFL. While that's not true, even TMZ has a level of integrity and responsibility that is far more than you see on some of these blogs. This really hurts the reputation and credibility of all of us."[35]

The increase of sports websites and blogs for fans to comment on, and often rant about, followed the model of sports talk radio. The first sports talk radio program is believed to have been on WNBC in New York City in March 1964.[36] Sports talk radio had moderate success until it rode the wave of popularity of political talk radio programs that proliferated in the 1980s because of deregulation, which loosened restrictions on content and on the number of broadcast stations and newspapers that could be owned by a single corporation.[37] The repeal of the FCC's Fairness Doctrine meant radio could now serve the commercial interests of the radio station or the corporation that owned it rather than the best interests of the public. Political talk radio became successful because it was relatively cheap to produce, and conservative talk-show hosts such as Rush Limbaugh used rhetoric that perpetuated many conservatives' dissatisfaction with liberal ideology, civil rights, and women's rights.[38]

Sports talk radio hosts learned from their conservative counterparts. The number of all-sports radio stations in the United States increased from 413 to 677 between 2002 and 2012 as sports talk radio programs "spread like an unchecked virus," according to a critic. "Sports talkers," as they were called, found success by being brash, confrontational, and provocative, often to the point of being offensive. Jim Rome, who has hosted one of the highest-rated sports programs for a few decades, famously chided NFL quarterback Jim Everett in 1994 for what he perceived as his lack of toughness, repeatedly calling the quarterback "Chris" after female tennis player Chris Evert. During an interview with the player on his television program, he again called him "Chris," and Everett responded by shoving him off his chair. Rome was widely criticized for his lack of professionalism, but the incident advanced his career.[39] This confirmed the belief that there was often no such thing as bad publicity in talk radio.

Sports talkers can influence whether coaches are fired, players are traded or signed, or fans go to a ballpark, a stadium, or an arena. In 1990 Don Imus, Mike Francesa, Chris "Mad Dog" Russo, and Steve Somers of WFAN in New York City engaged in relentless criticism of the home arena of the New York Islanders, the Nassau Veterans Memorial Coliseum on Long Island, which they called the "Nassau Mausoleum." The ridicule was based not on the personal observations of Francesa, Russo, or Imus, who were not hockey fans, but partly, according to an historian, on the fact that WFAN broadcast the games of the Islanders' rival, the New York Rangers.[40]

Such excesses are common in sports talk radio, where name-calling and bluster can substitute for information and discussion. In 2007 Imus was suspended after referring to the Rutgers University women's basketball team as "nappy-headed ho's."[41] Then, in 2015, ESPN fired radio host Colin Cowherd after he made derogatory comments about the intelligence of baseball players from the Dominican Republic.[42] Such comments—and others like them—appeared to have no negative impact on his career; if anything, the controversy may have helped him as Cowherd went to work for Fox Radio after losing his job at ESPN. He became cohost of a television program, *Speak for Yourself*, on Fox Sports with Jason Whitlock, who has frequently found himself criticized for comments that were considered offensive, such as calling civil rights leader Jesse Jackson a "domestic terrorist," blaming Michael Vick's dog fighting on hip-hop culture, and empathizing with white police officers who were accused of killing black suspects. ESPN selected Whitlock, who is black, to be the first editor of the Undefeated, or what the network called the "black Grantland." The network fired Whitlock after two years as editor, however, because the site had yet to be launched.[43]

The popularity of sports radio and television talk programs is reminiscent of a day when men went to their favorite bar and talked sports with the other regulars and the bartender, who would often moderate or dominate those discussions.[44] Now, such discussions were moderated—and dominated—by the host of a talk radio or television program. They provided listeners, who tended to be overwhelmingly male, a venue where they could talk about sports and anything else without being told to quit talking so much about sports or being told they should keep their opinions to themselves because others found them offensive. Therapist David Nylund wrote that the popularity of sports talk radio reflected fears among men that they were losing their status and power in society.[45]

In 2015 Sarah Spain, a Chicago-based sports journalist who is a reporter for ESPN and a writer for espnW, called for higher standards in "the conversation on sports talk radio." She cited sports talkers who referred to television sports reporter Erin Andrews as a "gutless bitch" who should "drop dead;" called NBA players "animals and wildebeests;" ridiculed the looks of female softball players; and used anti-gay slurs.[46] She appeared with Julie DiCaro, a sports journalist and sports radio personality in Chicago, on a viral video that exposed examples of the online harassment women in sports media received on Twitter and elsewhere on social media.[47]

Christine Brennan, among others, observed how social media, including Twitter, Facebook, and blogs, contributed to the coarsening of dialogue that rarely appeared in newspapers or on television:

> You certainly see from Twitter, from comments on blogs, the comments under my columns, that the Internet seems to foster this kind of Neanderthal reaction; they come out of the woodwork like cockroaches, but they seem to want to continue to show up on the Internet. Even on Facebook, where their name and picture have to be attached to the comment, they still do it. So I don't really look at the comments under my columns because I know that all that stuff exists there. The Internet has given them a forum that the traditional newspaper no longer did.
>
> No newspaper would ever publish letters with what these people say, but on the Internet it can be said and still be attached to your name. So that's where we see it. I mean you could go on my column, see my column, and right next to it see "top ten cheerleaders" or whatever, and that's just blatant sexism. The Internet has opened the world to sexism that otherwise did not exist on TV or print and that's unfortunate.[48]

Twitter has perpetuated such excesses. Critics say that too many journalists use it not to report news but to promote their own work and advertise how many followers they have.[49] In addition, Twitter, as Spain and Brennan acknowledged, appears to prompt those tweeting to say something that they would not probably write in a newspaper. The *Denver Post* fired its sports columnist after he tweeted that he was "very uncomfortable" about a Japanese driver winning the 2017

Indianapolis 500 on Memorial Day.[50] Previously ESPN suspended one of its baseball announcers, Curt Schilling, after he compared Muslims to German Nazis in a tweet in August 2015.[51] It had guidelines in place that said employees should avoid saying anything on social media that they would not say in print or broadcast. Other media outlets such as the *New York Times*, the *Washington Post*, and National Public Radio instituted similar guidelines.[52]

Twitter and other social media, whatever their shortcomings, revolutionized sports media by allowing journalists to break news in real time and engage with readers in a way that had never been possible with newspapers or television. Twitter is well suited to sports, which has an audience that appears to have an insatiable craving for news and commentary. Through Twitter sports journalists can report and comment on a game while it is being played or break news with commentary, video, or links to other stories.[53] Sportswriters also can update information in a story or correct mistakes without waiting until the next day.[54]

Before Twitter there was a one-way street from the journalist to the reader. Twitter changed that, allowing journalists to communicate directly with readers and other sports fans and, perhaps more importantly, allowing fans to communicate directly with athletes. This changed the fan-athlete relationship. It meant athletes could bypass the media and communicate what they wanted to say directly to a fan.[55] But this is not necessarily in the best interests of athletes, who express themselves before, after, and sometimes during games, criticizing teammates, coaches, opponents, and referees by using language that can be provocative, profane, or, at the very least, counterproductive. As one observer of Twitter noted: "Athletes aren't afraid to confront their opponents through Twitter. That is what the world of sports has become. It's less about what you bring to the field, and more about what you say in a tweet."[56]

In 2016 retired baseball great Derek Jeter introduced the Players Tribune, a website where professional athletes could share their thoughts and stories directly with readers without the filter of the media. Could this jeopardize the future of sports journalism? What happens to sports journalism, one writer asked, if athletes and perhaps fans think that reporters are no longer necessary?[57] While the Players Tribune has something to add to sports, it is an online sports site and not journalism—and certainly not the future of sports journalism. Contributors may offer personal, even compelling, insights into their lives as athletes, but what incentive do they have to share the grittier aspects of their lives or discuss a slump that they or their team is having? If a player does not want to speak to reporters after a bad game, will he or she be any more likely to write about it? What player will spend hours or days interviewing, researching, and writing a story to give it the accuracy and context it deserves? Players watch the game from a dugout or the bench, not from the distance of a press box, and they are no more likely to replace journalists than journalists are to replace them.

The Athletic, a subscriber sports website and app, was created in early 2016 with $30 million in venture capital and, as ESPN did, began luring sportswriters from newspapers by offering higher salaries. The Athletic hopes that subscribers will pay for analytical writing. By mid-2018, it said it had a hundred thousand subscribers. "Skeptics question if the company can bring in enough long-term subscriptions to fund its aggressive expansion," Benjamin Mullin wrote in the *Wall Street Journal*. To complicate its objective, The Athletic must create a niche in the crowded field of sports journalism, where consumers have seemingly countless options for reading and viewing sports for free.[58]

So, what is the future of sports journalism? That, of course, depends on whom you ask.

When asked in 2015 about the state of sports journalism, Bryant Gumbel, the host of *Real Sports* on HBO, summed up his frustration in six words: "There's so little of it practiced." He said that much of what passes for sports coverage is merely cheerleading because too many journalists serve as mouthpieces for the team and the sport about which they are writing. This can lead to failing to report the arrest of a college athlete, not investigating a story about a booster giving a car to a prized recruit, or saying little or nothing about steroid use or concussions because a reporter does not want to give bad publicity to the league that has a business relationship with his or her employer. Gumbel observed: "What passes for sports coverage is terribly sycophantic. The media tends not to ask the same difficult questions that they ask of politicians and businessmen. We give people in sports a pass. It's unfortunate, there are some abuses that go unreported and unaddressed."[59]

The failure of sports journalists to ask basic questions was particularly evident in the 2012 story involving Manti Teʻo, a Notre Dame linebacker and Heisman Trophy hopeful, and his extraordinary play after learning about the death of Lennay Kekua, his Stanford University girlfriend, of leukemia after she had survived a near-fatal car accident. The story became one of the most discussed stories of the college football season. But the story was a hoax. Kekua did not exist. The story was perpetuated because sportswriters and other journalists did not question its basic facts. Teʻo eventually admitted he had never met Kekua but had spoken to and texted her—or at least someone pretending to be her—hundreds of times. Until his admission, the story, as it was reported, was pure fantasy, "in the tradition of so much of Notre Dame's mythmaking and with the help of a compliant press," Timothy Burke and Jack Dickey wrote in a compelling account in Deadspin in early 2013:

> Her passing, recounted so many times in the national media, produces no obituary or funeral arrangement in the national media, produces no obituary or funeral announcement in Nexis, and no mention in the Stanford student newspaper. . . .
>
> The Stanford registrar's office has no record that a Lennay Kekua ever enrolled. There is no record of her birth in the news. Outside of a few Twitter and Instagram accounts, there's no online evidence that Lennay Kekua ever existed.
>
> The photographs identified as Kekua—in online tributes and on TV news reports—are pictures from the social-media

accounts of a 22-year-old California woman who is not named Lennay Kekua.[60]

The Te'o story, which served as a failure of both traditional and digital journalism, supports Gumbel's frustration with sports journalism. Another criticism is that much of what appears on ESPN or Fox Sports, sports websites, talk radio, and social media is little more than trivia, gossip, and the rehashing of old news. The decline in journalistic standards can be attributed to the decline of newspapers and the loss of reporters who had the training, sources, and often the time to follow up on stories. But it has more to do with the rise of social media and talk radio. Reporting requires hard work and a lot of time; talk is cheap, and controversy and soft interviews with athletes get ratings and website clicks. Mitch Albom, an award-winning sportswriter who became a best-selling author, said that gossip has become "sports news." Sports journalists used to ignore the off-field excesses of athletes, but now, he said, they cannot seem to write enough about it. "Once upon a time, we looked away from the other stuff. Now we never stop staring, following, snapping and gossiping. Maybe the old method wasn't telling the whole story. But at least we weren't manufacturing it," he wrote.[61]

Thus, the internet permanently changed how sports was reported and presented and changed the definition of who was a journalist. Anyone with a smartphone and an interest in sports can call themselves a sports journalist, which means more sports "journalists" are working today than ever before. But while there is more bad sports journalism than ever, good writing is found every day in the sports section of the *New York Times*, the *Washington Post*, and other newspapers and their online editions throughout the country. *Sports Illustrated* is not the magazine it once was, but it still publishes compelling and skillful stories in every issue. Thoughtful and provocative work also can be found in *ESPN: The Magazine* and on ESPN.com and other websites, such as Sporting News.com, SBNation.com, Bleacherreport.com, Deadspin .com, FoxSports.com, Yahoo! Sports.com, and TheUndefeated.com.

Gumbel criticized the state of sports journalism because he said there are so few investigative pieces. He is right. Much of this can be blamed on the decline of newspapers, where staffs and resources have been gutted and those journalists who remain have too many other demands to take on complex stories. Mark Fainaru-Wada's and Lance Williams's reporting in the *San Francisco Chronicle* in 2004 that exposed the use of steroids and performance-enhancing drugs in baseball and other sports may not have been possible a few years later, given the swift economic downturn of the newspaper industry, the *Chronicle*'s editor said.[62]

Sports journalists often are not as critical or inquisitive as they should be, but there are those who still ask hard questions and write stories that raise important questions. Because many of these journalists do not work for newspapers or websites, it is necessary to look harder to find them—such as on *Real Sports with Bryant Gumbel* on HBO or on ESPN's *Outside the Lines* and *30 for 30*. One of the *30 for 30* films, the eight-hour *O.J.: Made in America*, which told the story of the 1995 murder trial of football great O. J. Simpson, won a 2017 Academy Award for best documentary feature.[63] Taylor Branch, perhaps best known for his books chronicling the civil rights movement, wrote a searing indictment of the NCAA and college athletics, "The Shame of College Sports," in the *Atlantic* magazine in October 2011.[64] He concluded that the NCAA was a sham, "exploiting athletes in revenue sports like football and men's basketball to make hundreds of millions of dollars while expounding the virtues of amateurism."[65] Other writers—including journalists, academics, and even satirists—have exposed abuses, inequities, and discrimination in college athletics.[66]

For most of the history of American sports, journalists supported the sports establishment in America, participating in what one writer called "a conspiracy of silence" that perpetuated the color line in baseball.[67] Reporters also did not back away from the white-male hierarchy that discriminated against minorities and females, who not only wanted to play sports but also wanted to write about them. And finally, there has been little criticism from sports journalists, with the exception of Dave Zirin and a few others, of team owners who demand that cities pay for the construction of a new stadium or they might move their team to another city.[68]

In 2005 the *Nation* hired Zirin, making him the first sports editor in the 150-year history of the magazine.[69] Few journalists, in sports or elsewhere, are more provocative in engaging the politics of sports and calling for social justice as he does in his columns in the *Nation*, on his podcast, *Edge of Sports*, and in his many books. His work was described by a sports historian in 2008: "The politics of sport center Zirin's work. He concerns himself with labor relations and the corporatization of sport; the prejudices and biases of fans and sportswriters, especially racism, homophobia, and sexism; and the spectacles of nationalism. Wherever the mainstream media castigate athletes, often inciting moral panics and social outrage, Zirin champions the humanness and potential of players. In fact, Zirin often focuses on the athletes who resist, transgress, or reject prevailing norms and dominant ideologies. He takes hope in the resistance of past and present players, often calling out superstars who remain silent or compliant."[70]

News about sports used to be restricted to sports magazines and the sports pages of newspapers. But as Zirin has shown, sports are now viewed as something that is part of society rather than apart from it. Many of those writing about sports are doing so from perspectives as diverse as economics, sociology, history, economics, film, English, psychology, medicine, religion, law, business, technology, media, international relations, statistics, and civil and equal rights. For example, Michael Lewis's 2004 book, *Moneyball*, examined how Oakland A's general manager Billy Beane began in the late 1990s to use statistical analysis—or sabermetrics—to determine his roster, which enabled the A's to be competitive against teams with much higher payrolls.[71] Today every team in professional sports has an analytics department or an analytics expert on staff.[72] Not surprisingly, enterprising journalists, too, have seized upon sabermetrics as a way to better understand and report sports. In August 2017 Syracuse University introduced the first sports analytics bachelor's degree in the United States.[73] That was seven years after Deford accepted the Red Smith Award for Journalism and called for sports to be studied as a discipline in academia: "Whatever of sports journalism, in the future I would think that the discipline of sport—the study of it as art, sociology—may well be emphasized more in the classroom as a significant part of culture—just as sport has, in the past, been emphasized too much in academia as an amusement."[74]

Thus, sports and sports journalism are being taken more seriously than ever before. Colleges and universities offer courses in the study of sport in disciplines across the curriculum, and the number of under-graduate students majoring in sports journalism or sports communi-cation is increasing every year.[75] Indiana University-Purdue University Indianapolis (IUPUI) created what is believed to be the first graduate program in sports journalism in 2010.[76] Since then, other colleges and universities have added master's programs in sports journalism. In 2003 Penn State University created the John Curley Center for Sports Journalism, the first of its kind to offer opportunities for students to work with media organizations to cover sports events and sports-related issues; to sponsor campus lectures and panels on issues involving sports; and to offer a curriculum that focuses on sport and society.[77] A number of other colleges and universities, including IUPUI, the University of Maryland, the University of Georgia, and Arizona State University, have since created their own graduate sports journalism centers.

The creation and expansion of such programs have resulted in an increase in the hiring of sportswriters and sportscasters to teach and advise students interested in careers in sports journalism. Richard Deitsch, who writes a column about sports and the media for the Ath-letic, teaches sports journalism at Columbia University. In December 2016, when he was with *Sports Illustrated*, he discussed the future of sports journalists with a dozen sports editors from college newspapers in the United States for an article on SI.com. The conversation was no doubt quite different from what it would have been with college sports editors a generation earlier, when print journalism was a rela-tively healthy industry and social media did not exist. Most of those interviewed said they hoped for a career in sports journalism.[78]

But sometimes things do not change as dramatically as it might appear. That was the conclusion in 2015 when a researcher interviewed working sports journalists: "The interviews suggest that many core aspects of sports journalism remain very much the same as they were in the pre-digital age. Sports journalism revolves around covering professional, college, and popular high school sports; reporting game results and news about local teams; providing analysis of a team's success and failures; and giving commentary on the news of the day. It still revolves around going someplace where a reader is not and proving information that the reader did not know before."[79]

***

There will always be a need for sports journalists as long as athletes compete against each other in front of spectators and as long as people are interested in reading and hearing about a game or the lives of athletes. For almost three hundred years, Americans have been fascinated with sports and have turned to newspapers, magazines, radios, and televisions—and now websites, podcasts, and blogs—to satisfy that fascination. We are "sports junkies," to use the words of one of the ESPN founders. We crave news about sports—any news about sports. Technology will continue to change how we will receive that news, but we will continue to depend on journalists with the ability to interview, report, describe, and, particularly, write about sports. But that is about the only thing on which we can depend.

Sports journalism barely exists as it did for most of its history, when sportswriters relied for their information from players and coaches, were finished with their day's responsibilities when their story was written, and gave little thought to readers unless they called the sports department. Gone are the days when sports journalists could take their readers, listeners, and viewers for granted because newspapers and television monopolized sports content. Journalists still need to report and write, but they also need to take videos and blog and tweet several times a day or risk losing their audience. Gone are the days when you could consider yourself a sportswriter or sportscaster only if you had sports credentials and a press pass. Now, anyone, it seems, can call himself or herself a sports journalist.

Many veteran sports journalists have left the profession, either because they were laid off or because they grew disgruntled by the need to "break through the clutter" of sports, where news and opinion are presented all day, every day. Sportswriters once went to work for a newspaper when they were twenty or twenty-two years old and stayed with that paper until they retired. It was not long ago when you either worked as a sports journalist or you worked for a team. There was a firewall between sports journalism and public relations. No more.

Now, sports teams and organizations have their own reporters who produce content that promotes a team and disseminates it directly to fans, bypassing the scrutiny of skeptical journalists. In addition, what happens when a sports journalist works directly for the website of a team, a league, or a college athletic conference rather than a traditional media outlet, such as a newspaper, magazine, or a broadcast station? The journalist becomes less likely to criticize that team or organization. John McClain, who covers the Houston Texans for the *Houston Chronicle*, talked about a newspaper beat writer he knew who got a job working for the team and his work became more and more diluted. Journalists who work for team websites may "nibble on the hand that feeds," McClain said, "but you can't bite it." This raises the follow-up question: When does a sports journalist become more of a public relations practitioner than a journalist? John Cherwa, a special contributor to the *Los Angeles Times* and legal affairs chair for the Associated Press Sports Editors, said, "I will go to the grave thinking people find more credibility in the independent voice of the *Boston Globe* or *Boston Herald*, and believe it to be more factual than the people at MLB.com."[80]

As we know from the history of sports journalism, the profession has always had sportswriters and sportscasters who protected the players, the teams, and the sports they covered, and perpetuated discrimination against minorities and women. The sportswriters and sportscasters who distinguished themselves and advanced their profession were those with the ability to interview, to report, to describe, and, particularly, to write about sports; but they also recognized that sports reflected and affected society and revealed the worst qualities and the best qualities in us, whether as athletes, fans, or team owners. The best sports journalists in the future will continue to be the ones who can do that.

Notes

Introduction

1. See "Real Sports with Bryant Gumbel (1995)" themoviedb.org/tv/10471-real
-sports-with-bryant-gumbel, December 24, 2017; and "Real Sports with
Bryant Gumbel" hbo.com/real-sports-with-bryant-gumbel/cast-and-crew
/bryant-gumbel, December 24, 2017.
2. "Real Sports with Bryant Gumbel," narrated by Bryant Gumbel, HBO, September 15, 2009. A tape of the show is in the possession of Patrick S. Washburn.
3. Daniel Victor, "Frank Deford, a Literary Storyteller of Sport, Dies at 78,"
New York Times, May 29, 2017. http://www.nytimes.com/2017/05/29/sports
/frank-deford-sportswriter-dies-at-78.html.
4. "Real Sports with Bryant Gumbel," narrated by Gumbel, HBO, September
15, 2009.
5. Patnode, "Friend, Foe, or Freeloader?" 77, 79, 83.
6. Pew, "Radio Discussed as Press Threat or Promise," 7.
7. "Dedication of RCA Seen on Television," *New York Times*, April 21, 1939, 16.
8. See Sterling and Kittross, *Stay Tuned*, 209, 324, 369–70; MacCambridge,
The Franchise, 24; and "History: 1950s." *Advertising Age*, September 15, 2003,
adage.com/article/adage-encyclopedia-history-1950s/98701.
9. See Bill Molzon, "Television's Sports Heritage: The Early Days of TV
Sports," American Sportscasters Online, americansportscastersonline.com
/waynesbergarticle.html, accessed July 5, 2017"; and Schulberg, "A Fan Fights
Back," 63.
10. Michener, *Sports in America*, 333, 335.
11. For the first sports story in an American newspaper, see "London October
7, 9, 10," *Boston Gazette*, March 5, 1733, 2.
12. Kian and Zimmerman, "The Medium of the Future," 297.

13. Inabinett, *Grantland Rice and His Heroes*, ix.

14. Arthur Daley, "Sports of the Times," *New York Times*, July 15, 1954, 30.

15. See Arledge, *Roone*, 30–33; and Rader, *In Its Own Image*, 106–7.

16. Arledge, *Roone*, 57.

17. See Arledge, *Roone*, 7–8, 115; and Gunther, *The House That Roone Built*, 22.

18. See David Haugh, "Jeannie Morris Recognized for Pioneering Efforts," *Chicago Tribune*, March 6, 2014, http://articles.chicagotribune.com/2014-03 -06/sports/ct-jeannie-morris-haugh-spt-0307-20140307_1_johnny-morris -jeannie-morris-da-coach; and Lily Rothman, "This Is Why Female Sports- writers Can Go in Men's Locker Rooms," *Time*, http://time.com/4061122 /ludtke-kuhn-jaguars-colts/, accessed May 19, 2017.

19. Sherry Ricchiardi, "Offensive Interference." http://ajrarchive.org/Article .asp?id=3788, May 13, 2017.

20. Morrison, "Media Is Failing Women—Sports Journalism Particularly So."

21. See "Claire Smith Wins J.G. Taylor Spink Award, to be Honored During Hall of Fame Weekend," ESPN, http://www.espn.com/mlb/story/_/id/18217975 /claire-smith-wins-jg-taylor-spink-award-honored-hall-fame-weekend, accessed May 30, 2017 and "J.G. Taylor Spink Award," National Baseball Hall of Fame, baseballhall.org/discover-more/awards/jg-taylor-spink, accessed December 30, 2017.

22. Stout, "Introduction." xiv.

1. The Beginning of American Sportswriting

1. "London October 7, 9, 10," *Boston Gazette*, March 5, 1733, 2. Printers in the 1700s frequently used an "f" for an "s" in newspaper copy. To make it easier for readers of this book, the authors have replaced the "f" in words in quotations from that era with an "s" to make them more understandable and to avoid confusion. Thus, in the description of the fight, "Concourfe" has been changed to "Concourse."

2. Enriquez, "Coverage of Sports," 198. Although printed in a colonial news- sheet, this account was first published in a London newspaper. Reprinting English news was a common practice during America's colonial period.

3. McChesney, "Media Made Sport," 51.

4. "The King Majesties Declaration to His Subjects Concerning Lawfull Sports to Bee Vsed," 2–4. This was published in London by Thomas Barker in 1618.

5. See Gorn and Goldstein, *A Brief History of American Sports*, 10; Gorn, "Sports through the Nineteenth Century," 35; and Daniels, *Puritans at Play*, 166.

6. See Gorn, "Sports Through the Nineteenth Century," 36; Daniels, *Puritans at Play*, 165–66, 172; Griffin, *England's Revelry*, 42; and Altherr, *Sports in North America*, 59.

7. Altherr, *Sports in North America*, 59.

8. See Griffin, *England's Revelry*, 44–45, 49; and Daniels, *Puritans at Play*, 164–65.

9. "Observance of the Sabbath and Religious Holidays," 4. The spellings by Bradford are from the original.

10. Mather, "Cotton Mather Comments on Recreation," 15. This was published in Boston in 1726 as "A Serious Address to those who unnecessarily frequent the Tavern."

11. See Griffin, *England's Revelry*, 42; and Daniels, *Puritans at Play*, 166.

12. See Barney, "Physical Education and Sport in the United States of America," 166, 174; Gorn, "Sports through the Nineteenth Century," 40; Altherr, *Sports in North America*, 165; and Daniels, *Puritans at Play*, 167–69.

13. See Daniels *Puritans at Play*, 164, 167, 170–72; and Altherr, *Sports in North America*, 304–5.

14. See Daniels, *Puritans at Play*, 174; Gorn, "Sports through the Nineteenth Century," 42; and Altherr, "General Attitudes Toward Exercise and Sports," 2.

15. See Daniels, *Puritans at Play*, 174; and Rush, "Benjamin Rush Recommends Horseback Riding as Healthful Recreation," 15. Rush's statement was published in *Sermons to Gentlemen upon Temperance and Exercise* (Philadelphia: John Dunlap, 1772), 15.

16. Altherr, "General Attitudes Toward Exercise and Sports," 2.

17. See Daniels *Puritans at Play*, 166–67; and Gorn, "Sports through the Nineteenth Century," 36–37.

18. See Gorn, "Sports through the Nineteenth Century," 36, 39; and Barney, "Physical Education and Sport in the United States of America," 173.

19. Copeland, "The Colonial Press, 1690–1765," 35–36, 40.

20. Altherr, *Sports in North America*, 64, 114, 266, 430.

21. Altherr, *Sports in North America*, 114, 266.

22. Enriquez, "Coverage of Sports," 178.

23. "Account of a Cockfight," *Virginia Gazette*, March 23, 1755.

24. See "Notice of a Swimming Accident in Philadelphia," *South Carolina Gazette*, September 9–16, 1732; "Account of a Fishing Accident," *Boston News-Letter*, April 13–20, 1732; "Account of a Horse Racing Accident," *Boston News-Letter*, September 2–9, 1731; "Account of a Hunting Accident," *New*

York Gazette, 9– September 16, 1734; and "Account of a Skating Accident," *New York Gazette*, February 10–17, 1737.

25. "Account of a Goose Hunt," *Boston News-Letter*, November 15–23, 1733.

26. See "Advertisement for a Horse Race," *South Carolina Gazette*, March 24, 1739; "Advertisement for a Shooting Match," *South Carolina Gazette*, December 14–21, 1747; "Advertisement for a Cockfight," *South Carolina Gazette*, February 17–24, 1733; "Advertisements for Bull Baitings," [*Rivington's*] *Royal Gazette*, June 14, 1783; "Notice of a Cricket Match," *Maryland Gazette*, July 25, 1754; "Advertisements for Foot Races," *South Carolina Gazette*, November 21, 1743; and "Advertisements for a Horse Race," *South Carolina Gazette*, March 24, 1739.

27. "Advertisement for a Horse Race," *South Carolina Gazette*, March 24, 1739.

28. See Menna, "The Emergence of Sports Journalism and Writing," 34; and Gorn, "Sports through the Nineteenth Century," 44, 46.

29. Gorn, "Sports through the Nineteenth Century," 43, 46.

30. See Menna, "The Emergence of Sports Journalism and Writing," 35; and Gorn, "Sports through the Nineteenth Century," 46.

31. Gorn and Goldstein, *A Brief History of American Sports*, 81–82.

32. See "Muscular Christianity," Infed, infed.org/mobi/muscular-christianity/, accessed November 15, 2019; Gorn and Goldstein, *A Brief History of American Sports*, 82, 85; Gorn, "Sports through the Nineteenth Century," 45, 84–85; and McChesney, "Media Made Sports," 52.

33. See Gorn and Goldstein, *A Brief History of American Sports*, 49, 53; and Eisenberg, *The Great Match Race*, ix.

34. See Gorn and Goldstein, *A Brief History of American Sports*, 73; and Levine, "Prize Fighting," 30.

35. Gorn and Goldstein, *A Brief History of American Sports*, 65, 73.

36. Mee, *Bare Fists*, 133.

37. Kirsch, *Sports in North America*, 118–19.

38. Mee, *Bare Fists*, 134.

39. See Gorn and Goldstein, *A Brief History of American Sports*, 55; and Levine, "The Louisville Regatta," 27.

40. Robinson, *The World of Yachting*, 14, 16, 168.

41. See Henderson, *Ball, Bat, and Bishop*, 136, 138, 146; William Henry Nugent, "The Sports Section," *American Mercury*, March 1929, 333; Altherr, "'There Is Nothing Now Heard of, in our Leisure Hours, But Ball, Ball, Ball,'" 206; and Gorn and Goldstein, *A Brief History of American Sports*, 78, 80.

42. See Adelman, "The First Modern Sport in America," 108–9, 111; and Gorn and Goldstein, *A Brief History of American Sports*, 75.

43. See Bryant and Holt, "A Historical Overview of Sports and Media in the United States," 23; and Poore, "Biographical Notice of John S. Skinner," 15.

44. Poore, "Biographical Notice of John S. Skinner," 3, 5–7.

45. Poore, "Biographical Notice of John S. Skinner," 13.

46. Skinner, "Introduction to the *American Turf Register and Sporting Magazine*," 36–37.

47. Menna, "The Emergence of Sports Journalism and Writing," 34.

48. See Poore, "Biographical Notice of John S. Skinner," 1; Enriquez, "Coverage of Sports," 199; "Patronage of Sporting Works," 43 (this was published in *The American Turf Register and Sporting Magazine* in August 1838, and Skinner's premise about bloodline documentation proved true, which resulted in readers writing grateful letters to the editor); McChesney, "Media Made Sports," 51; and Bryant and Holt, "A Historical Overview of Sports and Media in the United States," 22.

49. Poore, "Biographical Notice of John S. Skinner," 15–16.

50. Poore, "Biographical Notice of John S. Skinner," 116–20.

51. Poore, "Biographical Notice of John S. Skinner," 1.

52. Yates, *William T. Porter and* The Spirit of the Times, 190–91, 194–95.

53. Yates, *William T. Porter and* The Spirit of the Times, 5, 8–9.

54. See Porter, "Prospectus of *The Spirit of the Times* and Life in New York, 1831," 39; and Porter, "To Our Friends," 40. Both articles originally appeared in *The Spirit of the Times* on December 10, 1831.

55. Yates, *William T. Porter and* The Spirit of the Times, 9, 11.

56. Yates, *William T. Porter and* The Spirit of the Times, 10.

57. Yates, *William T. Porter and* The Spirit of the Times, 11–12, 18.

58. See Yates, *William T. Porter and* The Spirit of the Times, 12; Hudson, *Journalism in the United States from 1690 to 1872*, 342; and Yates, *William T. Porter and* The Spirit of the Times, 9.

59. See Hudson, *Journalism in the United States from 1690 to 1872*, 341; and Nugent, "The Sports Section," 332.

60. See Yates, *William T. Porter and* The Spirit of the Times, 15, 19–20; and Menna "The Emergence of Sports Journalism and Writing," 35–36.

61. See Betts, "Sporting Journalism in Nineteenth-Century America," 41–42; and Menna, "The Emergence of Sports Journalism and Writing," 34.

62. Forester, "A Week in the Woodlands," 64.

63. Nugent, "The Sports Section," 333. Charging ten dollars for *The Spirit of the Times* raised its cost to more than three times what its competitors charged.

64. See Yates, *William T. Porter and* The Spirit of the Times," 28, 34; Bryant and Holt, "A Historical Overview of Sports and Media in the United States," 23; and Nugent, "The Sports Section," 333.

65. See Nugent, "The Sports Section," 332–33; Bryant and Holt, "A Historical Overview of Sports and Media in the United States," 23; and Betts, "Sporting Journalism in Nineteenth-Century America," 41.

66. Yates, *William T. Porter and* The Spirit of the Times, 191–92.

67. See Thompson, *The Penny Press*, 11–12; and Bryant and Holt, "A Historical Overview of Sports and Media in the United States," 23.

68. See Buchholz, "The Penny Press, 1833–61," 125; Bryant and Holt, "A Historical Overview of Sports and Media in the United States," 23; Menna, "The Emergence of Sports Journalism and Writing," 35; and Betts, "Sporting Journalism in Nineteenth-Century America," 43.

69. See Betts, "Sporting Journalism in Nineteenth-Century America," 45; Buchholz, "The Penny Press, 1833–61," 129, 133; and Nugent, "The Sports Section," 336.

70. See Nugent, "The Sports Section," 335; and Betts, "Sporting Journalism in Nineteenth-Century America," 43.

71. See Crouthamel, *Bennett's New York Herald and the Rise of the Popular Press*, 39; and Betts, "Sporting Journalism in Nineteenth-Century America," 43.

72. "The Great Contest: Fashion v. Peytona (1845)," 19–20.

73. "The Great Contest: Fashion v. Peytona (1845)," 21–23.

74. "The Great Contest: Fashion v. Peytona (1845)," 25.

75. See Betts, "Sporting Journalism in Nineteenth-Century America," 43–44; Nugent, "The Sports Section," 336; Evensen, "Sports Journalism: Longtime Staple for U.S. Publications," in Blanchard, *History of the Mass Media in the United States*, 621; and Crouthamel, *Bennett's* New York Herald *and the Rise of the Popular Press*, 39.

76. Betts, "Sporting Journalism in Nineteenth-Century America," 44.

77. Schiff, "The Father of Baseball," 5.

2. Sports Journalism Blossoms

1. Schiff, "The Father of Baseball," 11.

2. Chadwick, *The Game of Base Ball*, 10.

3. Schiff, "The Father of Baseball," 11–12.

4. Hodermarsky, *Baseball's Greatest Writers*, 12.

5. See Hodermarsky, *Baseball's Greatest Writers*, 7–8; and Schiff, "The Father of Baseball," 11–39, 45. In writing for newspapers, Chadwick was following his father, who had worked as a newspaper editor in England. See Tygiel, *Past Time*, 16.

6. See Schiff, "The Father of Baseball," 43–44; and Tygiel, *Past Time*, 18–19.

7. See Schiff, "The Father of Baseball," 14, 16; and Hodermarsky, *Baseball's Greatest Writers*, 8.

8. See Schiff, "The Father of Baseball," 45, 156; and Fedler, *Lessons from the Past*, 147. Fedler noted that typewriters were not common on metropolitan papers in the 1800s. "Some reporters thought typewriters would be too difficult to operate," he wrote. "Other reporters thought typewriters would be too difficult for them to do two jobs at once: fast mechanical work with their hands 'and equally fast and continuous exertion of the mind.'"

9. See Schiff, "The Father of Baseball," 59–64; Chadwick, *The Game of Base Ball*, 11; and Hodermarsky, *Baseball's Greatest Writers*, 9–10.

10. See Schiff, "The Father of Baseball," 64–70; Hodermarsky, *Baseball's Greatest Writers*, 9; and Chadwick, *The Game of Base Ball*, 11. For a concise discussion of Chadwick's impact on baseball statistics, see Tygiel, *Past Time*, 15–34.

11. See Chadwick, *The Game of Base Ball*, 12; Tygiel, *Past Time*, 19; Hodermarsky, *Baseball's Greatest Writers*, 9; and Schiff, "The Father of Baseball," 218.

12. See Hodermarsky, *Baseball's Greatest Writers*, 12–13; Schiff, "The Father of Baseball," 214, 224; and Emery and Emery with Roberts, *The Press and America*, 521.

13. E. Miklich, "Baseball History: 19th Century Baseball: The Leagues," http://www.19cbaseball.com/leagues.html, accessed April 16, 2010.

14. Riess, *City Games*, 70.

15. Riess, *City Games*, 68.

16. Juergens, *Joseph Pulitzer and the* New York World, 48–49.

17. Juergens, *Joseph Pulitzer and the* New York World, 119–21.

18. Juergens, *Joseph Pulitzer and the* New York World, vii, 120, 124, 129–30.

19. Juergens, *Joseph Pulitzer and the* New York World, 130–31.

20. Oriard, *Reading Football*, 66.

21. Oriard, *Reading Football*, 157–58.

22. See Mott, *A History of American Magazines, 1741–1850*, 342; and Tebbel and Zuckerman, *The Magazine in America, 1741–1990*, 57. Andrew Bradford of Philadelphia published the first magazine in North America in 1741, *American Magazine, or A Monthly View of the Political State of the British Colonies*. See Tebbel and Zuckerman, *The Magazine in America, 1741–1990*, 3–4.

23. See Tebbel and Zuckerman, *The Magazine in America, 1741–1990*, 57, 64–65; Vincent, *Mudville's Revenge*, 158; Sloan and Thompson, *The Media in America*, 257; "Bicycle," 410–11; Mott, *American Journalism*, 595; and Betts, *America's Sporting Heritage, 1850–1950*, 61. Mott noted (on page 579) that in the 1890s many of the top newspapers also paid close attention to the sport of bicycling and set up special departments, which carried race results along with news about "wheelmen's" clubs and new bicycle models.

24. Reel, *The National Police Gazette and the Making of the Modern American Man, 1879–1906*, 28–29.

25. Reel, *The National Police Gazette and the Making of the Modern American Man, 1879–1906*, 42–45.

26. Reel, *The National Police Gazette and the Making of the Modern American Man, 1879–1906*, 51, 54, 128–32.

27. Welky, "Culture, Media and Sport," 84.

28. Reel, *The National Police Gazette and the Making of the Modern American Man, 1879–1906*, 28, 54, 92, 115.

29. Reel, *The National Police Gazette and the Making of the Modern American Man, 1879–1906*, 109–10.

30. Reel, *The National Police Gazette and the Making of the Modern American Man, 1879–1906*, 113, 123.

31. See Van Every, *Sins of New York as "Exposed" by the* Police Gazette, 262–63; Isenberg, *John L. Sullivan and His America*, 6–10; and Reel, *The National Police Gazette and the Making of the Modern American Man, 1879–1906*, 124.

32. Reel, *The National Police Gazette and the Making of the Modern American Man, 1879–1906*, 124–25.

33. Reel, *The National Police Gazette and the Making of the Modern American Man, 1879–1906*, 94, 115–16, 125.

34. Reel, *The National Police Gazette and the Making of the Modern American Man, 1879–1906*, 137–38.

35. Dinan, *Sports in the Pulp Magazines*, 8.

36. Reel, *The National Police Gazette and the Making of the Modern American Man, 1879–1906*, 138–41.

37. Reel, *The National Police Gazette and the Making of the Modern American Man, 1879–1906*, 142–43.

38. "Richard K. Fox and His Sporting Representatives," *National Police Gazette*, August 25, 1883, 13.

39. Reel, *The National Police Gazette and the Making of the Modern American Man, 1879–1906*, 118.

40. Oriard, *Reading Football*, 226.

41. Oriard, *Reading Football*, 125.

42. Oriard, *Reading Football*, 127, 132.

43. Betts, *America's Sporting Heritage, 1850–1950*, 116.

44. "Lawlessness of Baseball Players," *Rochester (NY) Post-Express*, no date, in *Current Literature (1888–1912)*, Vol. 28 (New York: Current Literature Publishing, 1888–1912), 57.

45. Betts, *America's Sporting Heritage, 1850–1950*, 116–17.

46. Betts, *America's Sporting Heritage, 1850–1950*, 117–18

47. White, *The Autobiography of William Allen White*, 356.

48. See Betts, *America's Sporting Heritage, 1850–1950*, 79; and "Currier & Ives—The History of the Firm," http://currierandives.com/history.html, accessed May 18, 2010.

49. See Betts, *America's Sporting Heritage, 1850–1950*, 79; and Staebler, "The Stereograph," 28–30, 46, 68.

50. Staebler, "The Stereograph," 4–5.

51. See Staebler, "The Stereograph," 44; Jeremy Norman's HistoryofInformation .com, "The '*Daily Graphic*' of New York, Probably the First Illustrated Daily Newspaper, Begins Publication (March 4, 1873–September 23, 1889)," History of Information, www.historyofinformation.com/expanded.php?id=4389, accessed July 15, 2018; and Betts, *America's Sporting Heritage, 1850–1950*, 79.

52. See Sloan and Thompson, *The Media in America*, 246–47; and Cozens and Stumph, *Sports in American Life*, 116–17.

53. See Betts, *America's Sporting Heritage, 1850–1950*, 67; Cozens and Stumph, *Sports in American Life*, 114; Irwin, "The American Newspaper," January 21, 1911, 18; and Irwin, "*The American Newspaper*," March 4, 1911, 18. Historian Frank Luther Mott described the sportswriting which came out of the yellow journalism period as "slangy and facetious." See Mott, *American Journalism*, 579.

54. Irwin, "The American Newspaper," January 21, 1911, 18.

55. Cozens and Stumph, *Sports in American Life*, 115.

56. Michener, *Sports in America*, 285, 314–15.

57. *Editor & Publisher*, "The Baseball Graft," 12. The same issue about "free publicity" surfaced again in 1921 when the *Chicago Tribune* announced it was cutting back severely on how much it wrote about professional baseball in favor of more about amateur sports. *Editor & Publisher* applauded the move, noting that papers which followed the *Tribune*'s lead would not lose out on advertising money because they "cannot lose what they do not have."

It concluded, "[S]porting departments are not conducted for the purpose of exploiting any professional game at the newspapers' expense." See "*Chicago Tribune* Cuts Sports," 8; and "Sports Writers and Baseball Reports," 28.

58. Michener, *Sports in America*, 315.

59. Yardley, *Ring*, 25.

60. See Hodermarsky, *Baseball's Greatest Writers*, 15–16; and Scott Topping, "Lardnermania: The Life of Ring W. Lardner," Lardnermania, http://tridget .com/life.htm, May 31, 2010.

61. Hodermarsky, *Baseball's Greatest Writers*, 15.

62. Topping, "Lardnermania."

63. Quoted in Hodermarsky, *Baseball's Greatest Writers*, 18.

64. Yardley, *Ring*, 24–25.

65. See Emery and Emery with Roberts, *The Press and America*, 293; and Cozens and Stumph, *Sports in American Life*, 118.

66. Betts, *America's Sporting Heritage, 1850–1950*, 136–37.

67. Betts, *America's Sporting Heritage, 1850–1950*, 139.

68. Betts, *America's Sporting Heritage, 1850–1950*, 139.

3. Newspapers and Radio Begin to Coexist

1. Fountain, Sportswriter, 27.

2. Grantland Rice, "Notre Dame's Cyclone Beats Army, 13 to 7," *New York Herald Tribune*, October 19, 1924, 1.

3. Fountain, *Sportswriter*, 27–28.

4. Fountain, *Sportswriter*, 28–29.

5. Inabinett, *Grantland Rice and His Heroes*, 19.

6. Harper, *How You Played the Game*, 31–47. A number of authors have noted that Rice was known as the "Dean of American Sportswriters." For example, see Hodermarsky, *Baseball's Greatest Writers*, 23.

7. Fountain, *Sportswriter*, 56–57.

8. See Hodermarsky, *Baseball's Greatest Writers*, 23–24; and Inabinett, *Grantland Rice and His Heroes*, 7–8.

9. See Rice, *The Tumult and the Shouting*, xv; Fountain, *Sportswriter*, 4; and Harper, *How You Played the Game*, 15.

10. Barton, "Grantland Rice," xi.

11. See Inabinett, *Grantland Rice and His Heroes*, 3–5; and Fountain, *Sportswriter*, 6.

12. Fountain, *Sportswriter*, 4.

13. Inabinett, *Grantland Rice and His Heroes*, 21–22.

14. Roessner, *Inventing Baseball Heroes*, 3–4.

15. Inabinett, *Grantland Rice and His Heroes*, 104–5.

16. See Hodermarsky, *Baseball's Greatest Writers*, 23; and Harper, *How You Played the Game*, 18.

17. Hodermarsky, *Baseball's Greatest Writers*, 24.

18. Inabinett, *Grantland Rice and His Heroes*, ix.

19. Rice, *The Tumult and the Shouting*, xvi.

20. Grantland Rice, "Ruth Hits Three Home Runs as Yankees Win, 10–5," *New York Herald Tribune*, October 7, 1926, 1, 15.

21. Inabinett, *Grantland Rice and His Heroes*, ix, 1, 5–7.

22. Smith, "My Press-Box Memoirs," 202. Charles Fountain, in his 1993 biography of Rice, agreed with Smith that Rice might be looked down upon today because of the way he wrote, but his readers loved it. "Were he writing today his florid style and unfailingly upbeat assessment of all that he witnessed would doom him to deserved obscurity at some weekly newspaper buried deep in the bowels of the Heartland, writing high school sports in a way that would make the parents proud. Yet in his time—and one cannot separate Grantland Rice from his time—he was the best." See Fountain, *Sportswriter*, 3.

23. Inabinett, *Grantland Rice and His Heroes*, 21.

24. Harper, *How You Played the Game*, 16. Harper wrote (pages 502–3) that one indication of Rice's national stature came toward the end of his life in 1948 when Ralph Edwards's second-ever *This Is Your Life* television show was devoted to him.

25. Arthur Daley, "Sports of the Times," *New York Times*, July 15, 1954, 30.

26. Quoted in Harper, *How You Played the Game*, 518.

27. Inabinett, *Grantland Rice and His Heroes*, 104–5.

28. Emery and Emery with Roberts, *The Press and America*, 226. For a discussion of the increasing concerns with journalistic standards in the nineteenth century, see Dicken-Garcia, *Journalistic Standards in Nineteenth-Century America*.

29. The best discussion of the different types of complaints about the press is Rodgers, "An Untamed Force."

30. See Rodgers, "An Untamed Force," 28–29; and Emery and Emery with Roberts, *The Press and America*, 521.

31. Rodgers, "An Untamed Force," 10.

32. Kaszuba, "Ringside, Hearthside," 142.

33. Ross, *Ladies of the Press*, 145–47.

34. Ross, *Ladies of the Press*, 145. According to historian Nan Robertson, making Morgan's interview with Bigelow particularly memorable was not only her height but the "galumphing noise" that she made with her boots when she came up to his desk and the fact that she smelled like a horse stable. See Robertson, *The Girls in the Balcony*, 44.
35. Ross, *Ladies of the Press*, 147.
36. Rayne, *What Can a Woman Do*, 41–42.
37. Kroeger, *Nellie Bly*, 128–29.
38. Ross, *Ladies of the Press*, 242–43.
39. Creedon, "Women in Toyland," 72–73.
40. See Creedon, "Women in Toyland," 73–75; and Ross, *Ladies of the Press*, 470–71. A few women also began writing regularly about sports in magazines at the turn of the century. One of the first was Dr. Emma E. Walker, who in a health column for *Ladies' Home Journal* wrote about tennis, golf, and rowing and noted in 1902 that girls in New York City liked using a punching bag for indoor exercise. Then, in the 1920s, Agnes R. Wayman often talked about sports in *The American Girl*, which was the Girl Scout magazine. See Creedon, "From Whalebone to Spandex," 113–14.
41. Faber, *The Life of Lorena Hickok, E.R.'s Friend*, 66–67.
42. Martinelli and Bowen, "The Public Relations Work of Journalism Trailblazer and First Lady Confidante Lorena Hickok, 1937–45," 132.
43. Ross, *Ladies of the Press*, 193–94.
44. Kaszuba, "Ringside, Hearthside," 142, 144–45.
45. Kaszuba, "Ringside, Hearthside," 141.
46. Kaszuba, "Ringside, Hearthside," 144.
47. Kaszuba, "Ringside, Hearthside," 148.
48. See Asinof, *Eight Men Out*, 4, 61, 64, 119; and Tygiel, *Past Time*, 64, 66–68, 73. One of the most elaborate "scoreboards" was a Jackson Manikin Board during the 1915 World Series. Tygiel (page 67) noted that it had "mechanical athletes that moved in and out of dugouts, swung the bat left- and right-handed, and even argued with the umpire."
49. Gamache, "Evolution of the Sportscast Highlight Form," 48–49, 53–56, 63.
50. Gamache, "Evolution of the Sportscast Highlight Form," 82–83, 89, 93.
51. Gamache, "Evolution of the Sportscast Highlight Form," 93.
52. Harper, *How You Played the Game*, 313–14.
53. See Jolly, *Marconi*, 52–54; and Dunlap, *Marconi*, 60–61.
54. Smith, *Play by Play*, 13.

55. See Emery and Emery with Roberts, *The Press and America*, 271–72, 274; and Sterling and Kittross, *Stay Tuned*, 28–29, 40.

56. See Betts, *America's Sporting Heritage*, 271–72; Sterling and Kittross, *Stay Tuned*, 61–62; Emery and Emery with Roberts, *The Press and America*, 278; Lichty and Topping, *American Broadcasting*, 90; Raney and Bryant, *Handbook of Sports and Media*, 119–20; Cozens and Stumpf, *Sports in American Life*, 143; and Smith, *Play by Play*, 21. Listing the number of radio stations is problematic because the figure constantly changed. Sterling and Kittross noted (page 62), for example, that while more than six hundred stations broadcast in 1922, "many went off [the air] again in a few months, weeks, or even days." Thus, the numbers cited here are for a specific date during a year from one or more of the above sources.

57. See Chase, *Sound and Fury*, 303; and Raney and Bryant, *Handbook of Sports and Media*, 119.

58. See Raney and Bryant, *Handbook of Sports and Media*, 120; Betts, *America's Sporting Heritage*, 271; Lichty and Topping, *American Broadcasting*, 108–9; Sterling and Kittross, *Stay Tuned*, 61; and Smith, *Play by Play*, 19. Smith (pages 15–16) noted that a professor and an instructor broadcast the first college football games in 1912 on an experimental station at the University of Minnesota. They did all of the team's home games in Morse code. Then, in 1920, a Texas-Texas A&M game was broadcast with words.

59. See Raney and Bryant, *Handbook of Sports and Media*, 120; and Smith, *Play by Play*, 17.

60. See Harper, *How You Played the Game*, 312–13; and Fountain, *Sportswriter*, 194–96.

61. *Smith, Play by Play*, 25.

62. *Smith, Play by Play*, 20.

63. See Cozens and Stumpf, *Sports in American Life*, 144–45; Betts, *America's Sporting Heritage*, 272; and Raney and Bryant, *Handbook of Sports and Media*, 120–21.

64. Patnode, "Friend, Foe, or Freeloader?" 77, 79, 83.

65. Pew, "Radio Discussed as Press Threat or Promise," 7.

66. Harper, *How You Played the Game*, 313.

67. Ted Patterson, "Jack Graney, the First Player-Broadcaster," SABR Research Journals Archive, http://research.sabr.org/journals/jack-graney, accessed October 19, 2018.

68. "Rick Telander, American Sports Journalist," https://upclosed.com/people /rick-telander, accessed May 11, 2019.

4. Sportswriters and Black Athletes

1. Officially, the fight attendance was 70,043, but it was estimated at around 80,000 because of people who crowded into Yankee Stadium without seats. See Astor, ". . . *And a Credit to His Race*," 179.

2. Mead, *Champion*, 133–34, 145.

3. See Roberts, *Joe Louis*, 164, 169; and Margolick, *Beyond Glory*, 289.

4. Margolick, *Beyond Glory*, 301–2. When the fight ended McCarthy quickly handed the microphone to his assistant, Ed Thorgersen, a sports commentator for Fox Movietone News, to finish the broadcast and went through the ropes into the ring along with about fifty others, including the fighters' seconds and handlers, photographers, and policemen. See Margolick, *Beyond Glory*, 289, 301.

5. Carter, *An Hour Before Daylight*, 32–33.

6. See Hamburger, "Horse Racing" and "Oliver Lewis," 211; and Salisbury, "Isaac Murphy," 248.

7. See Elliott, "Frank Hart," 139–40; Binker, "William Henry Lewis," 211; and Heapey, "Marshall 'Major' Taylor," 361.

8. See Bond, "Ed Gordon, Jr.," and Hornbuckle, "William Dehart Hubbard," 161; and Elliott, "John Baxter Taylor," and Crawford, "Eddie Tolan," 369–70.

9. "Fritz Pollard Biography," Biography, http://www.biography.com/people /fritz-pollard-9443774, accessed February 17, 2014.

10. Gems, "'Duke' Slater," 332.

11. Roberts, *Papa Jack*, 2–4, 6, 10–11.

12. Roberts, *Papa Jack*, 19, 28–29, 31, 47, 49–50, 53, 56.

13. Gilmore, *Bad Nigger!*, 26–27.

14. Roberts, *Papa Jack*, 57–58.

15. Gilmore, *Bad Nigger!*, 26.

16. Roberts, *Papa Jack*, 61–65.

17. See Roberts, *Papa Jack*, 54, 65; and Gilmore, *Bad Nigger!*, 28–29.

18. Roberts, *Papa Jack*, 54.

19. Roberts, *Papa Jack*, 66.

20. Gilmore, *Bad Nigger!*, 29, 31–32.

21. Hutchison, "Usually White, But Not Always Great," 231–39.

22. Hutchison, "Usually White, But Not Always Great," 233.

23. Hutchison, "Usually White, But Not Always Great," 234.

24. Burns, *Unforgivable Blackness*.

25. Hutchison, "Usually White, But Not Always Great," 235.

26. Gilmore, *Bad Nigger!*, 38.

27. Burns, *Unforgivable Blackness*.

28. "Jack Johnson Biography," Biography, http://www.biography.com/people, accessed March 23, 2014. The money that Johnson received for the fight would be the equivalent today of about $3 million.

29. Hutchison, "Usually White, But Not Always Great," 235.

30. See Gilmore, *Bad Nigger!*, 41; Burns, *Unforgivable Blackness*; and Cressman, "From Newspaper Row to Times Square," 187.

31. See Roberts, *Papa Jack*, 108–10; Hietala, *The Fight of the Century*, 42; and Richard Hoffer, "The Great Black Mark," *Sports Illustrated*, July 5, 2010, 15.

32. "A Word to the Black Man," *Los Angeles Times*, July 6, 1910.

33. *The Advocate*'s statement appeared in an article in the *Baltimore Afro-American*. See "Views of the Afro American Press on the Johnson-Jeffries Fight," *Baltimore Afro-American*, July 16, 1910, 4.

34. Roberts, *Papa Jack*, 22–23, 111.

35. "Advice to Jack Johnson," *New York Age*, July 14, 1910, 4.

36. Isard, "Champion Jack," 25.

37. See "Jack Johnson Not Getting Fair Deal," *Baltimore Afro-American*, November 23, 1912, 6; and "Punishment for the Crime," *Washington Bee*, January 18, 1913, 4.

38. See Hutchison, "Usually White, But Not Always Great," 235; and Tony Langston, "Jack Johnson and American Sporting Writers," *Chicago Defender*, July 4, 1914, 4.

39. See Roberts, *Papa Jack*, 201–3; and Burns, *Unforgivable Blackness*.

40. Burns, *Unforgivable Blackness*.

41. Schaap, *Triumph*, 14–21.

42. Schaap, *Triumph*, 16–17.

43. Baker, *Jesse Owens*, 23.

44. Baker, *Jesse Owens*, 27, 30–32.

45. Baker, *Jesse Owens*, 26, 33–35, 38–39.

46. Baker, *Jesse Owens*, 44, 50, 52.

47. See Wiggins, "Racial Theories," 289–90; and Baker, *Jesse Owens*, 45.

48. Cobb, "Race and Runners," 52–54, 56. The wire services paid little attention to Cobb's findings. See Oriard, *King Football*, 313.

49. Baker, *Jesse Owens*, 63–64.

50. See Baker, *Jesse Owens*, 65; Schaap, *Triumph*, 57; and Schuyler, "Letters to the Sports Editor," *New York Times*, July 11, 1936, 8.

51. Schapp, *Triumph*, 90. The American Olympic Association went through several name changes in the 1940s before being renamed the United States Olympic Committee in 1961. See "History," Team USA, www .teamusa.org/About-the-USOC/Inside-the-USOC/History, accessed July 14, 2018.

52. Schapp, *Triumph*, 100–101.

53. See Schapp, *Triumph*, 126–31; and Shirley Povich, "This Morning . . . ," *Washington Post*, July 13, 1936, 15.

54. See Fred Farrell, "Fanning with Farrell," *Daily Worker*, August 2, 1936, 14; Schaap, *Triumph*, 157; and R. Walter Merguson, "Race Athletes Not Involved in Olympic Scandal Charges," *Pittsburgh Courier*, August 1, 1936, 1.

55. See Grantland Rice, "Dark Shadow Falls over Herr Hitler as Negro Athletes Dominate Olympics," *Los Angeles Times*, August 4, 1936, A13; Westbrook Pegler, "Fair Enough," *New York World-Telegram*, August 6, 1936, 17; "Jesse Owens Became a Sporting Legend for His Achievements at the 1936 Berlin Games," Jesse Owens, http://www.olympic.org/jesse-owens, accessed April 20, 2014; and Joe Williams, "Negro Stars Shine in Games, Give America Lead in Points, No More Hitler Greetings," *New York World-Telegram*, August 4, 1936, 22. For an in-depth treatment of Owens at the 1936 Olympics, see Schapp, *Triumph*, 159–229.

56. Drake, "Jesse Who?", 99.

57. Robert L. Vann, "Proud I'm an American, Owens Says," *Pittsburgh Courier*, August 8, 1936, 1.

58. See Margolick, *Beyond Glory*, 59–60; and Buni, *Robert L. Vann of the* Pittsburgh Courier, 252.

59. Margolick, *Beyond Glory*, 60–61, 63–64.

60. Margolick, *Beyond Glory*, 64–65. Johnson offered to help Louis prepare for his championship fight against Jim Braddock in 1937, but Louis' backers turned him down. As a result, he made the same offer to Braddock but was rebuffed again. Then, he controversially predicted that Braddock would win because Louis was "overrated." In reporting what he had said, the Associated Negro Press noted that Johnson was "taking the wrong way as usual" and claimed people had no interest in what he believed. "He should go off and keep his trap shut for a while at least," it concluded. See Hietala, *The Fight of the Century*, 180.

61. "Joe Louis," BoxRec, http://www.boxrec.com/listbouts.php?human_id=9027 &cat=boxer, accessed April 30, 2014. In his first twelve professional fights in 1934, Louis's earnings per bout increased from $59 to $2,750, which was

considerable money for someone who had been on relief recently. See Buni, *Robert L. Vann of the* Pittsburgh Courier, 252.

62. Hietala, *The Fight of the Century*, 180–82.

63. See Hietala, *The Fight of the Century*, 182; and Buni, *Robert L. Vann of the* Pittsburgh Courier, 252. The *Courier* apparently played up Louis's boxing career in the 1930s more than any other black newspaper, frequently pushing back deadlines so that articles about his Friday night fights could get in the next day's paper. This resulted frequently in large crowds of boxing fans waiting at the *Courier* for the paper to come off the presses at 6:00 a.m. so they could read about his most recent fight. Publisher Robert Vann also assigned Chester Washington, because he was a fast typist, to be Louis's secretary at his training camp, and he would reply to seventy-five to a hundred letters a day from the boxer's fans. This quickly led to him becoming a confidante to Louis. See Buni, *Robert L. Vann of the* Pittsburgh Courier, 252–53.

64. Hietala, *The Fight of the Century*, 183.

65. See Hietala, *The Fight of the Century*, 183, 185; and Margolick, *Beyond Glory*, 321–22, 324.

66. Laucella, "Jesse Owens, A Black Pearl Amidst an Ocean of Fury," 17, 20, 23, 32–33. Commenting on the press's frequent linking of Owens with Africa, newspaper columnist Westbrook Pegler said: "It is a doubtful compliment to a Negro athlete who is qualified to attend college to attempt to account for his proficiency on the field by suggesting that he is still so close to the primitive that whenever he runs a foot-race in a formal meet between schools his civilization vanishes and he becomes again for the moment an African savage in breechcloth and nose ring legging it through the jungle." See Oriard, *King Football*, 314.

67. Mead, *Champion*, 106.

68. Fountain, *Sportswriter*, 246–48.

69. Laucella, "Jesse Owens, A Black Pearl Amidst an Ocean of Fury," 34.

70. See Fountain, *Sportswriter*, 250; and Hutchison, "Usually White, But Not Always Great," 236. The most extensive treatment of nationalism, resulting in Owens's popularity and positive press coverage in the Olympics, is in Schaap, *Triumph*, 150–229.

71. Buni, *Robert L. Vann of the* Pittsburgh Courier, 253–54.

72. Wiggins, "The Notion of Double-Consciousness and the Involvement of Black Athletes in American Sport," 142.

73. Rodgers, "An Untamed Force," 10. The "Canons of Journalism" did not specifically single out sportswriters for criticism.

74. At the 1930 annual meeting of the American Society of Newspaper Editors, a report by Don Maxwell, the sports editor of the *Chicago Tribune*, discussed the ethics of sports departments. He noted many staffs had no ethics twenty years before, but that had slowly changed because of the hiring "of better men—better trained men, real newspaper men" to cover sports. "If athletics and sports are to be the wholesome influence on young people that they are capable of being," he continued, "then the sports editors and reporters ought to have some of that wholesome quality impossible without integrity." While Maxwell did not mention sports coverage becoming less racist, it was something that changed markedly in the twenty years to which he was referring. See American Society of Newspaper Editors, *Proceedings of the Annual Meeting of the American Society of Newspaper Editors*, 175–79.

75. See Tygiel, *Baseball's Great Experiment*, 10–11; and Wiggins, "Baseball," 22.

76. Tygiel, *Baseball's Great Experiment*, 13–15.

77. Tygiel, *Baseball's Great Experiment*, 24.

78. See "Negro League History 101," Negro League Baseball, www.negroleaguebaseball.com/history101.html, accessed February 26, 2015; and Carroll, *When to Stop the Cheering?*, 8–11.

79. "Negro League History 101."

80. Lamb, *Conspiracy of Silence*, 10–11, 15–16.

81. Tygiel, *Baseball's Great Experiment*, 42. For an in-depth discussion of the black newspapers' coverage of black baseball and the campaign for integration, see chapters 2 through 6 in Carroll, *When to Stop the Cheering?*

82. Lamb, *Conspiracy of Silence*, 14, 24.

83. See Lamb, *Conspiracy of Silence*, 85–88; and Carroll, *When to Stop the Cheering?*, 104–5. The *Daily Worker's* drive to integrate baseball not only included stories in the paper but picketing and petitions. See Richard Goldstein, "Bill Mardo Dies at 88; Championed Integration," *New York Times*, January 27, 2012, B16.

84. Lamb, *Conspiracy of Silence*, 102–3.

85. Lamb, *Conspiracy of Silence*, 14, 26, 55–56.

86. Lamb, *Conspiracy of Silence*, 60–61.

87. Reisler, *Black Writers/Black Baseball*, 2.

88. Tygiel, *Baseball's Great Experiment*, 65. Rickey spent $25,000 in 1945 for three scouts (Sukeforth was one of them) to scour the Negro Leagues for talent, presumably for the creation of another black baseball league. The scouts were not told that he was considering signing a black to a Dodgers

contract. See Weaver, "The Black Press and the Assault on Professional Baseball's 'Color Line,' October, 1945–April, 1947," 305.

89. See Dave Anderson, "Clyde Sukeforth, 98, Is Dead; Steered Robinson to Majors," *New York Times*, September 6, 2000, C24; and Weaver, "The Black Press and the Assault on Professional Baseball's 'Color Line,' October, 1945–April, 1947," 305.

90. For an in-depth examination of Robinson's 1946 spring training and the racism that he faced, see Lamb, *Blackout*.

91. Louis Effrat, "Dodgers Purchase Robinson, First Negro in Modern Major League Baseball," *New York Times*, April 11, 1947, 20.

92. Kahn, *The Boys of Summer*, xvii.

93. Robinson, *Baseball Has Done It*, 53.

94. See Washburn, "New York Newspaper Coverage of Jackie Robinson in His First Major League Season," 187–89; and Blanchard, "The Hutchins Commission, the Press and the Responsibility Concept," 25.

95. See Carroll, *When to Stop the Cheering?*, 160; and Lamb, *Blackout*, 331.

96. Chris Lamb and Glen Bleske, "Covering the Integration of Baseball—A Look Back," *Editor & Publisher*, January 27, 1996, 48–49.

97. Weaver, "The Black Press and the Assault on Professional Baseball's 'Color Line,' October, 1945–April, 1947," 315. Robinson had a huge impact on attendance. In July, Brooklyn became the first major league team that season to have one million paid fans at home games, and it set a National League mark of 1.8 million by the end of the season. The same was true on the road, where a league record of 1.9 million came to see the Dodgers play. See Carroll, "'This Is IT!,'" 158.

98. Carroll, "'This Is IT!,'" 154, 156.

99. Email, Brian Carroll to Patrick S. Washburn, March 6, 2015.

100. Carroll, "'This Is IT!,'" 151–62.

101. Tygiel, *Baseball's Great Experiment*, 9.

5. *Sports Illustrated* and ABC Television

1. See "Regency TR-1 Transistor Radio History—An Essay," Regencytr1, www .regencytr1.com, accessed March 20, 2015; "A Brief History of the Transistor Radio;" Vintage Radios, www.vintageradios.com/a-brief-history-of -the-transistor-radio, accessed March 20, 2015; Joseph Stromberg, "The Transistor Radio Launches the Portable Electronic Age," Smithsonian, www.smithsonianmag.com/smithsonian-institution/the-transistor-radio -launches-the-portable-electronic-age-1107617, accessed March 20, 2015;

and "Transistor Radios," PBS, www.pbs.org/transistor/backgroundl/events /tradio.html, accessed March 20, 2015. Also see "Seven Ways to Compute the Relative Value of a U.S. Dollar Amount—1774 to Present," Measuring-Worth, www.measuringworth.com/calculators/uscompare/relativevalue .php, accessed January 28, 2017. A prototype of a transistor radio was demonstrated at a radio fair in Düsseldorf, Germany, in 1953, but it was never sold to the public.

2. "Regency TR-1 Transistor Radio History—An Essay."

3. Rushin, "There and Back," 59.

4. Rushin, "There and Back," 59, 62, 64.

5. See "*Sports Illustrated* First Issue August 16, 1954" www.sportshistorytoday .com/sportsllustrated-issue-August-16-1954, accessed March 5, 2017; and MacCambridge, *The Franchise*, 44–46. The first cover of *Sports Illustrated* was dated August 16, but it appeared on newsstands four days earlier.

6. *Sports Illustrated*, August 16, 1954.

7. Phillips, "Memo from the Publisher," *Sports Illustrated*, August 16, 1954, 13. The italics and capitals are in the original.

8. MacCambridge, *The Franchise*, 17–19. *Sport* magazine continued publishing until August 2000.

9. MacCambridge, *The Franchise*, 14.

10. MacCambridge, *The Franchise*, 15–16.

11. MacCambridge, *The Franchise*, 19–23.

12. See MacCambridge, *The Franchise*, 24; and Geltner, *Last King of the Sports Page*, 69.

13. See MacCambridge, *The Franchise*, 24, 38; and "Wonderful Moneyed World of Sports," *Business Week*, August 7, 1954, 58.

14. Geltner, *Last King of the Sports Page*, 70.

15. See Geltner, *Last King of the Sports Page*, 241, n. 27; and MacCambridge, *The Franchise*, 4.

16. Rushin, "There and Back," 59.

17. Geltner, *Last King of the Sports Page*, 70.

18. Rushin, "There and Back," 59.

19. "New Heraldry," *Sports Illustrated*, August 16, 1954, 130–31.

20. Phillips, "Memo from the Publisher," *Sports Illustrated*, November 22, 1954, 1. The italics are in the original.

21. Chris J. Ohmer, "Sporting Look—A 20-Year History," 5–6, 10. This paper was written in the spring quarter of 1987 for an undergraduate honors tutorial class on journalism history in the E. W. Scripps School of Journalism at

Ohio University. It is in the possession of Patrick S. Washburn, who taught the course.

22. Ohmer, "Sporting Look—A 20-Year History," 11–12.

23. Ohmer, "Sporting Look—A 20-Year History," 13–14.

24. See MacCambridge, *The Franchise*, 71; and Geltner, *Last King of the Sports Page*, 74.

25. Deford, "Sometimes the Bear Eats You: Confessions of a Sportswriter," 79–80.

26. Rushin, "There and Back," 65.

27. Michener, *Sports in America*, 322.

28. MacCambridge, *The Franchise*, 158–200.

29. Volk, "Letter from the Publisher," 4.

30. MacCambridge, *The Franchise*, 163.

31. Smith, "*Sports Illustrated*'s African American Athlete Series as Socially Responsible Journalism," 374–75.

32. Smith, "*Sports Illustrated*'s African American Athlete Series as Socially Responsible Journalism," 375–77.

33. Associated Press, "Time Warner Illustrated for Women," *Sporting Goods Business*, February 10, 1997, 54.

34. Furrow, "A Struggle for Identity," 157–58.

35. Furrow, "A Struggle for Identity," 159–160.

36. Bailey, "From the Editor," 12. This was not the first sports magazine for women. In May 1974, tennis star Billie Jean King and her husband began publishing *womenSports*, and it soon had a monthly circulation of two hundred thousand. Before ceasing publication in 2000, it was renamed three times, becoming *Women's Sports* in 1979, *Women's Sports and Fitness* in 1984, and *Condé Nast Women's Sports and Fitness* in 1998. See "WomenSports," Revolvy .com, www.revolvy.com/topic/WomenSports, accessed October 27, 2018.

37. Furrow, "A Struggle for Identity," 160.

38. Furrow, "A Struggle for Identity," 163–64.

39. Bogart, "Magazines Since the Rise of Television," 162.

40. See "Dedication of RCA Seen on Television," *New York Times*, April 21, 1939, 16; and Conway, *The Origins of Television News in America*, 12–16, 39.

41. See "Dedication of RCA Seen on Television," *New York Times*, April 21, 1939, 16; and Orrin E. Dunlap Jr., "Today's Eye Opener," *New York Times*, April 30, 1939, sec. 11, 12.

42. "Dedication of RCA Seen on Television," 16.

43. Conway, *The Origins of Television News in America*, 14.

44. Walker and Bellamy, *Center Field Shot*, 6–9.

45. Walker and Bellamy, *Center Field Shot*, 11, 68, 78, 84, 86.

46. Bill Molzon, "Television's Sports Heritage: The Early Days of TV Sports," American Sportscasters Online, americansportscastersonline.com /waynesbergarticle.html, accessed July 5, 2017. In 1949, a poll of sixty-four TV stations showed they devoted an average of 16 percent of their programming to sports coverage. Twenty sports were broadcast with the highest amount of coverage given to baseball, basketball, boxing, football, and wrestling. See Cozens and Stumpf, *Sports in American Life*, 152.

47. Sterling and Kittross, *Stay Tuned*, 209, 255, 258, 324, 369–70.

48. See MacCambridge, *The Franchise*, 24; and Rushin, "There and Back," 60.

49. Schulberg, "A Fan Fights Back," 63.

50. Michener, *Sports in America*, 333, 335.

51. See "Timeline Events in the History of Broadcasting," Illinois School of Information Sciences, people.ischool.illinois.edu/~chip/projects/timeline /1951moses.html, accessed July 9, 2017; Rushin, "There and Back," 58; "The Color Revolution: Television in the Sixties," Television Obscurities, www .tvobscurities.com/articles/color60s, accessed July 13, 2018; and Sterling and Kittross, *Stay Tuned*, 298, 399.

52. Christopher Klein, "The Birth of Satellite TV, 50 Years Ago," History, July 23, 2012, history.com/news/the-birth-of-satellite-tv-50-years-ago.

53. Bruce Weber, "Tony Verna, Who Started Instant Replay and Remade Sports Television, Dies at 81," *New York Times*, January 21, 2015.

54. Endres and Ferraro, "From War Hero to Sports Icon," 17–19.

55. Phinizy, "Go-Go Slow," 68, 74, 76.

56. See Arledge, *Roone*, 1; and Gunther, *The House That Roone Built*, 22.

57. See Arledge, *Roone*, 7–8; and Rader, *In Its Own Image*, 104.

58. Arledge, *Roone*, 30–33.

59. Rader, *In Its Own Image*, 106–7.

60. See Arledge, *Roone*, 45, 57–58; and Gunther, *The House That Roone Built*, 19.

61. Arledge, *Roone*, 50–57, 65.

62. Arledge, *Roone*, 58.

63. Arledge, *Roone*, 46, 57–58.

64. Gunther, *The House That Roone Built*, 19.

65. Rader, *In Its Own Image*, 116.

66. Hoffer, "What a Wonderful World," 12–13.

67. See ABC Sports Online, "History of ABC's Monday Night Football," January 15, 2003, espn.com/abcsports/mnf/s/2003/0115/1493105.html; and Arledge, *Roone*, 120.

68. See ABC Sports Online, "History of ABC's Monday Night Football;" and Rader, *In Its Own Image*, 107.

69. Arledge, *Roone*, 115.

70. Rader, *In Its Own Image*, 57.

71. "Dizzy Dean Quotes," *Baseball Almanac*, baseball-almanac.com/quotes /quodean.shtml, accessed July 16, 2017.

72. Arledge, *Roone*, 101, 111.

73. See Arledge, *Roone*, 108–10; and Rader, *In Its Own Image*, 132.

74. Arledge, *Roone*, 113–14.

75. Arledge, *Roone*, 116–17, 120.

76. See Rader, *In Its Own Image*, 113; Rushin, "There and Back," 59; and Mac-Cambridge, *The Franchise*, 8.

6. ESPN and Women Sportswriters and Broadcasters

1. Freeman, *ESPN*, 25–26.

2. ESPN is an acronym for Entertainment and Sports Programming Network.

3. Freeman, *ESPN*, 7.

4. Josh Krulewitz, "SportsCenter to Air 50,000th Episode in September," ESPN, http://www.espnfrontrow.com/2012/08/sportscenter-to-air-50000th-episode -in-september-revisit-episode-no-1/, accessed May 17, 2017.

5. See, Freeman, *ESPN*; Miller and Shales, *Those Guys Have All the Fun*; Smith and Hollihan, *ESPN*; and Vogan, *ESPN*.

6. *Sports Night*, a half-hour television program, ran from 1998 to 2000, on ABC.

7. Freeman, *ESPN*, 55–56, 58.

8. Freeman, *ESPN*, 51–52.

9. Freeman, *ESPN*, 75, 85.

10. Freeman, *ESPN*, 28, 98, 116, 121, 123.

11. Kay Koplovitz, "How Muhammad Ali, Joe Frazier and Satellites Changed History," Media Village, https://www.mediavillage.com/article/how -muhammed-ali-joe-frazier-and-satellites-changed-the-course-of-television -history/, accessed May 15, 2017.

12. Siedlecki, "Sports Anti-Siphoning Rules for Pay Cable Television," 821.

13. 567 F. 2nd 9 (D.C. Cir. 1977), *cert. denied* 434 U.S. 829 (1977).

14. Turner's cable station was originally called WTCG ("Watch this channel grow").

15. "The Rise of Cable Television," Encyclopedia.com, http://www.encyclopedia .com/arts/newswires-white-papers-and-books/rise-cable-television, accessed July 29, 2017.

16. Freeman, *ESPN*, 103–4.

17. Freeman, *ESPN*, 102.

18. Ed Sherman, "ESPN's Chris Berman Has Seen NFL Draft's Popularity Soar," *Chicago Tribune*, http://www.chicagotribune.com/sports/columnists/ct-nfl -draft-espn-sherman-media-spt-0427-20150426-column.html, accessed May 15, 2017.

19. Freeman, *ESPN*, 104, 108.

20. Ben Zimmer, "Marching Madly into Brackets," *Wall Street Journal*, https:// www.wsj.com/articles/sb10001424052702304256404579449831528247714, accessed, May 17, 2017.

21. Freeman, *ESPN*, 100–101.

22. Freeman, *ESPN*, 110.

23. See Freeman, *ESPN*, 139; and Miller and Shales, *Those Guys Have All the Fun*, 178.

24. Freeman, *ESPN*, 235.

25. Freeman, *ESPN*, 185–86, 227.

26. Sandomir, "Reynolds and ESPN Settle Lawsuit."

27. "Report: ESPN Settles Sexual Harassment Claim Involving Chris Berman," NBC Sports, http://profootballtalk.nbcsports.com/2015/11/10/report-espn -settles-sexual-harassment-claim-involving-chris-berman/, accessed May 18, 2017.

28. John Koblin, "The Most Sexless Sex Scandal that Shook ESPN," Deadspin, http://www.nytimes.com/2008/04/16/sports/baseball/16reynolds.html, accessed May 18, 2017.

29. Shelley Smith, "ESPN Host: A Trailblazer for Women," *Chicago Tribune*, August 28, 1987, http://articles.chicagotribune.com/1987-08-28/sports /8703050481_1_espn-reporter-and-weekend-sports-phyllis-george.

30. Milton Kent, "Gardner Proves that Hard Work Has Its Rewards," *Baltimore Sun*, December 24, 1992, http://articles.baltimoresun.com /1992-12-24/sports/1992359166_1_gardner-broadcasting-sports-women -working.

31. David Haugh, "Jeannie Morris Recognized for Pioneering Efforts," *Chicago Tribune*, http://articles.chicagotribune.com/2014-03-06/sports/ct-jeannie -morris-haugh-spt-0307-20140307_1_johnny-morris-jeannie-morris-da -coach, accessed May 12, 2017.

32. ESPN, "Let Them Wear Towels," YouTube, https://www.youtube.com/watch ?v=mqMXDQYNZPQ, accessed April 30, 2017.

33. Freeman, *ESPN*, 216.

34. See Robert McG. Thomas Jr., "Women in the Locker Room: Struggles Are Similar to Those of the 1970s," *New York Times*, October 3, 1990, http://www .nytimes.com/1990/10/03/sports/women-in-the-locker-room-1990-struggles -are-similar-to-those-of-the-70-s.html; and ESPN, "Let Them Wear Towels."

35. Lynn Zinser, "The First Woman Through the Locker Room Door, 35 Years Ago," *New York Times*, January 21, 2010.

36. ESPN, "Let Them Wear Towels."

37. Canadian Broadcasting Corporation, "40 Years after Winning the Right to Report from Men's Locker Rooms, Melissa Ludtke Still Sees Work to be Done," Canadian Broadcasting Corporation, https://www.cbc.ca/radio /day6/episode-409-kavanaugh-and-rape-reporting-getting-gritty-women -in-sports-journalism-saving-haida-and-more-1.4839202/40-years-after -winning-the-right-to-report-from-men-s-locker-rooms-melissa-ludtke -still-sees-work-to-be-done-1.4839285, accessed October 12, 2019.

38. ESPN, "Let Them Wear Towels."

39. Canadian Broadcasting Corporation, "40 Years after Winning the Right to Report from Men's Locker Rooms."

40. Lily Rothman, "This Is Why Female Sportswriters Can Go in Men's Locker Rooms," *Time*, http://time.com/4061122/ludtke-kuhn-jaguars-colts/, accessed May 19, 2017.

41. Lincoln, "Locker Rooms: Equality with Integrity."

42. Eleanor Clift, "'Let Them Wear Towels': The Women Who Changed Sports Forever," Daily Beast, http://www.thedailybeast.com/let-them-wear-towels -the-women-who-changed-american-sports-forever?source=dictionary, accessed May 2, 2017.

43. Creedon, "Women in Toyland," 89.

44. ESPN, "Let Them Wear Towels."

45. Baccellieri, "The Everlasting Legacy of Melissa Ludtke Who Dared to Join the Boys Club of the Baseball Press."

46. Sherry Ricchiardi, "Offensive Interference," *American Journalism Review*, http://ajrarchive.org/Article.asp?id=3788, accessed May 13, 2017.

47. Maxwell Strachem, "37 Years Ago, a Female Journalist Won the Right to Do Her Job," Huffington Post, http://www.huffingtonpost.com/entry/melissa -ludtke-locker-rooms-sports-journalism_us_56057c26e4b0dd8503074f2e, accessed May 21, 2017.

48. Clift, "'Let Them Wear Towels.'"

49. Clift, "'Let Them Wear Towels.'"

50. ESPN, "Let Them Wear Towels."

51. Hoffarth, "Title IX, 40 Years Later: Broadcasters Continue to Give a Voice to the Legacy," *Daily News*, June 27, 2012, http://www.dailynews.com/article /zz/20120621/NEWS/120627112.

52. "Winners of 31st Annual Sports Emmy Awards Announced," Emmyonline, http://emmyonline.com/sports_31st_winners, accessed July 28, 2017.

53. U.S. Department of Justice, Title IX, https://www.justice.gov/crt/title-ix -education-amendments-1972, accessed May 2, 2017.

54. Vecsey, "Sports of The Times: The Grace of Steve Garvey," *New York Times*, October 10, 1984, http://www.nytimes.com/1984/10/10/sports/sports-of-the -times-the-grace-of-steve-garvey.html.

55. Vecsey, "Sports of The Times."

56. The J. G. Taylor Spink Award, which is named for the late editor of *The Sporting News*, honors a baseball writer for "meritorious contributions to baseball writing" and is presented during the Hall of Fame Weekend. Each honoree is included in the writers' wing of the Baseball Hall of Fame.

57. "Claire Smith Wins J. G. Taylor Spink Award, to be Honored During Hall of Fame Weekend," ESPN, http://www.espn.com/mlb/story/_/id/18217975/claire-smith -wins-jg-taylor-spink-award-honored-hall-fame-weekend, accessed May 30, 2017. In 1987, the nonprofit organization, Association of Women in Sports Media, was created as an advocacy group for women who work in sports. See Association for Women in Sports Media, http://awsmonline.org, accessed July 15, 2018.

58. ESPN, "Let Them Wear Towels."

59. Dexter, "The Time a Baseball Player Sent a Rat to a Female Sportswriter."

60. Ricchiardi, "Offensive Interference."

61. Creedon, "Women in Toyland," 92–93.

62. Sally Jenkins, "Who Let Them In?" *Sports Illustrated*, June 17, 1991, https://www .si.com/vault/1991/06/17/124373/who-let-them-in-women-have-invaded-the -mens-club-of-tv-sportscasters-but-they-get-less-airtime-pay-and-prestige.

63. ESPN, "Let Them Wear Towels."

64. Kunen and Brown, "Sportswriter Lisa Olson Calls the New England Patriots Out of Bounds for Sexual Harassment."

65. See Ricchiardi, "Offensive Interference;" and Kessel, "An AWSM Experience for Merrill Students," The Shirley Povich Center for Sports Journalism, http://awsmonline.org/tag/lisa-olson/, accessed July 18, 2017.

66. "Bengals Coach Bans Female Writer," SI.com.

67. George Vecsey, "Sam Wyche Needs Some Time Off," *New York Times*, October 3, 1990, http://www.nytimes.com/1990/10/03/sports/sports-of-the-times -sam-wyche-needs-some-time-off.html.

68. Creedon, "Women in Toyland," 95.

69. Jenkins, "Who Let Them in?"

70. "Augusta Forced to Apologize after Female Reporter Is Barred from Masters Locker Room," *Daily Mail*, http://www.dailymail.co.uk/news/article-1375718 /Augusta-National-apologises-female-reporter-barred-Masters-locker-room .html, accessed June 1, 2017.

71. Michael Margulis, "Welcome to Augusta: Home of Racism, Classism, Sexism . . . and Golf," Medium, https://medium.com/@michaelmargulis /welcome-to-augusta-home-to-racism-classism-sexism-and-golf -23cda988f391, accessed June 1, 2017.

72. Christine Brennan, "In Her Own Words," The Shirley Povich Center for Sports Journalism, http://povichcenter.org/still-no-cheering-press-box /chapter/Christine-Brennan/index.html, accessed May 3, 2017.

73. Sara Morrison, "Media Is Failing Women—Sports Journalism Particularly So," Poynter Institute, http://www.poynter.org/2014/media-is-failing-women -sports-journalism-particularly-so/240240, accessed May 7, 2017.

74. Laura Wagner, "ESPN Hires Mendoza for Sunday Night Baseball," National Public Radio, January 13, 2016, http://www.npr.org/sections/thetwo-way /2016/01/13/462930401/espn-hires-jessica-mendoza-for-sunday-night -baseball.

75. Garcia, "Beth Mowins on Being the First Woman in 30 Years to Call the NFL," CNN Business, May 16, 2017, http://money.cnn.com/2017/05/16/media /beth-mowins-espn-nfl-game/index.html.

76. Deitsch, "Uphill Battle for Women in NFL Play-by-Play Roles May Soon Reach a Turning Point."

77. See Isaac Stanley Becker, "'I Prefer to Hear a Male Voice': Female Commentators Find Harsh Judgment at World Cup," *Washington Post*, June 26, 2018, www.washingtonpost.com/video/sports/segments/women-reporters-face -sexism-and-sexual-harassment-at-world-cup/2018/06/26/612e4414-7919 -11e; Vanessa Romo, "World Cup: Third Female Journalist Sexually Harassed on Camera," National Public Radio, June 26, 2018, www.npr.org/2018/06 /26/623441842/world-cup-a-third-female-journalist-sexually-harassed-on -camera-because; and James Masters, "The World Cup Sexism that Won't Go Away—And the Female Reporters on the Front Line," CNN Sports, July 5, 2018, www.cnn.com/2018/07/04/football/world-cup-female-journalist -harassment-spt-intl/index.html.

78. Becker, "'I Prefer to Hear a Male Voice.'"

79. Romo, "World Cup."

80. Becker, "'I Prefer to Hear a Male Voice.'"

81. Steve Wulf, "Melissa Ludtke: 'Sorry, Guys. You Couldn't Stop Us Then. You Can't Stop Us Now,'" ESPN, http://www.espn.com/espnw/voices/article /24793238/sorry-guys-stop-us-stop-us-now, accessed October 19, 2018.

82. Tom Schad, "Andrea Kremer, Hannah Storm to Become First All-Female Broadcasting Pair to Call NFL Game," *USA Today*, September 25, 2018, https://www.usatoday.com/story/sports/media/2018/09/25/andrea-kremer -hannah-storm-broadcasting-nfl-history/1421546002/.

83. Freeman, *ESPN*, 95, 269.

84. Joe Drape and Brooks Barnes, "ESPN Layoffs: The Struggling Industry Giant Sheds On-Air Talent," *New York Times*, April 26, 2017, https://www.nytimes .com/2017/04/26/sports/espn-layoffs.html?_r=0.

85. "ESPN Inc. Fact Sheet," ESPN, http://espnmediazone.com/us/espn-inc-fact -sheet/, accessed May 2, 2017.

86. Badenhausen, "Why ESPN Is Worth $40B as the World's Most Valuable Media Property."

87. Richard Perez-Pena, "The Top Player in This League? It May Be the Sports Reporter," *New York Times*, December 24, 2007, C1, 6.

88. Freeman, *ESPN*, 164, 195–201, 271.

89. "Rush Limbaugh's 'Racist' Quotes List," Snopes, http://www.snopes.com /politics/quotes/limbaugh.asp, accessed May 30, 2017.

90. "Limbaugh's Comments Touch off Controversy," ESPN, http://www.espn .com/nfl/news/story?id=1627887, accessed May 10, 2017.

91. Hartmann, "Rush Limbaugh, Donovan McNabb, and 'a Little Social Concern,'" 45–60.

92. Lamb, *From Jack Johnson to LeBron James*, 501–21.

93. Lamb, *From Jack Johnson to LeBron James*, 503.

94. Lamb, *From Jack Johnson to LeBron James*, 511.

95. Gillis, "Rebellion in the Kingdom of Swat," 45–68.

96. Scott Fowler, "Stick to Sports? Stephen Curry, Other Athletes Should Continue to Make Opinions an Asset," *Charlotte Observer*, http://www .charlotteobserver.com/sports/spt-columns-blogs/scott-fowler /article132025374.html, accessed June 6, 2017.

97. See Freeman, *ESPN*, 243; and David Carr, "Tiger Woods' Apology," NDTV, http://www.ndtv.com/world-news/tiger-woods-apology-mea-culpa-at-arms -length-411432, accessed June 12, 2017.

98. Roger Pielke Jr., "Measuring the "Tiger Effect"—Doubling of Tour Prizes, Billions into Players' Pockets," Sporting Intelligence, http://www

.sportingintelligence.com/2014/08/06/measuring-the-tiger-effect-doubling-of-tour-prize-money-billions-extra-into-players-pockets-060801/, accessed June 12, 2017.

99. Maureen Callahan, "The Night Tiger Woods Was Exposed as a Serial Cheater," *New York Post*, November 24, 2013, http://nypost.com/2013/11/24/the-night-tiger-woods-was-exposed-as-a-serial-cheater/.

100. Jon Hurdle and Richard Perez-Pena, "Former Penn State President Gets Jail Time in Child Molestation Scandal," *New York Times*, June 2, 2017, https://www.nytimes.com/2017/06/02/us/penn-state-graham-spanier-child-molestation-sentence.html.

101. Ivey DeJesus, "Sara Ganim, *Patriot-News* Staff, Awarded Pulitzer Prize for Coverage of Jerry Sandusky Case," Penn Live, http://www.pennlive.com/midstate/index.ssf/2012/04/sara_ganim_patriot-news_staff.html, accessed July 28, 2017.

102. Ed Sherman, "Sportswriters Snubbed by the Pulitzer Committee Again," Poynter Institute, http://www.poynter.org/2015/sports-writers-snubbed-by-the-pulitzer-committee-again/338465/, accessed June 15, 2017.

103. "Meyer Lucas Group Listing and Jupiter Home of MLB Pitcher and Outfielder Rick Ankiel Used as Setting for HBO's Real Sports with Bryant Gumbel," *Business Insider*, http://markets.businessinsider.com/news/stocks/Meyer-Lucas-Group-Listing-and-Jupiter-Home-of-MLB-Pitcher-and-Outfielder-Rick-Ankiel-Used-as-Setting-for-HBOs-Real-Sports-with-Bryant-Gumbel-490416, accessed December 15, 2017.

104. "Real Sports With Bryant Gumbel Recognized with Overseas Press Club Award for 2016 Exposé on International Olympic Committee," Medium, https://medium.com/hbo-cinemax-pr/real-sports-with-bryant-gumbel-recognized-with-overseas-press-club-award-ba90021a2b45, accessed June 15, 2017.

105. Fainaru-Wada and Williams, *Game of Shadows*, xii.

106. Nicholas Martinez, "The Steroid Era's Destruction of Baseball," *Bleacher Report*, http://bleacherreport.com/articles/480826-the-steroid-eras-destruction-of-major-league-baseball, accessed June 16, 2017.

107. "The Steroids Era," ESPN, http://www.espn.com/mlb/topics/_/page/the-steroids-era, accessed June 16, 2017.

108. John Erik Koslosky, "How the Steroid Era Saved Baseball," Motley Fool, January 14, 2014, https://www.fool.com/investing/general/2014/01/14/we-cant-ignore-the-steroid-era-it-just-might-have.aspx.

109. "SI 60 Q&A: How Tom Verducci Blew the Lid off Baseball's Steroid Era."

110. "The Mitchell Report," MLB.com, http://mlb.mlb.com/mlb/news/mitchell/, accessed June 7, 2017.

111. Jeff Pearlman, "Pee No Evil," Slate, http://www.slate.com/articles/sports /sports_nut/2006/06/pee_no_evil.html, accessed June 8, 2017.

112. Reilly, "Gutless Wonders."

113. Fainaru-Wada and Williams, *Game of Shadows*.

114. Bob Egelko, "Lawyer Admits Leaking Balco Testimony," SFGate, http:// www.sfgate.com/bayarea/article/LAWYER-ADMITS-LEAKING-BALCO -TESTIMONY-He-agrees-2617522.php, accessed June 18, 2017.

115. Fainaru-Wada and Fainaru, *League of Denial*.

116. "League of Denial: The NFL's Concussion Crisis," *Frontline*, http://www .pbs.org/wgbh/frontline/film/league-of-denial/transcript/, accessed June 17, 2017."

117. "League of Denial."

118. Richard Sandomir, "Partly by Shunning Documentary, ESPN Lifts It," *New York Times*, October 10, 2013, http://www.nytimes.com/2013/10/10/sports /football/by-shunning-concussion-documentary-espn-gives-it-a-lift.html.

119. Richard Sandomir, "Football Star Is Accused," *New York Times*, July 23, 2009, http://www.nytimes.com/2009/07/23/sports/football/23espn.html.

120. Aaron Gordon, "Playmakers, the Show the NFL Killed for Being Too Real," Vice, April 22, 2015, https://sports.vice.com/en_us/article/bmee43 /playmakers-the-show-the-nfl-killed-for-being-too-real.

121. Freeman, *ESPN*, 271.

122. See Ratchford, "'Black Fists and Fool's Gold,'" 49–59.

123. Sydney Smith, "Was ESPN's LeBron Decision OK by Media Ethics Standards?" imediaethics.org, http://www.imediaethics.org/was-espns-lebron -decision-ok-by-media-ethics-standards/, accessed June 20, 2017.

124. Leonard Shapiro, "Coverage of LeBron James's Decision Brings ESPN's Integrity into Question Again," *Washington Post*, July 13, 2010, http://www.washington post.com/wp-dyn/content/article/2010/07/13/AR2010071305908.html.

125. Tom Kludt, "ESPN Ends DraftKings-Sponsored Segments," *Money*, October 6, 2015, http://money.cnn.com/2015/10/06/media/espn-draftkings-ads/.

7. The State of Sports Journalism

1. Joe Drape and Brooks Barnes, "ESPN Layoffs: The Struggling Industry Giant Sheds On-Air Talent," *New York Times*, April 26, 2017, https://www.nytimes .com/2017/04/26/sports/espn-layoffs.html? r=0.

2. Drape and Barnes, "ESPN Layoffs."

3. See Richard Deitsch, "Media Circus: Looking at the Aftermath and Impact of ESPN's Layoffs," *Sports Illustrated*, May 7, 2017, http://www.si.com/tech -media/2017/05/07/espn-layoffs-impact-media-circus; Derek Thompson, "ESPN Is Not Doomed," *Atlantic*, May 1, 2017, http://www/theatlantic.com /business/archive/2017/05/espn-layoffs-future/524922/; and Allie Stoneberg, "New State-of-the-Art Home for SportsCenter," ESPN Press Room, May 19, 2014, http://espnmediazone.com/us/press-releases/2014/05/new-state-of -the-art-home-for-sportscenter.

4. John Ourand, "Amazon Scores with Live Streaming Rights for NFL 'RNF' Package," Sports Business Daily, April 4, 2017, http://www.sportsbusinessdaily .com/Daily/Closing-Bell/2017/04/04/NFL-TNF.aspx,

5. Meg James, "The Rise of Sports TV Costs and Why Your Bill Keeps Going Up," *Los Angeles Times*, November 28, 2016, http://www.latimes.com/business /hollywood/la-fi-ct-sports-channels-20161128-story.html.

6. "Sports in the Digital Age," *International Business Times*, http://www.ibtimes .com/sportsnet/sports-journalism-digital-age-1090350, accessed June 23, 2017.

7. Drape and Barnes, "ESPN Layoffs."

8. Dave Zirin, "Why the ESPN Layoffs Are So Disappointing," *Nation*, http:// www.thenation.com/article/why-the-espn-layoffs-are-so-disappointing/, accessed June 23, 2017.

9. Neil Best, "ESPN Proved Vulnerable to Economics of a Changing Indus- try," *Newsday*, http://www.newsday.com/sports/columnists/neil-best/espn -proved-vulnerable-to-economics-of-a-changing-industry-1.13538497, accessed June 23, 2017.

10. Michael Long, "Around the World in ESPN," SportsPro, http://www .sportspromedia.com/from-the-magazine/around_the_world_in_espn, accessed July 5, 2018.

11. Dan Kennedy, "Print Is Dying, Digital Is No Savior: The Long, Ugly Decline of the Newspaper Business Continues," WGBH, January 26, 2016, http://news .wgbh.org/2016/01/26/local-news/print-dying-digital-no-savior-long-ugly -decline-newspaper-business-continues.

12. Kian and Zimmerman, "The Medium of the Future," 285–87.

13. Kian and Zimmerman, "The Medium of the Future," 285.

14. Jack O'Dwyer, "Web Journalism Jobs Won't Replace Lost Print Jobs," O'Dw- yer's, March 31, 2014, http://www.odwyerpr.com/story/public/2156/2014-03 -31/web-journalism-jobs-wont-replace-lost-print-jobs.html.

15. Kian and Zimmerman, "The Medium of the Future," 299.

16. Max Schudel, "Frank Deford, Who Wrote about Sports with Panache and Insight, Dies at 78," *Washington Post*, May 29, 2017, http://www .washingtonpost.com/national/frank-deford-who-wrote-about-sports -with-style-and-insight-dies-at-78/2017/05/29/02c5331c-448e-11e7-bcde -624ad94170ab_story.html?utm_term=.c2eb15d64a1a.

17. Schudel, "Frank Deford, Who Wrote about Sports with Panache and Insight, Dies at 78."

18. Daniel Victor, "Frank Deford, a Literary Storyteller of Sport, Dies at 78," *New York Times*, May 29, 2017, http://www.nytimes.com/2017/05/29/sports /frank-deford-sportswriter-dies-at-78.html.

19. Deford, "Sportswriter Is One Word," University of Notre Dame, https:// journalism.nd.edu/assets/46541/frankdeford.pdf, accessed May 20, 2019.

20. Brennan, "The Evolution of Bill Simmons."

21. Peter Kafka, "Sports Guy Bill Simmons Helped Make Podcasts a Thing," Recode, January 3, 2014, http://www.recode.net/2014/1/3/11621882/sports -guy-bill-simmons-helped-make-podcasts-a-thing-next-up-a.

22. Grierson, "Welcome Back, 30 for 30: In Praise of ESPN's Documentary Series," Deadspin, http://deadspin.com/5946977/welcome-back-30-for-30 -in-praise-of-espns-documentary-series, accessed July 1, 2017.

23. Tom Kludt, "Grantland's Audience Grows Despite Loss of Bill Simmons," *Money*, October 14, 2015, http://money.cnn.com/2015/10/14/media/bill -simmons-grantland/index.html.

24. Will Brinson, "ESPN Suspends Bill Simmons for Calling Roger Goodell 'a Liar,'" CBS Sports, http://www.cbssports.com/nfl/news/espn-suspends-bill -simmons-for-calling-roger-goodell-a-liar/, accessed July 1, 2017.

25. Justin Block, "ESPN Closing Grantland Is the Dumbest Smart Business Decision," Huffington Post, http://www.huffingtonpost.com/entry/espn -grantland-dumb-business-decision_us_5633bd2ae4b00aa54a4e1aa0, accessed July 1, 2017.

26. John Koblin, "Bill Simmons' HBO Program Is Canceled," *New York Times*, November 5, 2016, https://www.nytimes.com/2016/11/05/business/media /bill-simmons-hbo-programcanceled.html.

27. Eric Jackson, "The Ringer and Bill Simmons Get a Second Chance with Vox," CNBC, June 1, 2017, http://www.cnbc.com/2017/06/01/the-ringer-and -bill-simmons-get-a-second-chance-with-vox.html.

28. Telander, *The Best American Sports Writing.*

29. Moritz, "The Story Versus the Stream," 398.

30. Moritz, "The Story Versus the Stream," 397.

31. Moritz, "The Story Versus the Stream," 403.

32. Kian and Zimmerman, "The Medium of the Future," 295.

33. Moritz, "The Story Versus the Stream," 403.

34. Kian and Zimmerman, "The Medium of the Future," 297.

35. Kian and Zimmerman, "The Medium of the Future," 297.

36. Neil Best, "First Time, Long Time for Bill Mazer," *Newsday*, http://www
.newsday.com/sports/columnists/neil-best/first-time-long-time-for-bill
-mazer-1.2962262, accessed June 29, 2017.

37. Nylund, "When in Rome," 138.

38. "Overview: The Rise of Talk Radio," POV, http://www.pbs.org/pov
/thefirenexttime/overview-the-rise-of-talk-radio/, accessed June 29, 2017.

39. See "Number of Dedicated Sports Radio Stations Grew Each Year from '02–
10," Sports Business Daily, February 14, 2012, http://www.sportsbusinessdaily
.com/Daily/Issues/2012/02/14/Research-and-Ratings/Sports-radio.aspx; John
Tuscano, "Sports Talk Radio Continues to Expand in Popularity Around
the Country," Penn Live, http://www.pennlive.com/sports/index.ssf/2013/07
/sports_talk_radio_continues_to.html, accessed June 29, 2017; and Nylund,
"When in Rome," 138, 142.

40. Hirshon, "The Myth of the Nassau Mausoleum," 2–3.

41. Bill Carter, "Radio Host Is Suspended Over Racial Remarks," *New York
Times*, April 10, 2007, http://www.nytimes.com/2007/04/10/business/media
/10imus.html.

42. "Colin Cowherd No Longer on ESPN Air after Comments about Domini-
cans," ESPN, http://www.espn.com/espn/story/_/id/13314040/colin-cowherd
-no-longer-espn-air-comments-dominican-republic-players, accessed July
2, 2017.

43. Ross, "The Defeat of Jason Whitlock."

44. Nylund, "When in Rome," 143.

45. See Nylund, "When in Rome," 141; and Nylund, *Beers, Babes, and Balls*.

46. Sarah Spain, "C'mon, Guys. It's Time to Elevate the Conversation on Sports
Talk Radio," ESPN, http://www.espn.com/espnw/news-commentary/article
/12612828/cmon-guys-time-elevate-conversation-sports-talk-radio, accessed
June 21, 2017.

47. Shannon Ryan, "WSCR's Julie DiCaro a Lightning Rod on Local Sports
Media Scene," *Chicago Tribune*, June 20, 2016, http://www.chicagotribune
.com/sports/ct-julie-dicaro-wscr-spt-0621-20160620-story.html.

48. Brennan, "In Her Own Words."

49. Sheffer and Schultz, "Paradigm Shifting or Passing Fad?" 480.

50. Cindy Boren, "Columnist Fired over Tweet about Japanese Driver's Indy 500 Win, Says It Wasn't 'Based in Racism,'" *Washington Post*, June 1, 2017, http:// www.washingtonpost.com/news/early-lead/wp/2017/06/01/columnist-fired -over-tweet-about-japanese-drivers-indy-500-win-says-it-wasnt-based-in -racism/?utm_term=.91566d43369d.

51. Steve Almasy, "Curt Schilling Suspended by ESPN after Controversial Tweet," CNN, August 25, 2015, http://www.cnn.com/2015/08/25/us/curt-schilling -insensitive-tweet/index.html.

52. Sheffer and Schultz, "Paradigm Shifting or Passing Fad?" 476.

53. Sheffer and Schultz, "Paradigm Shifting or Passing Fad?" 474–75.

54. Kian and Zimmerman, "The Medium of the Future," 297.

55. Sheffer and Schultz, "Paradigm Shifting or Passing Fad?" 475–76.

56. Brittany Johnson, "How Twitter Is Impacting Professional Athletes and Their Sports," *Bleacher Report*, http://bleacherreport.com/articles/1546676-how -twitter-is-impactin%20g-professional-athletes-and-their-sports, accessed June 17, 2017.

57. Matt McCue, "Will the Future of Sports Reporting Include Sports Reporters?" Fast Company, http://www.fastcompany.com/3036764/will-the-future -of-sports-reporting-include-sports-reporters, accessed June 17, 2017.

58. Benjamin Mullin, "Website 'The Athletic' Makes Aggressive Play," *Wall Street Journal*, June 5, 2018, B3.

59. Ken Fang, "HBO Real Sports' Bryant Gumbel Notes the Lack of Sports Journalism," Awful Announcing, http://awfulannouncing.com/2015/hbo-real -sports-bryant-gumbel-notes-the-lack-of-sports-journalism.html, accessed June 29, 2017.

60. Timothy Burke and Jack Dickey, "Manti Te'o's Dead Girlfriend, the Most Heartbreaking and Inspirational Story of the College Football Season, Is a Hoax," Deadspin, http://deadspin.com/manti-teos-dead-girlfriend-the -most-heartbreaking-an-5976517, accessed October 12, 2016.

61. Mitch Albom, "Nothing Sporting about Gossip as 'News,'" *Athens (OH) Messenger*, December 29, 2009, 4.

62. Deford, "Sportswriter Is One Word."

63. "*O.J. : Made in America* Wins Best Documentary Feature Oscar," ESPN, http://www.espn.com/espn/story/_/id/18776042/made-america-wins-best -documentary-feature-oscar, accessed July 11, 2017.

64. Branch, "The Shame of College Sports."

65. Jorge Castillo, "After Leaving Football, a Historian Emerges as an NCAA Critic," *New York Times*, October 26, 2011, http://www.nytimes.com/2011

/10/26/sports/ncaafootball/historian-taylor-branch-delivers-critical-view
-of-ncaa.html.

66. See Gaul, *Billion-Dollar Ball*; Clotfelter, *Big-Time Sports in American Univer-sities*; Zimbalist, *Unpaid Professionals*; and Dave Zirin, "Why Not Even the Mighty John Oliver Can Shame the NCAA," *Nation*, http://www.thenation .com/article/why-not-even-mighty-john-oliver-can-shame-ncaa/, accessed July 8, 2017.

67. Lamb, *Conspiracy of Silence*, 14.

68. "Dave Zirin on Bad Sports: How Owners are Ruining the Games We Love," *Democracy Now*, July 30, 2010, http://www.democracynow.org/2010/7/30 /dave_zirin_on_bad_sports_how.

69. "Introducing 'Edge of Sports,' A New Nation Podcast with Dave Zirin," *Nation*, http://www.thenation.com/article/introducing-edge-of-sports-a -new-nation-podcast-with-host-dave-zirin/, accessed July 7, 2017.

70. King, "Toward a Radical Sport Journalism," 334.

71. Lewis, *Moneyball*.

72. Steinberg, "Changing the Game: The Rise of Sports Analytics."

73. Reimer, "Syracuse University Will Launch the First Sports Analytics Degree in the U.S."

74. Deford, "Sportswriter Is One Word."

75. "Schools Across Country Increase Focus on Sports Communication," Penn State University, January 23, 2012, http://news.psu.edu/story/152329/2012/01 /23/schools-across-country-increase-focus-sports-communication.

76. "Journalism and Public Relations," IUPUI, http://liberalarts.iupui.edu/jour /pages/graduate-studies-folder/ma-sports-journalism.php, accessed July 10, 2017.

77. "Schools Across Country Increase Focus on Sports Communication."

78. Deitsch, "Sports Journalists Discuss the Future of Sports Media."

79. Moritz, "The Story Versus the Stream," 407.

80. Justin Rice, "When the League Owns the Network—and Pays the Journalists: A New Set of Ethical Questions Arise," NiemanLab, http://www.niemanlab .org/2009/07/when-the-league-owns-the-network-and-pays-the-journalists -a-new-set-of-ethical-questions-arise/, accessed October 25, 2018.

Bibliography

Adelman, Melvin L. "The First Modern Sport in America: Harness Racing in New York City, 1825–1870." In *The Sporting Image: Readings in American Sport History*, edited by Paul J. Zingg, 107–38. Lanham MD: University Press of America, 1988.

Altherr, Thomas L. "General Attitudes Toward Exercise and Sports." In *Sports in North America: A Documentary History*, Vol. 1, Part I, *Sports in the Colonial Era, 1618–1783*, edited by Thomas L. Altherr, 1–19. Gulf Breeze FL: Academic International Press, 1997.

———, ed. *Sports in North America: A Documentary History*, Vol. 1, Part I, *Sports in the Colonial Era, 1618–1783*. Gulf Breeze FL: Academic International Press, 1997.

———. "'There Is Nothing Now Heard of, in our Leisure Hours, But Ball, Ball, Ball': Baseball and Baseball-Type Games in the Colonial Era, Revolutionary War, and Early American Republic." In *The Cooperstown Symposium on Baseball and American Culture, 1999*, edited by Peter M. Rutkoff, 187–213. Jefferson NC: McFarland & Co., 2000.

American Society of Newspaper Editors. *Proceedings of the Annual Meeting of the American Society of Newspaper Editors*. Washington DC: ASNE, 1930.

Arledge, Roone. *Roone: A Memoir*. New York: HarperCollins, 2003.

Asinof, Eliot. *Eight Men Out: The Black Sox and the 1919 World Series*. 1963. Reprint. New York: Henry Holt and Co., 1987.

Astor, Gerald. *". . . And a Credit to His Race": The Hard Life and Times of Joseph Louis Barrow, a.k.a. Joe Louis*. New York: Saturday Review Press [distributed by] E. P. Dutton, 1974.

Badenhausen, Kurt. "Why ESPN Is Worth $40B as the World's Most Valuable Media Property." *Forbes*, May 13, 2017. https://www.forbes.com/sites/kurtbadenhausen/2012/11/09/why-espn-is-the-worlds-most-valuable-media-property-and-worth-40 billion/#4cdc67436527.

Bailey, Sandy. "From the Editor." *Sports Illustrated for Women*," Spring 1999, 12.

Baker, William J. *Jesse Owens: An American Life*. New York: Free Press, 1986.

Barney, Robert Knight. "Physical Education and Sport in the United States of America." In *History of Physical Education and Sport*, edited by Earle F. Zeigler, 171–227. Champaign IL: Stipes Publishing Co., 1988.

Barton, Bruce. "Grantland Rice." In *The Tumult and the Shouting: My Life in Sport*, by Grantland Rice, xi–xiii. New York: A. S. Barnes & Co., 1954.

"The Baseball Graft." *Editor & Publisher*, May 20, 1911, 12.

"Bengals Coach Bans Female Writer." *Sports Illustrated*, October 15, 1990. https://www.si.com/vault/1990/10/15/122874/curtain-call-bengal-coach-sam-wyche-tested-the-nfls-equal-access-rule—and-paid-for-it.

Betts, John Rickards. *America's Sporting Heritage, 1850–1950*. Reading MA: Addison-Wesley Publishing, 1974.

———. "Sporting Journalism in Nineteenth-Century America." *American Quarterly* 5, no. 1 (Spring 1953): 39–56.

"Bicycle." In *Funk & Wagnalls New Encyclopedia*, Vol. 3, 410–11. 1971. New York: Funk & Wagnalls, 1975.

Binker, Mary Jo. "William Henry Lewis." In *African Americans in Sports*, Vol. 1, edited by David K. Wiggins, 211–12. Armonk NY: M. E. Sharpe, 2004.

Blanchard, Margaret A., ed. *History of the Mass Media in the United States: An Encyclopedia*. Chicago: Fitzroy Dearborn, 1998.

———. "The Hutchins Commission, the Press and the Responsibility Concept." *Journalism Monographs* 49 (May 1977).

Bogart, Leo. "Magazines Since the Rise of Television." *Journalism Quarterly* 33, no. 2 (Spring 1956): 153–66.

Bond, Gregory. "Ed Gordon, Jr." In *African Americans in Sports*, Vol. 1, edited by David K. Wiggins, 125–26. Armonk NY: M. E. Sharpe, 2004.

Branch, Taylor. "The Shame of College Sports." *The Atlantic*, August 31, 2016. http://www.theatlantic.com/magazine/archive/2011/10/the-shame-of-college-sports/308643/.

Brennan, Matt. "The Evolution of Bill Simmons." *The Week*, June 22, 2017. http://theweek.com/articles/631188/evolution-bill-simmons.

Bryant, Jennings, and Andrea M. Holt. "A Historical Overview of Sports and Media in the United States." In *Handbook of Sports and Media*, edited by Arthur A. Raney and Jennings Bryant, 21–43. Mahwah NJ: Lawrence Erlbaum Associates, 2006.

Buchholz, Michael. "The Penny Press, 1833–61." In *The Media in America: A History*, edited by Wm. David Sloan and Susan Thompson, 123–43. Northport AL: Vision Press, 2008.

Buni, Andrew. *Robert L. Vann of the* Pittsburgh Courier: *Politics and Black Journalism*. Pittsburgh: University of Pittsburgh Press, 1974.

Burns, Ken, dir. *Unforgivable Blackness: The Rise and Fall of Jack Johnson*. Washington DC: WTEA, 2004.

Carroll, Brian. "'This Is IT!': The PR Campaign by Wendell Smith and Jackie Robinson." *Journalism History* 37, no. 3 (Fall 2011): 151–62.

———. *When to Stop the Cheering? The Black Press, the Black Community, and the Integration of Professional Baseball*. New York: Routledge, 2007.

Carter, Jimmy. *An Hour Before Daylight: Memories of a Rural Boyhood*. New York: Simon & Schuster, 2001.

Chadwick, Henry. *The Game of Base Ball: How to Learn It, How to Play It, and How to Teach It*. 1868. Reprint. Columbia SC: Camden House, 1983.

Chase, Francis, Jr. *Sound and Fury*. New York: Harper & Brothers, 1942.

"*Chicago Tribune* Cuts Sports." *Editor & Publisher*, August 27, 1921, 8.

Clotfelter, Charles. *Big-Time Sports in American Universities*. Cambridge UK: Cambridge University Press. 2011.

Cobb, W. Montague. "Race and Runners." *Journal of Health and Physical Education* 7, no. 1 (January 1936): 3–7, 52–56.

Conway, Mike. *The Origins of Television News in America: The Visualizers of CBS in the 1940s*. New York: Peter Lang, 2009.

Copeland, David A. "The Colonial Press, 1690–1765." In *The Media in America: A History*, edited by Wm. David Sloan and Susan Thompson, 35–50. Northport AL: Vision Press, 2008.

Cozens, Frederick W., and Florence Scovil Stumph. *Sports in American Life*. Chicago: University of Chicago Press, 1953.

Crawford, Scott A. G. M. "Eddie Tolan," In *African Americans in Sports*, Vol. 2, edited by David K. Wiggins, 369–70. Armonk NY: M. E. Sharpe, 2004.

Creedon, Pamela J. "From Whalebone to Spandex: Women and Sports Journalism in American Magazines, Photography and Broadcasting." In *Women, Media and Sport: Challenging Gender Values*, edited by Pamela J. Creedon, 108–58. Thousand Oaks CA: Sage Publishing, 1994.

———. "Women in Toyland: A Look at Women in American Newspaper Sports Journalism." In *Women, Media and Sport: Challenging Gender Values*, edited by Pamela J. Creedon, 67–107. Thousand Oaks CA: Sage Publishing, 1994.

———. ed. *Women, Media and Sport: Challenging Gender Values*. Thousand Oaks CA: SAGE, 1994.

Cressman, Dale. "From Newspaper Row to Times Square: The Dispersal and Contested Identity of an Imagined Journalistic Community." *Journalism History* 34, no. 4 (Winter 2009): 182–93.

Crouthamel, James L. *Bennett's* New York Herald *and the Rise of the Popular Press.* Syracuse NY: Syracuse University Press, 1989.

Daniels, Bruce C. *Puritans at Play: Leisure and Recreation in Colonial New England.* New York: St. Martin's Press, 1995.

Deford, Frank. "Sometimes the Bear Eats You: Confessions of a Sportswriter." *Sports Illustrated,* March 28, 2010, 77–87.

Deitsch, Richard. "Uphill Battle for Women in NFL Play-by-Play Roles May Soon Reach a Turning Point." *Sports Illustrated,* August 24, 2016. https://www.si.com/nfl/2016/08/24/nfl-women-announcers-beth-mowins-kate-scott.

———. "Media Circus: Looking at the Aftermath and Impact of ESPN's Layoffs." *Sports Illustrated,* May 7, 2017. http://www.si.com/tech-media/2017/05/07/espn-layoffs-impact-media-circus.

———. "Sports Journalists Discuss the Future of Sports Media." *Sports Illustrated,* December 12, 2016. http://www.si.com/tech-media/2016/12/12/media-circus-student-sports-journalists.

Dicken-Garcia, Hazel. *Journalistic Standards in Nineteenth-Century America.* Madison: University of Wisconsin Press, 1989.

Dinan, John. *Sports in the Pulp Magazines.* Jefferson NC: McFarland & Co., 1998.

Drake, Robert. "Jesse Who? Race, the Southern Press, and the 1936 Olympic Games." *American Journalism* 28, no. 4 (Fall 2011): 81–110.

Dunlap, Orrin E., Jr. *Marconi: The Man and His Wireless.* 1937. Reprint. New York: Macmillan, 1941.

Eisen, George, and David K. Wiggins, eds. *Ethnicity and Sport in North American History and Culture.* Westport CT: Greenwood Press, 1994.

Eisenberg, John. *The Great Match Race.* Boston: Houghton Mifflin, 2006.

Elliott, Sara A. "Frank Hart." In *African Americans in Sports,* Vol. 1, edited by David K. Wiggins, 139–40. Armonk NY: M. E. Sharpe, 2004.

———. "John Baxter Taylor." In *African Americans in Sports,* Vol. 2, edited by David K. Wiggins, 159–60. Armonk NY: M. E. Sharpe, 2004.

Emery, Michael, and Edwin Emery, with Nancy L. Roberts. *The Press and America: An Interpretive History of the Mass Media.* 8th ed. Boston: Allyn & Bacon, 1996.

Endres, Kathleen L., and Andrea M. Ferraro. "From War Hero to Sports Icon: The Transformation of the Goodyear Blimp." Paper presented at the annual meeting of the American Journalism Historians Association, St. Paul MN: October 2014.

Enriquez, Jon. "Coverage of Sports." In *American Journalism: History, Principles, Practices*, edited by W. David Sloan and Lisa Mullikin Parcell, 198–208. Jefferson NC: McFarland & Co., 2002.

Evensen, Bruce. "Sports Journalism: Longtime Staple for U.S. Publications." In *History of the Mass Media in the United States: An Encyclopedia*, edited by Margaret A. Blanchard, 621–23. Chicago: Fitzroy Dearborn, 1998.

Faber, Doris. *The Life of Lorena Hickok, E.R.'s Friend*. New York: William Morrow, 1980.

Fainaru-Wada, Mark, and Steve Fainaru, *League of Denial: The NFL, Concussions, and the Battle for Truth*. New York: Crown Archetype, 2013.

Fainaru-Wada, Mark, and Lance Williams. *Game of Shadows: Barry Bonds, BALCO, and the Steroids Scandal that Rocked Professional Sports*. New York: Gotham Books, 2007.

Fedler, Fred. *Lessons from the Past: Journalists' Lives and Work, 1850–1950*. Long Grove IL: Waveland Press, 2000.

Forester, Frank. "A Week in the Woodlands: Or Scenes on the Road, in the Field and Round the Fire, 1839." In *Sports in North America: A Documentary History*, Vol. 2, *Origins of Modern Sports, 1820–1840*, edited by Larry K. Menna, 60–68. Gulf Breeze FL: Academic International Press, 1995.

Fountain, Charles. *Sportswriter: The Life and Times of Grantland Rice*. New York: Oxford University Press, 1993.

Freeman, Michael. *ESPN: The Uncensored History*. New York: Taylor Trade, 2001.

Furrow, Ashley D. "A Struggle for Identity: The Rise and Fall of *Sports Illustrated Women*." *Journalism History* 38, no. 3 (Fall 2012): 156–65.

Gamache, Raymond W. "Evolution of the Sportscast Highlight Form: From Peep Show to Pathe to Pastiche." PhD dissertation, University of Maryland, 2008.

———. *A History of Sports Highlights: Replayed Plays from Edison to ESPN*. Jefferson NC: McFarland & Co., 2010.

Gaul, Gilbert M. *Billion-Dollar Ball: A Journey Through the Big-Money Culture of College Football*. New York: Viking Press, 2015.

Geltner, Ted. *Last King of the Sports Page: The Life and Career of Jim Murray*. Columbia MO: University of Missouri Press, 2012.

Gems, Gerald R. "'Duke' Slater." In *African Americans in Sports*, Vol. 2, edited by David K. Wiggins, 332–33. Armonk NY: M. E. Sharpe, 2004.

Gillis, William. "Rebellion in the Kingdom of Swat: Sportswriters, African American Athletes, and Coverage of Curt Flood's Lawsuit against Major League Baseball." *American Journalism* 23, no. 2 (Spring 2009): 45–68.

Gilmore, Al-Tony. *Bad Nigger! The National Impact of Jack Johnson*. Port Washington NY: Kennikat Press, 1975.

Gorn, Elliott, and Warren Goldstein. *A Brief History of American Sports*. New York: Hill and Wang, 1993.

Gorn, Elliot J. "Sports through the Nineteenth Century." In *The New American Sport History: Recent Approaches and Perspectives*, edited by S. W. Pope, 33–57. Urbana: University of Illinois Press, 1997.

Griffin, Emma. *England's Revelry: A History of Popular Sports and Pastimes, 1660–1830*. Oxford UK: Oxford University Press, 2005.

Gunther, Marc. *The House That Roone Built: The Inside Story of ABC News*. Boston: Little, Brown and Co., 1994.

Hamburger, Susan. "Horse Racing." In *African Americans in Sports*, Vol. 1, edited by David K. Wiggins, 159–60. Armonk NY: M. E. Sharpe, 2004.

———. "Oliver Lewis." In *African Americans in Sports*, Vol. 1, edited by David K. Wiggins, 211. Armonk NY: M. E. Sharpe, 2004.

Harper, William A. *How You Played the Game: The Life of Grantland Rice*. Columbia MO: University of Missouri Press, 1999.

Hartmann, Douglas. "Rush Limbaugh, Donovan McNabb, and 'a Little Social Concern.'" *Journal of Sport and Social Issues* 31, no. 1 (February 2007): 45–60.

Heapey, Leslie A. "Marshall 'Major' Taylor." In *African Americans in Sports*, Vol. 2, edited by David K. Wiggins, 361–62. Armonk NY: M. E. Sharpe, 2004.

Henderson, Robert W. *Ball, Bat, and Bishop: The Origin of Ball Games*. Urbana: University of Illinois Press, 2001.

Hietala, Thomas R. *The Fight of the Century: Jack Johnson, Joe Louis, and the Struggle for Racial Equality*. Armonk NY: M. E. Sharpe, 2002.

Hirshon, Nicholas. "The Myth of the Nassau Mausoleum: Two-Step Flow at the First All-Sports Radio Station." Paper presented at the annual meeting of the American Journalism Historians Association, St. Paul MN, October 2014.

Hodermarsky, Mark. *Baseball's Greatest Writers*. Dubuque IA: Kendall Hunt, 2003.

Hoffer, Richard. "What a Wonderful World," *Sports Illustrated*, May 9, 2011, 12–13.

Home Box Office v. FCC. 567 F.2nd 9 (D.C. Cir. 1977), *cert. denied* 434 U.S. 829 (1977).

Hornbuckle, Adam R. "William Dehart Hubbard." In *African Americans in Sports*, Vol. 1, edited by David K. Wiggins, 161. Armonk NY: M. E. Sharpe, 2004.

Hudson, Frederic. *Journalism in the United States from 1690 to 1872*. New York: Haskell House, 1968.

Hutchison, Phillip J. "Usually White, But Not Always Great: A Journalistic Archaeology of White Hopes, 1908–2013." *Journalism History* 39, no. 4 (Winter 2014): 231–40.

Inabinett, Mark. *Grantland Rice and His Heroes: The Sportswriter as Mythmaker in the 1920s*. Knoxville: University of Tennessee Press, 1994.

Irwin, Will. "The American Newspaper." *Collier's*, January 21, 1911, 15–18.

——. "The American Newspaper." *Collier's*, March 4, 1911, 18–22.

Isard, Carrie Teresa. "Champion Jack: Celebrity and Collective Representation in the Early 20th Century Black Press." Paper presented at the annual meeting of the American Journalism Historians Association, Kansas City MO, October 2011.

Isenberg, Michael T. *John L. Sullivan and His America*. Urbana: University of Illinois Press, 1988.

Jolly, W. P. *Marconi*. New York: Stein and Day, 1972.

Juergens, George. *Joseph Pulitzer and the* New York World. Princeton NJ: Princeton University Press, 1966.

Kahn, Roger. *The Boys of Summer*. 1971. Reprint. New York: New American Library, 1973.

Kaszuba, Dave. "Ringside, Hearthside: Sports Scribe Jane Dixon Embodies Struggle of Jazz Age Women Caught Between Two Worlds." *Journalism History* 35, no. 3 (Fall 2009): 141–50.

Kian, Edward, and Matthew Zimmerman. "The Medium of the Future: Top Sports Writers Discuss Transitioning from Newspapers to Online Journalism." *International Journal of Sport Communication* 5, no. 3 (September 2012): 285–304.

King, C. Richard. "Toward a Radical Sport Journalism: An Interview with Dave Zirin." *Journal of Sport and Social Issues* 32, no. 4 (November 2008): 333–44.

"The King Majesties Declaration to His Subjects Concerning Lawfull Sports to Bee Vsed." In *Sports in North America: A Documentary History*, Vol. I, Part I, *Sports in the Colonial Era, 1618–1783*, edited by Thomas L. Altherr, 2–4. Gulf Breeze FL: Academic International Press, 1997. This originally was published in London by Thomas Barker in 1618.

Kirsch, George B., ed. *Sports in North America: A Documentary History*, Vol. 3, *The Rise of Modern Sports, 1840–1860*. Gulf Breeze FL: Academic International Press, 1992.

Kroeger, Brooke. *Nellie Bly: Daredevil, Reporter, Feminist*. New York: Times Books, 1994.

Kunen, James S., and S. Avery Brown. "Sportswriter Lisa Olson Calls the New England Patriots Out of Bounds for Sexual Harassment." *People*, May 29, 2017. http://people.com/archive/sportswriter-lisa-olson-calls-the-new-england-patriots-out-of-bounds-for-sexual-harassment-vol-34-no-15/.

Lamb, Chris. *Blackout: The Untold Story of Jackie Robinson's First Spring Training*. Lincoln: University of Nebraska Press, 2004.

——. *Conspiracy of Silence: Sportswriters and the Long Campaign to Desegregate Baseball*. Lincoln: University of Nebraska Press, 2012.

——, ed. *From Jack Johnson to LeBron James: Sports, Media, and the Color Line*. Lincoln: University of Nebraska Press, 2016.

Laucella, Pamela C. "Jesse Owens, A Black Pearl Amidst an Ocean of Fury: A Case Study of Press Coverage of the 1936 Berlin Olympic Games." Paper presented at the annual meeting of the Association for Education in Journalism and Mass Communication, Miami Beach FL, August 2002.

Levine, Peter, ed. *American Sport: A Documentary History*. Englewood Cliffs NJ: Prentice Hall, 1989.

——. "The Louisville Regatta." In *American Sport: A Documentary History*, edited by Peter Levine, 27–28. Englewood Cliffs NJ: Prentice Hall, 1989.

——. "Prize Fighting." In *American Sport: A Documentary History*, edited by Peter Levine, 29–30. Englewood Cliffs NJ: Prentice Hall, 1989.

Lewis, Michael. *Moneyball: The Art of Winning an Unfair Game*. New York: W. W. Norton, 2004.

Lichty, Lawrence W., and Malachi C. Topping. *American Broadcasting: A Source Book on the History of Radio and Television*. 1975. Reprint, New York: Hastings House, 1976.

MacCambridge, Michael. *The Franchise: A History of* Sports Illustrated *Magazine*. New York: Hyperion Books, 1997.

Margolick, David. *Beyond Glory: Joe Louis vs. Max Schmeling, and a World on the Brink*. New York: Alfred A. Knopf, 2005.

Martinelli, Diana Knott, and Shannon A. Bowen. "The Public Relations Work of Journalism Trailblazer and First Lady Confidante Lorena Hickok, 1937–45." *Journalism History* 35, no. 3 (Fall 2009): 131–40.

Mather, Cotton. "Cotton Mather Comments on Recreation." In *Sports in North America: A Documentary History*, Vol. 1, Part I, *Sports in the Colonial Era, 1618–1783*, edited by Thomas L. Altherr, 15. Gulf Breeze FL: Academic International Press, 1997. This originally was published in Boston in 1726 as "A Serious Address to those who unnecessarily frequent the Tavern."

McChesney, Robert W. "Media Made Sport: A History of Sports Coverage in the United States." In *Media, Sports, and Society*, edited by Lawrence Wenner, 49–69. Newbury Park CA: SAGE, 1989.

McCue, Matt. "Will the Future of Sports Reporting Include Sports Reporters?" *Fast Company*, June 17, 2017. http://www.fastcompany.com/3036764/will-the -future-of-sports-reporting-include-sports-reporters.

Mead, Chris. *Champion: Joe Louis, Black Hero in White America*. New York: Charles Scribner's Sons, 1985.

Mee, Bob. *Bare Fists: The History of Bare-Knuckle Prize Fighting*. Woodstock NY: Overlook Press, 2001.

Menna, Larry K. "The Emergence of Sports Journalism and Writing." In *Sports in North America: A Documentary History*, Vol. 2, *Origins of Modern Sports, 1820–1840*, edited by Larry K. Menna, 34–36. Gulf Breeze FL: Academic International Press, 1995.

———, ed. *Sports in North America: A Documentary History*, Vol. 2, *Origins of Modern Sports, 1820–1840*. Gulf Breeze FL: Academic International Press, 1995.

Michener, James A. *Sports in America*. New York: Random House, 1976.

Miller, James Andrew, and Tom Shales. *Those Guys Have All the Fun: Inside the World of ESPN*. New York: Little, Brown and Company, 2011.

Moritz, Brian. "The Story Versus the Stream: Digital Media's Influence on Newspaper Sports Journalism." *International Journal of Sport Communication* 8, no. 4 (December 2015): 397–410.

Mott, Frank Luther. *A History of American Magazines, 1741–1850*. 1930. Reprint. Cambridge MA: Harvard University Press, 1957.

———. *American Journalism: A History of Newspapers in the United States Through 250 Years, 1690 to 1940*. 1941. Reprint. New York: Macmillan, 1947.

Nylund, David. *Beers, Babes, and Balls: Masculinity and Sports Talk Radio*. Albany: State University of New York Press, 2007.

———. "When in Rome: Heterosexual, Homophobia, and Sports Talk Radio." *Journal of Sport and Social Issues* 28, no. 2 (May 2004): 136–68.

"Observance of the Sabbath and Religious Holidays." In *Sports in North America: A Documentary History*, Vol. 1, Part I, *Sports in the Colonial Era, 1618–1783*, edited by Thomas L. Altherr, 4–12. Gulf Breeze FL: Academic International Press, 1997.

Oriard, Michael. *King Football: Sport and Spectacle in the Golden Age of Radio and Newsreels, Movies and Magazines, the Weekly & the Daily Press*. Chapel Hill: University of North Carolina Press, 2001.

————. *Reading Football: How the Popular Press Created an American Spectacle.* Chapel Hill: University of North Carolina Press, 1993.

Patnode, Randall. "Friend, Foe, or Freeloader? Cooperation and Competition between Newspapers and Radio in the Early 1920s." *American Journalism* 28, no. 1 (Winter 2011): 75–95.

"Patronage of Sporting Works." In *Sports in North America: A Documentary History*, Vol. 2, *Origins of Modern Sports, 1820–1840*, edited by Larry K. Menna, 43–45. Gulf Breeze FL: Academic International Press, 1995. This originally was published in *The American Turf Register and Sporting Magazine* in August 1838.

Pew, Marlen. "Radio Discussed as Press Threat or Promise," *Editor & Publisher*, February 9, 1924, 7.

Phillips, H. H. S., Jr. "Memo from the Publisher." *Sports Illustrated*, August 16, 1954, 13.

————. "Memo from the Publisher." *Sports Illustrated*, November 22, 1954, 1.

Phinizy, Coles. "Go-Go Slow." *Sports Illustrated*, March 17, 1969, 68, 74, 76.

Poore, Ben Perley. "Biographical Notice of John S. Skinner." *The Plough, the Loom and the Anvil* 7, no. 1 (July 1854): 1–20.

Pope, S. W., ed. *The New American Sport History: Recent Approaches and Perspectives.* Urbana: University of Illinois Press, 1997.

Porter, William T. "Prospectus of *The Spirit of the Times* and Life in New York, 1831." In *Sports in North America: A Documentary History*, Vol. 2, *Origins of Modern Sports, 1820–1840*, edited by Larry K. Menna, 39. Gulf Breeze FL: Academic International Press, 1995. This originally was published in *The Spirit of the Times* on December 10, 1831, 38–39.

————. "To Our Friends." In *Sports in North America: A Documentary History*, Vol. 2, *Origins of Modern Sports, 1820–1840*, edited by Larry K. Menna, 40. Gulf Breeze FL: Academic International Press, 1995. This originally was published in *The Spirit of the Times* on December 10, 1831, 39–40.

Rader, Benjamin G. *In Its Own Image: How Television Has Transformed Sports.* New York: Free Press, 1984.

Raney, Arthur A., and Jennings Bryant, eds. *Handbook of Sports and Media.* Mahwah NJ: Lawrence Erlbaum Associates, 2006.

Ratchford, Jamal L. "'Black Fists and Fool's Gold: The 1960s Black Athletic Revolt Reconsidered': The LeBron James Decision and Self-Determination in Post-Racial America." *The Black Scholar* 42, no. 1 (Spring 2012): 49–59.

Rayne, M. L. *What Can a Woman Do: Or Her Position in the Business and Literary World.* 1884. Reprint. Albany NY: Eagle Publishing, 1893.

Reel, Guy. *The* National Police Gazette *and the Making of the Modern American Man, 1879–1906*. New York: Palgrave Macmillan, 2006.

Reilly, Rick. "Gutless Wonders." *Sports Illustrated*, June 8, 2017. https://www.si.com/vault/2005/08/15/8270108/gutless-wonders.

Reimer, Alex. "Syracuse University Will Launch the First Sports Analytics Degree in the U.S." *Forbes*, May 11, 2016. http://www.forbes.com/sites/alexreimer/2016/05/11/syracuse-university-will-launch-first-sports-analytics-degree-in-the-u-s/#568422d73b49.

Reisler, Jim. *Black Writers/Black Baseball: An Anthology of Articles from Black Sportswriters Who Covered the Negro Leagues*. Jefferson NC: MacFarland & Co., 1994.

Rice, Grantland. *The Tumult and the Shouting: My Life in Sport*. New York: A. S. Barnes, 1954.

Riess, Steven A. *City Games: The Evolution of American Urban Society and the Rise of Sports*. Urbana: University of Illinois Press, 1989.

Roberts, Randy. *Joe Louis: Hard Times Man*. New Haven CT: Yale University Press, 2010.

———. *Papa Jack: Jack Johnson and the Era of White Hopes*. New York: Free Press, 1983.

Robertson, Nan. *The Girls in the Balcony: Women, Men, and the* New York Times. New York: Random House, 1992.

Robinson, Bill. *The World of Yachting*. New York: Random House, 1966.

Robinson, Jackie. *Baseball Has Done It*. New York: J. B. Lippincott, 1964.

Rodgers, Ronald R. "An Untamed Force: Magazine and Trade Journal Criticism of the New Journalism and the Rise of Professional Standards, 1890s to 1920s." PhD dissertation, Ohio University, 2005.

Roessner, Amber. *Inventing Baseball Heroes: Ty Cobb, Christy Mathewson, and the Sporting Press in America*. Baton Rouge: Louisiana State University Press, 2014.

Ross, Betsy. *Playing Ball with the Boys: The Rise of Women in the World of Men's Sports*. Covington KY: Clerisy Press, 2010.

Ross, Ishbel. *Ladies of the Press: The Story of Women in Journalism by an Insider*. 5th ed. New York: Harper & Brothers, 1936.

Ross, Winston. "The Defeat of Jason Whitlock." *Newsweek*, September 13, 2015. http://www.newsweek.com/defeat-jason-whitlock-371758.

Rush, Benjamin. "Benjamin Rush Recommends Horseback Riding as Healthful Recreation." In *Sports in North America: A Documentary History*, Vol. 1, Part I, *Sports in the Colonial Era, 1618–1783*, edited by Thomas L. Altherr, 15. Gulf Breeze FL: Academic International Press, 1997. Rush's statement originally was published in *Sermons to Gentlemen upon Temperance and Exercise* (Philadelphia: John Dunlap, 1772), 15–16.

Rushin, Steve. "There and Back," *Sports Illustrated*, August 11, 2014, 59.

Rutkoff, Peter M., ed. *The Cooperstown Symposium on Baseball and American Culture, 1999*. Jefferson, North Carolina: McFarland & Co., 2000.

Salisbury, Tracey M. "Isaac Murphy." In *African Americans in Sports*, Vol. 2, edited by David K. Wiggins, 247–48. Armonk NY: M. E. Sharpe, 2004.

Schaap, Jeremy. *Triumph: The Untold Story of Jesse Owens and Hitler's Olympics*. Boston: Mariner Books, 2008.

Schiff, Andrew J. *"The Father of Baseball": A Biography of Henry Chadwick*. Jefferson NC: McFarland & Co., 2008.

Schulberg, Budd. "A Fan Fights Back." *Sports Illustrated*, October 11, 1954, 63.

Sheffer, Mary Lou, and Brad Schultz, "Paradigm Shifting or Passing Fad? Twitter and Sports Journalism." *International Journal of Sport Communication* 3, no. 4 (December 2010): 472–84.

"SI 60 Q&A: How Tom Verducci Blew the Lid off Baseball's Steroid Era." *Sports Illustrated*, September 9, 2014. https://www.si.com/mlb/2014/09/09/si-60-qa -tom-verducci-steroid-era-ken-caminiti-totally-juiced.

Siedlecki, M. Agnes. "Sports Anti-Siphoning Rules for Pay Cable Television: A Public Right to Free TV?" *Indiana Law Journal* 53, no. 4 (Spring 1978): 821–40.

Skinner, John S. "Introduction to the *American Turf Register and Sporting Magazine*." In *Sports in North America: A Documentary History*, Vol. 2, *Origins of Modern Sports, 1820–1840*, edited by Larry K. Menna, 36–38. Gulf Breeze FL: Academic International Press, 1995. This originally was published in *The American Turf Register and Sporting Magazine* in September 1829.

Sloan, W. David, and Lisa Mullikin Parcell, eds. *American Journalism: History, Principles, Practices*. Jefferson NC: McFarland & Co., 2002.

Sloan, Wm. David, and Susan Thompson, eds. *The Media in America: A History*. 7th ed. Northport AL: Vision Press, 2008.

Smith, Anthony F., and Keith Hollihan. *ESPN: The Company: The Story and Lessons Behind the Most Fanatical Brand in Sports*. Hoboken NJ: Wiley, 2009.

Smith, Red. "My Press-Box Memoirs." *Esquire*, October 1975, 202.

Smith, Reed. "*Sports Illustrated*'s African American Athlete Series as Socially Responsible Journalism." In *From Jack Johnson to LeBron James: Sports, Media, and the Color Line*, edited by Chris Lamb, 357–82. Lincoln: University of Nebraska Press, 2016.

Smith, Ronald A. *Play by Play: Radio, Television, and Big-Time College Sport*. Baltimore: Johns Hopkins University Press, 2001.

"Sports Writers and Baseball Reports." *Editor & Publisher*, September 10, 1921, 28.

Staebler, James. "The Stereograph: The Rise and Decline of Victorian Virtual Reality." Master's thesis, Ohio University, 2000.

Steinberg, Leigh. "Changing the Game: The Rise of Sports Analytics." *Forbes*, August 18, 2015. http://www.forbes.com/sites/leighsteinberg/2015/08/18/changing-the-game-the-rise-of-sports-analytics/#3d7608894c1f.

Sterling, Christopher H., and John M Kittross, *Stay Tuned: A Concise History of American Broadcasting*. Belmont CA: Wadsworth, 1978.

Stout, Glenn, ed. *Everything They Had: Sports Writing from David Halberstam*. New York: Hyperion Books, 2008.

——. "Introduction." In *Everything They Had: Sports Writing from David Halberstam*, edited by Glenn Stout, xiii–xxv. New York: Hyperion Books, 2008.

Tebbel, John, and Mary Ellen Zuckerman. *The Magazine in America, 1741–1990*. New York: Oxford University Press, 1991.

Telander, Rick, ed. *The Best American Sports Writing*. Boston: Houghton Mifflin Harcourt, 2016.

Thompson, Derek. "ESPN Is Not Doomed." *The Atlantic*, May 2017. http://www.theatlantic.com/business/archive/2017/05/espn-layoffs-future/524922/.

Thompson, Susan. *The Penny Press: The Origins of the Modern News Media, 1883–1861*. Northport AL: Vision Press, 2004.

Tygiel, Jules. *Baseball's Great Experiment: Jackie Robinson and His Legacy*. New York: Vintage Books, 1983.

——. *Past Time: Baseball as History*. New York: Oxford University Press, 2000.

Van Every, Edward. *Sins of New York as "Exposed" by the Police Gazette*. New York: Frederick A. Stokes, 1930.

Vincent, Ted. *Mudville's Revenge: The Rise and Fall of American Sport*. New York: Seaview Books, 1981.

Vogan, Travis. *ESPN: The Making of a Sports Media Empire*. Champaign: University of Illinois Press, 2015.

Volk, Garry. "Letter from the Publisher," *Sports Illustrated*, July 1, 1968, 4.

Walker, James R., and Robert V. Bellamy Jr. *Center Field Shot: A History of Baseball on Television*. Lincoln: University of Nebraska Press, 2008.

Washburn, Pat. "New York Newspaper Coverage of Jackie Robinson in His First Major League Season." *Western Journal of Black Studies* 4, no. 3 (Fall 1980): 183–92.

Weaver, Bill L. "The Black Press and the Assault on Professional Baseball's 'Color Line,' October, 1945-April, 1947." *Phylon* 40, no. 4 (Fourth Quarter 1979): 303–17.

Welky, David B. "Culture, Media and Sport: The *National Police Gazette* and the Creation of an American Working-Class World." *Culture, Sport, Society* 1, no. 1 (May 1998): 78–100.

Wenner, Lawrence, A., ed. *Media, Sports, and Society*. Newbury Park CA: SAGE, 1989.

White, William Allen. *The Autobiography of William Allen White*. New York: Macmillan, 1946.

Wiggins, David K., ed. *African Americans in Sports*. 2 vols. Armonk NY: M. E. Sharpe, 2004.

———. "Baseball." In *African Americans in Sports*, Vol. 1, edited by David K. Wiggins, 21–23. Armonk NY: M. E. Sharpe, 2004.

———. "The Notion of Double-Consciousness and the Involvement of Black Athletes in American Sport." In *Ethnicity and Sport in North American History and Culture*, edited by George Eisen and David K. Wiggins, 133–55. Westport CT: Greenwood Press, 1994.

———. "Racial Theories." In *African Americans in Sports*, Vol. 2, edited by David K. Wiggins, 289–92. Armonk NY: M. E. Sharpe, 2004.

Yardley, Jonathan. *Ring: A Biography of Ring Lardner*. New York: Random House, 1977.

Yates, Norris W. *William T. Porter and* The Spirit of the Times: *A Study of the Big Bear School of Humor*. Baton Rouge: Louisiana State University Press, 1957.

Zeigler, Earle F., ed. *History of Physical Education and Sport*. Champaign IL: Stipes Publishing Co., 1988.

Zimbalist, Andrew. *Unpaid Professionals: Commercialism and Conflict in Big-Time Sports*. Princeton NJ: Princeton University Press, 2001.

Zingg, Paul J., ed. *The Sporting Image: Readings in American Sport History*. Lanham MD: University Press of America, 1988.

Index